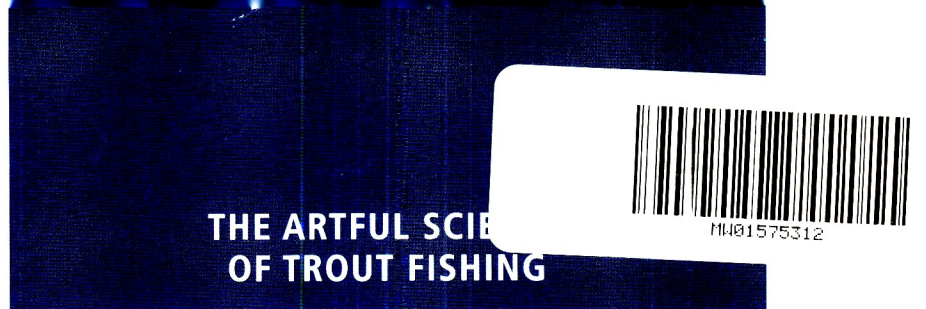

THE ARTFUL SCIENCE
OF TROUT FISHING

UNIVERSITY OF CANTERBURY
Te Whare Wānanga o Waitaha
CHRISTCHURCH NEW ZEALAND

First published in 2005 by
CANTERBURY UNIVERSITY PRESS
University of Canterbury
Private Bag 4800
Christchurch
NEW ZEALAND

www.cup.canterbury.ac.nz

Copyright © 2005 John W. Hayes and Les Hill
The moral rights of the authors have been asserted

ISBN 1-877257-19-2

A catalogue record for this book is available from
the National Library of New Zealand

This book is copyright. Except for the purpose of fair review, no part may be stored or transmitted in any form or by any means, electronic or mechanical, including recording or storage in any information retrieval system, without permission in writing from the publishers.
No reproduction may be made, whether by photocopying or by any other means, unless a licence has been obtained from the publisher or its agent.

Designed by Richard King at Canterbury University Press
Printed through Bookbuilders, China

All photographs are by Les Hill, unless otherwise credited

Watercolour paintings by Maggie Atkinson
Todd Bush Road, RD1, Nelson, New Zealand
toddsvalley@xtra.co.nz

Half-title photo by Darryl Torckler

CONTENTS

Acknowledgements	8
Preface	9

PART ONE: THE FISH

Chapter 1	*Behaviour, origins and distribution of trout*	17
Chapter 2	*Life cycle and movements of trout*	21
Chapter 3	*Trophy trout*	45
Chapter 4	*Senses*	57

PART TWO: THE HABITAT

Chapter 5	*General habitat features*	75
Chapter 6	*Running water*	79
Chapter 7	*Still water*	101

PART THREE: FEEDING BEHAVIOURS AND FISHING STRATEGIES

Chapter 8	*Feeding behaviours in rivers and fishing strategies*	123
Chapter 9	*Feeding behaviours in lakes and fishing strategies*	157

PART FOUR: CONSERVATION AND MANAGEMENT

Chapter 10	*Sports fishery management in New Zealand*	179
Chapter 11	*Conserving the habitat*	189
Chapter 12	*Indigenous conservation and trout fisheries management: an uneasy tension*	203
Chapter 13	*Managing angling*	219
Selected References		247
Index		251

*This book is dedicated to our fathers,
Bill Hayes and Jim Hill,
for introducing us to the joys of fishing.*

ACKNOWLEDGEMENTS

John Hayes

MIKE BRADSTOCK, former managing editor of Canterbury University Press, came up with the concept of a popular fishing book with scientific content and asked me to write *The Artful Science of Trout Fishing*. His infectious enthusiasm got me hooked on the idea and was a vital source of encouragement over several years until the book's completion. Mike also had a hand in editing the manuscript. Later, Richard King took over responsibility for publishing the book. He was a pleasure to work with, and the book's design and layout is a credit to him.

Producing this book with Les Hill initiated our friendship. By collaborating on this project we have ended up with a product that is far better than either Les or I could have achieved on our own. We also made a good decision in asking Maggie Atkinson to produce the splendid watercolours for the book.

There are several other people to whom I am grateful for contributing information, advice, photos and assistance, including: Neil Deans, Bob McDowall, Peter Williams, Rob Pitkethly, Mike Britton, John Gibbs, Bev Abbot, Tony Entwistle, Rowan Strickland, Aaron Quaterman, Karen Shearer, Roger Young, Nick Hughes, Mark Sherburn, Maurice Rodway, Jay Graybill, Mark Webb, Ross Millichamp, Richard Fitzpatrick, Peter Taylor, Peter Hamill, and Darryl Torckler.

Finally, I am indebted to my wife, Sue Hallas, for her support over the several years that this project has been simmering. Sue also ran her editor's eye over an early draft of the text.

Les Hill

THE PEOPLE who appear in the photographs in a book like this add immeasurably to the quality, meaning and balance of the images. I am most grateful to the following people (in the order that they appear) who are subjects of my photos and willingly helped me take the pictures: John Taylor, Oliver Varley, Tim Varley, John Cornish, Tony Allan, Brian Smith, the two anglers in a boat on Lake Alexandrina, Bob Worley, Howard Hill, Peter Sanford, Jack Taylor, Len Cook, Alan Pannett, Alistair Garland, Kiyoshi Suzaki, John McDowell, Chappie Chapman, Dave Lyttle, Kirsten Brown and Philip Sanford. There are some photographs of me taken by my brother Ho or Jack Taylor. I thank them for their assistance and obvious skill with my camera. I would also like to thank Jack Taylor for editing some of my writing when we first began 'penning' this book, and Graeme Marshall for checking page proofs.

PREFACE

THE FASCINATION OF TROUT FISHING for me is that it is multi-faceted. Its rewards span social, physical, intellectual, artistic and spiritual dimensions. Any one, or combination, of these resonates with an individual's particular character.

Angling has had an important influence in shaping my character and the course of my life. It has encouraged an independent and adventurous spirit, and a love of wild places. It has influenced the friendships I have made and steered me into my fisheries research career.

My attitude to trout fishing has been shaped by a lifelong interest in the sport and a research career that has encouraged an enquiring mind. Now, when I stand on the bank of river or lake, my mind often wanders beyond the immediate interest of catching trout to what is happening beneath the water's surface. How vibrant is the trout population? What is the food chain that supports it? How good is the habitat and how might it be affecting the numbers and distribution of trout? What governs the size of the trout? What motivates my fellow anglers and how are we all affecting the trout resource and each other? Some of this thought can pay rewards in terms of the number of fish caught, but much is simply aimed at making sense of what is masked beneath the silver surface.

Yet there are times when it is enough that angling simply tends my spirit: just to sit beside clear, flowing waters and hear the melodic call of a bellbird – and to see a trout rise.

This book covers some of these facets of trout fishing. It is not just a selection of techniques, nor simply of fishing yarns. Angling literature already abounds with such works. An important reason for writing this book was to popularise some of the wealth of information available from research on trout and angling in New Zealand and elsewhere. This is what has imparted so much depth of interest to my own angling journey and now, I hope, also to you, the reader.

The artful science of trout fishing

SINCE THE EARLIEST DAYS OF ANGLING, and the first published fly-fishing literature such as *De nimalium Natura* (Claudius Aelianus, third century), *A Treatyse of Fysshynge with an Angle* (Dame Juliana Berners, 1496) and *The Compleat Angler* (Isaak Walton, 1653), anglers have demonstrated a thirst for knowledge of their sport. The early writers showed an interest in the process of fly fishing, flies, tackle and tactics. Their thinking and writing influenced all who followed.

The very nature of the sport and its environmental focus directed thinking towards science. Fish biologists and entomologists try to unravel the intricate relationships between fish, their environment and their food. It is only natural therefore that anglers, too, look towards science and try to think and reason in scientific ways.

Anglers are avid readers about their sport. Many of them have a sizeable library of favourite books, most of which have been reread many times. Some read purely for enjoyment, but probably the majority seek information to improve their knowledge and gain more from their sport. Many actually endeavour to practise what they read. They correlate the observations of others with what they observe, assimilate much and undoubtedly become better anglers as a result.

Some anglers enjoy the solitude that fishing can offer. On a river or lake the pace and direction of thought lead to relaxation whether fish are actively sought or merely contemplated. Others, like me, prefer the company of another angler to share the fun. The time that company is most valued is on a trip of several days' duration, when the only way to a favourite stream involves an arduous walk, backs burdened with heavy packs.

Several years ago Len Cook and I undertook such a journey, the trek leading us first steadily uphill and over a divide before descending into the river we sought. From the top of the divide, high above the river, we could survey a considerable length of the valley. The valley floor, wide and flat, accommodated a river, at first seemingly devoid of direction. The main channel hugged a rock outcrop on the near side, then the entire flow spread towards the opposite side of the valley, branching as it went on its journey of many hundreds of metres. Near the far side many of the side streams joined again to cut a deep channel along a wooded bank. Then, dividing once more, the river headed our way across debris-strewn gravels and around little islands of pasture.

Our elevated position gave us a valuable perspective. The river looked most promising where it ran along the valley fringes, directly below and some distance away on the other side of the valley. These places, we decided, should be our immediate objective.

The great promise ahead made our journey seem eternal. We spoke little while our speed and resolve increased, our heads pushed forward. Finally we emerged from the bush on the valley floor, shed our packs and sorted and assembled our tackle. As we approached the first run our hopes soared even higher when we saw swallows swooping along the margins of the stream, their activity signalling the presence of insects.

The far edge of the immediate channel was bare, flood-swept gravel and sand, featureless and uninviting. Our side, though, the deeper of the two, was punctuated by large boulders, some submerged and others exposed. Among these rocks the swallows dived continually.

Len took the lead, rod held low and trailing, eyes alert. Looking towards a pocket ahead, a short reach between two boulders, he commented, 'According to theory there should be a fish right there.' Barely had he spoken when a shape rose to the surface, rolled briefly then descended from sight.

We stooped instinctively, then knelt low to watch, hoping to see the fish again, looking for anything that might increase our chances of catching it. Close to the water we could see why the swallows were so excited. Hosts of mayfly duns were appearing, then drifting along easily before alighting. This, too, accounted for the trout's activity. Up it came again, disturbed the surface then sank, not completely from sight – we could just discern its form about a metre below.

Len needed little encouragement to try his luck. He sneaked back downstream, well away from the fish, to change his fly. His intention was to try to match as closely as possible the hatching insects. He chose a small Dad's Favourite, the colour and size of which looked reasonable. From my better elevation I could see the fish, but Len, being lower and further away, could not. It mattered little because two boulders stood out, delineating the pocket. Between these lay Len's target. Windless days are few in this country, and particularly in the mountains. Yet on this occasion there was not even a hint of a breeze, so casting was relatively easy. Len's fly floated down, as he had hoped, a short distance upstream of where the trout waited.

When trying to 'match the hatch' with an artificial fly, one is made aware of the difficulties faced by fly tiers. Almost invariably, despite the best intentions otherwise, the imitation stands out among nearby naturals (often it's the first selected too). Len's fly this time stood a little more upright, appeared slightly larger. The colour, though, looked similar. As it rode over the fish, I expected at least a response, an inspection. But the fish stayed down. Len tried again, but the result was the same. It would have been reasonable to think immediately that the fish had become wary, aware of something different. Such inclinations were soon dispelled. The fish rose once more, and this time I noted the take with more interest. Several duns drifted close, above the trout, but instead it took something not visible to me. The take, too, was different, not one of those nose-and-tail rises, but more a bulge and nudge at the surface. This I relayed to Len, suggesting he try a small unweighted nymph, one that would lodge in the surface film.

Before casting, Len doused the nymph in the river to ensure that it would sink slightly, not float on top. Then he lengthened his line and cast. With such a light nymph, its drop into the water was almost imperceptible. Sure that Len could not see the trout, I watched closely. Up it came, nosed the surface and then turned down. 'Hit him!' I yelled. Up whipped Len's rod, then bent forward as the trout responded. I'm sure Len and I had equal enjoyment from this success.

Securing any fish involves an element of luck. That's one of the attractions of angling. But as any of the most successful anglers can tell you, luck isn't paramount. Len's fish was caught largely through experience — meaning a series of decisions based on observations and related to past success and failure.

In essence, ours was a scientific approach, based on knowledge and reason. From our initial hilltop observations we had recognised the most likely pools in the river, the ones with stable beds, greater depth and a more permanent look to them. The bird activity signalled not only an insect hatch but also where there was a concentration of food. It also hinted at what was taking place below the water surface in terms of emerging insects.

When we actually began our stalk upstream, a multitude of predetermined strategies were involved, including our demeanour, speed of approach, clothing and so on (showing appreciation of a trout's senses). But most of all Len showed an understanding of the river when he located the likely lie. Understanding the trout's feeding helped too. In all, a whole raft of knowledge and experience was involved.

No matter where or how you pursue trout, a thoughtful reasoned approach will assure you of more success. Science pervades all aspects of fishing. Hence a greater knowledge of the biology and habitat of trout, while satisfying in itself, will help in the endless pursuit that is angling.

PART ONE

The fish

The artful science of trout fishing

THE ENTHUSIASTIC EFFORTS of sports-minded forebears in acclimatising trout have provided New Zealand anglers with some of the best brown and rainbow trout sports fisheries in the world. The two species contrast in character and provide the angler with different challenges. Often they occupy different lies, their feeding habits may vary, but most of all they behave differently. For this reason I have quite catholic tastes and particularly enjoy fishing rivers that hold both species. In such places more surprises await. And rainbow trout are full of surprises.

One of my most outstanding memories was the day my friend Philip Sanford hooked the same fish three times. We were stalking together up a small stream when we spotted a nymphing rainbow in midstream. It fed most actively, as rainbows do, and was not holding in a quiet pocket or off the main flow, but right in a torrent: ideal nymph-and-indicator water. Any take would be translated quickly to the indicator. The timing of the strike in such conditions is relatively easy.

Philip used a weighted nymph that would sink quickly in the fast flow. It plopped ahead and to the side of the fish. The response was immediate: the fish lifted sideways and had hardly turned when the indicator dipped sharply. Philip hit hard.

One of the attractions of catching rainbows is their immediate power. This fish headed straight for the far bank, then turned downstream, clearly in view all the time. Just when Philip was beginning to relax, his rod sprang back. The fish was free. We watched it drift a little further downstream, then turn and quite aggressively push back up. It continued until, to our amazement, it stopped right where it had been feeding previously. That wasn't the last surprise. Within moments it started feeding again.

Not one to avoid a challenge, Philip changed his nymph and positioned himself to cast again. I don't think I held the same hope this time, but still the trout rose to the first cast. The leader straightened rapidly, the indicator stopped as before. Philip's lift in response met with a resistance and there was an immediate flurry on the water's surface. Then despondency again. The line went slack. One would reasonably expect that a trout firmly hooked twice would flee to deeper waters, but not this one. Like Philip, it was not easily deterred. Once more it began to feed.

Philip changed his nymph for a second time and began casting. Third time lucky? Maybe, but now surely we were dealing with a well-alerted fish. As the first nymph passed by, the fish looked closely but did not take. It continued to feed. Philip tried another pattern, but this too was refused.

At a time like this, a quite different offering will sometimes induce the desired response. With this in mind, Philip tied on a dry fly. The fish eagerly took this and again sped downstream. But alas, the hook failed to hold yet again and – believe it or not – again our rainbow swam upstream to its undoubted home.

What did we have to do to scare this fish? In fact it took very little. All the time that Philip had been casting he had managed to avoid hooking an overhanging branch. His line had fallen short, pitched to the left or perhaps to the right. Overhanging branches rarely remain untouched. In a final desperate bid to secure this fish he inevitably snared the foliage. To free his nymph, which was hanging just above the fish, he twitched his line and shook the branch at the same time. At this the trout fled, not to be seen again.

That was not the only time I've witnessed a rainbow being hooked three times before being either scared or landed. It has happened to me twice before.

In other ways, too, I've witnessed rainbow trout behaving in a manner belying the cautious reputation of trout. One day, as I stalked up a small stream, I scared a fish out into midstream. I avoided stepping on it by just a metre or two. More from reflex than real commitment, I flicked a nymph to the fish's new station. To my surprise it rose and took my half-hearted 'offering'.

Rainbows often seem to feed very actively. In their hurry they can be less discerning than browns, accepting a wide variety of fly patterns. Only once, in more than thirty-five years of fishing, have I lost a brown and then rehooked it immediately. I can also recall several browns that continued feeding after having a fly wrenched from their expectant jaws. Once I hooked and landed a three-and-a-half-kilogram brown on a fly that had dragged quite alarmingly across the tail of a pool. But usually they refuse a fly with even marginal drag.

Most often brown trout are conservative in all they do, particularly as a fishing season proceeds and some angler contact has been established. They acknowledge the presence of an angler given any small signal. They refuse clumsily selected or presented flies, and they soon focus single-mindedly on self-preservation.

Making generalisations about fish can be misleading, however. I think it is important to note that, in some respects, rainbow and brown trout are subtly different. Rainbows may be less discerning, but I would not like to convey the idea that they were invariably stupid and quite easy to catch. Nor would I like to suggest that all browns require an artist to catch them. It's merely the inclinations that are being compared here.

The only real certainty about the nature of trout is that each one is different. That's what makes trout fishing such a challenge.

CHAPTER ONE

Behaviour, origins and distribution of trout

IN THE INTRODUCTION to this section Les discussed some of the differences between brown and rainbow trout. Generally, the rainbow is considered the easier of the two to catch, and it has a reputation as a flashy, more acrobatic fighter. The brown trout is renowned as the most difficult to catch of all the salmonids. In order to understand these general perceptions, it is useful to compare the origins of these fish and how those origins have fashioned their behaviours, which are products of millennia of evolution in foreign lands.

New Zealand's brown trout are descended from stocks in England, Scotland, Germany and Italy. They are predominantly river-resident fish, although a component of many populations is migratory and may include sea-runners. River-resident fish are exposed to predators all around them, particularly from the banks, and over time evolutionary forces have honed their senses.

Our rainbows are descended mainly from Californian steelhead – sea-run rainbows, famous for their fighting ability. Steelhead and all other rainbows belong to the Pacific salmon genus, *Oncorhynchus*, and like salmon they spend most of their adult and subadult life at sea, using rivers only for spawning and rearing juveniles. For most of their lives steelhead are voracious predators in the open ocean and have relatively little to fear from predators outside that environment. Only juveniles and adults returning to fresh water to spawn are exposed to bank-side predators in the confines of the river environment. Perhaps this underlies the comparatively bold and undiscerning feeding behaviour of rainbow trout.

While brown trout migrate to some degree, they are much more river-resident than rainbows (or at least, more than steelhead). Their body form and behaviour are highly adapted to the river environment and to constant threats from land and air. The pectoral fins of brown trout are much larger than those of rainbow trout, so they can use the current to hug the river bed and avoid the full force of the flow.

The artful science of trout fishing

A fat young brown trout – like the rest of its kind, adaptable and supremely suited to the river environment.

Although rainbows eat more and grow faster than browns, they are less energy-efficient. They feed higher in the water column, where they must constantly battle the current. The brown is much more wary than the rainbow, readily using cover to advantage, and generally is sensitive to the slightest movement on the bank. On the other hand, the rainbow often allows its appetite for food to override caution.

Rainbow trout have been most successful in lake systems in New Zealand, particularly in those of the central North Island, where they give full rein to their voracious appetites and gorge on the abundant smelt. The rainbows' migratory tendencies, a legacy of their steelhead ancestry, may lie behind their association with lakes in this country. Repeated efforts at establishing river-resident rainbows, or even steelhead runs, in rivers unhindered by lakes or waterfalls have been relatively unsuccessful. This generalisation is less true in the northern half of the North Island, and there are some notable exceptions such as the Rangitikei, Ngaruroro and Mohaka Rivers in the central North Island, and the Pelorus–Rai catchment in the South Island. Nevertheless, compared with browns, the success of rainbow releases in rivers running freely to the sea has been low. It is possible that the young fish simply migrate out to sea and become lost if there is not a low-gradient, stable river section or lake downstream to halt them. The rivers in which rainbows have become established tend to be some of the most stable. Research also suggests that rainbow trout may not be able to withstand floods as well as brown trout can.

Rainbow trout predominate north of a line between southern Hawke's Bay and northern Taranaki. The northern limit of brown

A rainbow trout just netted from a Fiordland stream. Descendants of the steelhead, these migratory fish thrive best in New Zealand where they have access to lakes.

trout is about Coromandel. These limits are primarily set by water temperature. Brown trout prefer lower summer temperatures than rainbow trout but, more significantly, winter water temperatures exceeding 11°C will kill their eggs. This explains the northern limit of brown trout. The warmer waters of the north are the strongholds of the rainbow, and the cooler southern waters are the strongholds of the brown, but there are exceptions to this generalisation. The North Island hosts some excellent brown trout fisheries in regions such as Hawke's Bay, Manawatu and Taranaki. Conversely, rainbow trout thrive in some of the lakes on the eastern side of the Southern Alps and in the southernmost lakes.

These are the contrasting natures of the two most sought-after fish in New Zealand fresh waters: one dour, cautious and supremely adapted to the riverine environment; the other bold, voracious and flashy, seemingly more at home in the deep blue waters of inland 'seas' and their tributaries. For the angler, brown and rainbow trout complement each other, providing a wealth of fishing opportunities and challenges throughout the country.

CHAPTER TWO

Life cycle and movements of trout

THE SIGNIFICANCE of the trout's life cycle to the angler is that it dictates where fish can be found at different stages in their lives, how abundant and how large they will be, and what they will be doing at different times of the year. Understanding the life cycle can increase the size and the number of fish you catch.

The life cycle can be broken into four stages: spawning, incubation, fry and juvenile rearing, and maturity.

Spawning season

Basically, brown trout are autumn to early winter spawners, and rainbow trout are late winter to spring spawners. However, variations do occur, particularly with rainbows. They may begin spawning in April, along with brown trout, but can continue as late as October or November depending on the location. There even is a small summer run of rainbows into the Tongariro River. Most brown trout, on the other hand, usually have finished spawning by late July.

The eggs of brown trout require colder water, and autumn spawning ensures they will develop over winter and hatch long before the water exceeds lethal temperature (11°C) in the spring.

A female rainbow trout digging a redd (nest), with a male waiting in the background.
Darryl Torckler

Rainbow eggs survive temperatures up to 15 °C, which may explain the species' wider spawning season.

Spawning runs and other migrations

Because trout often spend their adult life far from the spawning grounds, they must migrate to spawn. For some brown trout in stable, gravelly spring creeks, the spawning 'migration' may simply involve swimming to the nearest suitable patch of gravel – possibly within a few hundred metres of their feeding territories. In his famous 1951 study of the Horokiwi Stream near Wellington, K. Radway Allen found that some brown trout dug their redds within metres of their home pool.

At the other extreme, steelhead in North America migrate hundreds or thousands of kilometres. New Zealand has nothing to compare to this, though there are several records of trout moving considerable distances. Most stay within the same river system, but a few go to sea and end up in other river catchments.

Tag returns of fish passing through the Glenariffe salmon trap in the headwaters of the Rakaia River, ninety-five kilometres from the sea, provide some of the best long-term records of movements between catchments. Of a hundred brown trout tagged at the Glenariffe trap, seventy-one were recaptured at the trap in subsequent spawning seasons, six were caught by anglers in the main Rakaia River and sixteen were caught near the mouth, in the Rakaia lagoon. Seven more were caught in other catchments, including the Ashburton and Rangitata Rivers and tributaries of Lake Ellesmere. These locations ranged from fifteen to sixty-five kilometres along the coast from the Rakaia mouth.

The most impressive recorded movement by a trout in New Zealand was of a brown trout tagged in the Selwyn River in 1969 that turned up in the Mataura River, some five hundred kilometres away.

Recent research in North America has changed the way that fisheries biologists view movement in river-resident trout populations. It was once thought that river-resident trout did not move much at all, because tagged fish usually were recaptured very close by – more often than not within the same pool. However, it is now known that many of the tagged trout that apparently vanish after tagging have not died, as was usually assumed, but have moved to other parts of the river, often many kilometres away. It is now accepted that a part of most populations is transient, and not necessarily composed of the same fish all of the time. If a trout finds good vacant habitat that meets its food and cover needs, it is likely to stay put. But if it outgrows its favourite spot or is displaced by

The need to spawn is a strong stimulus for trout to migrate upstream and surmount some surprisingly difficult obstacles in their path.

Fish & Game NZ – Wellington Region

Tagged trout provide information on movement within and between river catchments.
Cawthron Institute

competitors, floods or habitat change, it may become a wanderer until it finds another home.

New technologies such as radio tagging have revealed that trout do indeed move a lot in some rivers. Such was the case with a radio-tracking study of sixty adult brown trout that a colleague and I undertook in the Wairau River, Marlborough. Over a period of nine months, 34 per cent of the tagged trout moved more than ten kilometres and 17 per cent moved twenty kilometres, in both upstream and downstream directions. The Wairau is a large, unstable, braided river in which trout habitat changes frequently in response to floods and seasonal low flows, thus it is perhaps not surprising that the trout move extensively and frequently.

Tagging programmes often turn up surprises. A brown trout that my research team tagged in the Owen River in March 2000 was caught seventy-three kilometres away in the upper Matakitaki River in October 2001. The most direct journey by water would entail swimming four kilometres down the Owen River, twenty-three kilometres down the Buller River and forty-six kilometres up the Matakitaki River.

The best-known spawning migrations in this country occur in rivers that flow into lakes that provide extensive, often very productive feeding habitat for trout, which must eventually return en masse to the tributaries to spawn. In most regions the fishing season is closed when trout are spawning. Notable exceptions are waters of the central North Island and some of the southern lakes. The central North Island lake fisheries are unique in having a tradition of fishing for spawning trout, which are easier to catch because they are concentrated, but are also vulnerable to overfishing. Consequently, these fisheries require very careful management, especially where wild stocks are involved.

Anglers who are interested in winter fishing for spawning trout can benefit from knowledge of the environmental factors that influence spawning runs. Temperature controls the general timing of spawning migrations. Brown trout spawning migrations take place during a falling-temperature regime (autumn–early winter), whereas generally most rainbow trout migrate during a rising-temperature regime (late winter–spring). These patterns are in keeping with the respective water temperatures that the eggs of each species require. Brown trout spawn when the water is 6–10°C, and their eggs incubate in a declining- or steadily-cold-temperature regime. Rainbows are a little more variable, generally spawning when water temperatures are 5–11°C, and their eggs incubate in an increasing-temperature regime – over spring. As mentioned previously, these generalisations do not always hold for rainbow trout because, in New Zealand, these fish have a particularly variable spawning season.

When the temperature is suitable, spawning trout are stimulated to run upriver primarily by river freshes and floods. However, in practice it can be difficult to isolate the influence of freshes from the drop in water temperature that usually accompanies them. The best time to fish is when floodwaters are receding, as soon as the water is clear enough for the trout to see the lure.

While the water is turbid, trout migrate during both day and night, but in clear water they migrate mainly at night, often in the early evening. In small shallow streams, trout are particularly reluctant to migrate during the day. More trout migrate on cloudy than on clear frosty nights. During the coldest part of the winter this pattern of nocturnal migration may, however, be modified by cold nights.

Very low temperatures (below the ranges given above) can cause trout to delay migration. I believe I once saw this happen in a rainbow trout spawning run that I trapped during the winter of 1980 in a spawning tributary of Lake Alexandrina, near Tekapo. Because this spawning tributary is clear and shallow, the trout generally entered the trap at night. However, for a few days at the end of July, I began getting runs of up to seventy fish at a time in the middle of the afternoon. This coincided with the coldest winter water temperatures (5 –6°C). One afternoon I hid and watched the trap to see just when the trout were migrating. Nothing happened until the water temperature reached its daily maximum of 10°C, and then about fifty trout moved purposefully up from the lake and entered the trap.

Spawning

Brown and rainbow trout are primarily stream/river spawners, although they will spawn on gravel beaches in lakes if no suitable stream is available. The female digs a redd, or nest, in the gravel of the stream with vigorous movements of her flanks and tail. The number of eggs she lays depends on her size – as a rule of thumb, a trout lays about 1,500 eggs per kilogram of body weight. The male plays no part in digging the redd but spends most of his time defending the female from the amorous attentions of other males.

As the female gets close to finishing the redd, the male begins to nudge her and quivers beside her to stimulate her to shed her eggs. Finally, the female presses her vent close to the gravel at the bottom of the depression she has dug and releases her eggs. At the same time the male pulls up alongside the female and sheds his sperm (also called milt) among the eggs. As they are fertilised, most of the eggs fall among the spaces in the gravel. The few eggs that are swept downstream are eagerly snapped up by yearling trout, which hang around spawning pairs in anticipation of the feast to come. The female immediately covers the eggs with gravel, which she digs up just upstream from the egg pocket so the current carries the gravel over the eggs. Often she will lay more eggs in this new depression. When the redd is finished the eggs lie safely buried about seven to fifteen centimetres beneath the gravel. The outline of the redd remains visible for some weeks because the slime that normally covers the stream bed is washed away by the digging activity of the trout.

Trout are quite selective when it comes to choosing a spawning site. They prefer sites with clean, loose gravel one to seven centimetres in diameter (from pea gravel to medium-sized stones). They choose sites where the stream bed rises in the direction of the water flow and ensures a good flow of well-oxygenated water through the redd. These conditions often, but not always, occur in the tails of pools. However, despite a great deal of research, scientists still puzzle over the exact cues that trout use to select a spawning site. Often the fish will be found spawning only in a small section of a stream or river, though, to the human observer, there are kilometres of apparently similar habitat available.

On the spawning grounds male trout become extremely aggressive as they compete for mates. Fights constantly break out and males inflict horrendous injuries on each other. I once saw two male rainbows have a spectacular battle in a shallow creek about half a metre wide. Each fish in turn would furiously smash into the other with enough force to toss it flapping onto the bank. Once back in the water the recipient of the blow would do the same to

A good spawning stream with stable banks and bed.

Lake-edge spawning gravel with clean loose stones of the right size.

the other fish. On other occasions I have seen male trout lunge headlong at each other and lock jaws. I suspect that such battles cause the dislocated jaws often seen in male rainbows.

Because male trout are so aggressive, they are more likely to be caught around the time of spawning than are female trout. In Lake Tarawera, for instance, there is intense fishing selection for large, aggressive male rainbows as they congregate off stream mouths to spawn. This contributed to a decline in trophy fish in the population and in the angler catch. Female trout are focused on finding a spawning site and digging a redd. However, once the hen has laid her eggs she will, for a short time, defend the redd site from other females, presumably to guard against her eggs being dug up again – a serious problem in some spawning streams (see page 28).

Males have a greater tendency to take up residence in headwater tributaries following spawning. Anglers catch many more large mature males than females in headwater fisheries, and the incidence of males increases with the age of the fish. For example, in eight back-country rivers that Roger Young and I studied, about half of the anglers' catch of trout less than eight years old were males, but 80 per cent of the older fish were males. Some scientists think that because female trout use up more energy when spawning, they may need to migrate to the lower reaches of rivers to recover where growing conditions are better.

Incubation and fry behaviour

Trout eggs take twenty to a hundred days to hatch, depending on the temperature. The colder the water, the longer the eggs take to hatch. Once hatched, the trout embryo still has about two or three weeks before it becomes a free-swimming fry. During this time it remains buried in the gravel and feeds off the yolk sac that formed much of the bulk of the egg. At this stage it is called an alevin. As it develops, the alevin moves away from the egg pocket and up through the gravel. When the yolk sac is nearly all used up, the young trout emerges as a free-swimming fry.

The behaviour of emerging fry is fascinating. Most fry emerge from the gravels at night, and all emerge about the same time. Most emerge in the first few hours after dark but, if the moon is full, they stay in the gravel. A full moon can delay emergence for up to a week; then, on the first dark night the fry may emerge in thousands. This minimises predation at a particularly vulnerable stage. Emerging at night, the fry avoid daytime predators such as birds. By emerging en masse they derive some benefit from safety in numbers because the nocturnal predators, which are mainly bigger fish, soon have their fill of the unlucky fry and the others go unharmed.

Rainbow trout fry.
Rowan Strickland

The fish

Shoal of juvenile rainbow trout.
Rowan Strickland

As soon as they emerge, the fry passively drift downstream in the dark, but at dawn they stop. They may continue this nocturnal migration for a few nights but eventually they stop and take up residence. In this manner successive waves of fry colonise the stream bed. This downstream migration ensures that fry become well dispersed throughout the stream and not bunched up together all competing for the limited resources of living space and food.

In some lake tributaries used for spawning by rainbow trout, vast numbers of these migrating fry enter the lake soon after they emerge and spend no time growing in the stream.

Early in my research career I operated a fry trap on one such stream draining into Lake Alexandrina. The stream is only a couple of metres wide and one and a half kilometres long, yet it hosts over 3,000 spawning trout, mostly rainbows. On a dark night in late November, when the rainbow fry migration was nearing its peak, I wandered down to the trap to check it before I went to bed. I turned the headlamp on and peered into the collecting box. I was confronted by a seething mass of fry filling the box, wriggling along the screen mesh wings of the trap, and milling about in the creek further upstream. That night I trapped over 15,000 fry.

Survival and causes of mortality

Survival of eggs and alevins up to the free-swimming fry stage is extremely variable. Survival during incubation very much depends upon the quality of the spawning gravels: whether they are clogged with silt that could cause the eggs and alevins to suffocate. However, in some situations it is the *quantity* of spawning gravels that can be critical.

When a large number of trout congregate to spawn on limited spawning grounds, many eggs can be lost because of trout digging up each others' redds. This is called redd superimposition. Where brown and rainbow trout occur together, the later-spawning rainbow trout can be particularly damaging to brown trout redds made earlier in the season. I began my research career studying this in the small spawning creek of Lake Alexandrina mentioned earlier. About 3,000 rainbow trout and up to a hundred brown trout crowded into the small stream over the six-month spawning season. I found that redd superimposition by late-spawning rainbow trout killed more than 95 per cent of the eggs of brown trout and early-spawning rainbow trout.

Floods can destroy large numbers of eggs and alevins through scouring the stream bed and silting the spawning gravel.

Careless wading by anglers can also take its toll. A study in North America showed that a single disturbance by wading just before hatching could kill 43 per cent of the eggs in a redd, and repeated disturbance of this kind could kill up to 96 per cent of eggs and pre-emergent fry. The lesson is clear: in those waters in which winter fishing is legal, anglers should learn to recognise trout redds and be careful to avoid wading over them. In many spawning streams around New Zealand, cattle are allowed to roam freely. It is well known that cattle cause much damage to stream banks, but perhaps the unseen damage to trout eggs also needs tighter control.

Generally, the most critical time for survival is within the first few months of a trout's life as a free-swimming fry, particularly soon after emergence. In K. Radway Allen's study of the Horokiwi Stream, 44 per cent of fry died before beginning to feed, and only 2 per cent survived the first six months. An English study found that only 2.5 per cent of fry lived a year or more. Survival rate improves as fish get bigger, generally running at between 20 and 50 per cent a year.

What happens to all these fish? These low survival figures may give the impression that we should see dead and dying trout throughout our rivers and lakes. In fact, they simply seem to vanish. Anglers occasionally see dead trout, but these are barely the 'tip of the iceberg'. Under the water's surface the struggle for survival is going on, and the agents of mortality are diseases, predators of various kinds and the rigours of the variable stream environment brought about by flood and drought.

Predatory birds undoubtedly take their toll of trout. Herons prowl the shallow margins of spawning and nursery waters, picking off fry, and black shags pursue adult trout underwater. (The black shag should not to be confused with the little black shag, which does not prey on trout.) Acclimatisation societies once relentlessly hunted black shags, but today the birds are protected under the Wildlife Act and their presence on rivers and lakes is vigorously defended by the Department of Conservation (DOC) and avid bird lovers on the basis that they are part of the native fauna. Some claim that predatory birds bestow health and vigour on trout populations by weeding out sick and weak fish. I regard this as a rather lame argument. I have no doubt that shags consume healthy as well as weak trout. In the confines of a small river, the chances of a trout being eaten by a shag may have more to do with luck than the health and speed of the fish.

In many New Zealand rivers trout populations are kept well below carrying capacity by regular floods, so I cannot see how additional losses to predators can benefit the trout population. The argument only makes sense where trout reach such high densities that their growth could be stunted owing to shortage of food. Then, predators such as shags (and anglers) may harvest the population without reducing the stock; the harvested fish are simply replaced by others that, because of limited living space and food, would have died anyway.

There is also the argument that shags do not prey so heavily on trout, concentrating more on small native fish such as bullies and smelt. In fact, research shows that black shags are opportunistic predators – they take whatever they can get – and sometimes trout form a large part of their diet. A 1945 study carried out for the New Zealand Acclimatisation Society Association found 15,805 trout in 2,883 shag stomachs – a little more than five per shag.

Another infamous predator of trout is the eel. There are two common species in New Zealand waters: shortfin and longfin. The latter is the main predator of trout, and penetrates further inland into most rivers and lakes supporting trout, unless prevented by barriers to upstream migration such as large dams. Trout up to almost two kilograms have been reported from the stomachs of very large eels. I have seen one grasping a yearling trout in its jaws, and I have twice encountered large longfin eels harassing trout that I, or my fishing buddy, was trying to land, apparently attracted by distress chemicals or vibrations from the struggling trout.

As with shags, eels also have been the subject of concerted campaigns of destruction by the acclimatisation societies in years gone by. In more recent years, commercial fishing has caused a dramatic decline in the numbers of large eels in waterways throughout New Zealand.

Despite their proven appetite for trout, I have a soft spot for eels. New Zealand's rivers and lakes would be the poorer for their absence. Eels impart a mystery to deep, dark water and undercut

The heron is one of several birds that prey on young trout.

The longfin eel is a significant trout predator.
Rowan Strickland

banks. They provide an endless supply of humorous and hair-raising anecdotes, and a storehouse of childhood memories of slimy leviathans squirming on the banks of creeks and streams.

I HAVE FREQUENTLY witnessed eels showing aggressive interest in trout that were being played and landed by anglers. Whether this is a chemical or physical attraction I am not certain, but it may be chemical, as the following story illustrates.

As a lad I learnt the skills of spin and bait fishing from my father. As I approached the teenage years it became a challenge to catch more fish, occasionally at least, than my teacher.

One day Dad and I were fishing the Oreti River, between Winton and Mossburn. I had been lucky enough to land the first fish and it lay secure in my bag. My father was working the water some distance away, within shouting distance but far enough ahead that he could not see every detail of what I was doing.

The urge to emphasise my one–nil advantage became too great. I discreetly took the dead trout from my bag and attached it to my line once more. When my father's head was turned I heaved the fish back into the water then proceeded to 'play' it with enthusiasm, shouting loudly in my father's direction, 'Got another one!' – with emphasis on 'another'.

My father's eyes swung my way. He nodded his approval, then continued his pursuit. Content that the deceit had been successful, I turned my attention back to the trout. However, satisfaction soon turned to despair because, as I began to retrieve it, a huge eel emerged from nearby deep water and clamped its jaws around my trout's body. A brief tug-of-war ensued and the hook pulled free. This was a cruel blow to a young lad, particularly one who valued catching trout so highly. I remember the feeling of helplessness as the eel disappeared with my fish. The day's competition was lost at that point.

TROUT ALSO EAT their own kind. Large browns are often said to be 'cannibals', but I doubt that many specialise in this behaviour; most simply take the opportunity when an easy meal swims by. It may in fact be yearling fish that present the greatest threat to new season's fish. This is because yearlings often occur in large numbers in shallow water near where the fry live. Large trout spend most of their time in deeper water but may invade the shallows, where they can prey on fry at night.

Severe floods scour eggs from the stream bed and can deposit silt in the spawning gravels, thereby smothering eggs. Floods also sweep away the aquatic invertebrates that trout feed on, and this has been shown to lower growth rate of the trout. Recently emerged trout fry are particularly vulnerable to being swept downstream by high flows, and floods may wash them out to sea or strand them as the waters recede. Fry and larger trout may also be injured by rubble and flood debris moving along the river bed.

Anglers frequently report poor fishing after severe flood years, and it can take a surprisingly long time to recover. In Allen's study of the Horokiwi Stream, severe floods during the 1941 spawning depressed angling for four years. A trout population would take even longer to recover from successive bad spawning years if floods hit a river two or more winters in succession.

This suggests perhaps the impact of angling on the numbers of adults should be considered, as it may impair the speed of population recovery during good years. Especially in small flood-prone rivers it may help if anglers returned more of the adult trout that they catch.

A cannibal brown trout from the Hollyford River.
John Hayes

The rigours of spawning cause many trout to die. Rainbows in particular lose condition once they begin spawning. About a third of the rainbows in Lake Rotorua die after spawning each year. More males die than females. Although the female loses more body weight during spawning, mainly through producing eggs, the male draws even more heavily on his energy reserves. Males also have higher levels of stress hormones, which makes them more prone to disease and illness.

Trout can produce impressive numbers of young if spawning conditions are favourable. But how many are left by the time the trout grow large enough to interest an angler? K. Radway Allen answered this question elegantly in his study of the Horokiwi Stream. A 1.1-kilogram trout might lay 1,100 eggs and, in good spawning gravel, these might give rise to about a thousand fry. Of these, perhaps only two legal-sized fish – twenty-five centimetres (0.35 kilogram) – would remain after two years, and at two and a half years only one may be left, weighing about 0.45 kilogram (see page 32).

The trout in the Horokiwi during Allen's study grew to about twenty-five centimetres in two years, and a maximum of forty centimetres in four years. In better waters, where trout grow faster, they reach legal size at an earlier age (say, one and a half years), so more trout are available to be caught. Nevertheless, it is a pretty sobering thought that for every legal-sized trout landed on the bank, at least 300 more have already died. Thinking of trout populations in this manner is helpful for understanding what happens over the long haul, but does not mean that numbers are constant from year to

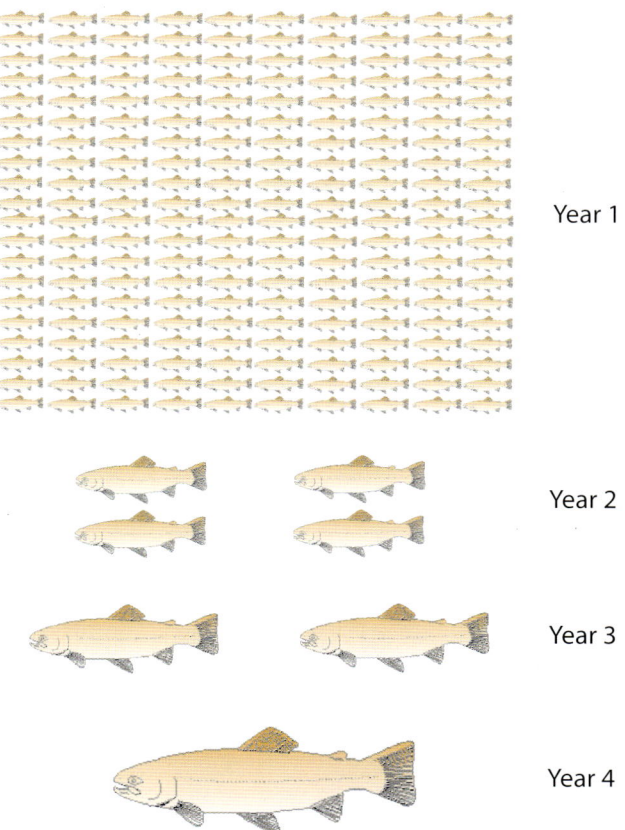

The sieve of natural mortality: numbers of trout surviving from an initial population of 200 fry.

year. As we have already seen, year-class failures owing to flooding at the egg and fry stages can produce gaps in the age structure of a trout population. On the other hand, good egg incubation and fry-rearing conditions can see strong year-classes provide pulses of exceptional fishing as the fish reach takable size and grow through to maturity in subsequent years. Even in lakes numbers can vary greatly from year to year.

How long do trout live?

In New Zealand, few trout live longer than about ten years. Brown trout tend to live longer than rainbows, probably because they recover better from spawning. Few rainbows live longer than six years, although one I examined from the upper Rangitikei River was eleven years old. Rainbows from this river are renowned for their large size, and it appears that longevity contributes to this.

Unlike rainbows, brown trout regularly live for six years or more. I have recorded brown trout up to fifteen years old in back-country rivers. In one remote wilderness river that a colleague and I studied,

60 per cent of trout caught by anglers were older than seven years. This contrasts with the age structure of trout in back-country rivers accessible by road, where only a third of the fish were as old as that. In two lowland rivers we studied, where access was easier still, only 2–12 per cent of trout were more than seven years old. In some heavily fished streams in France, brown trout rarely live longer than three years, partly as a result of high angling pressure.

Trout and salmon are known to make growth versus longevity trade-offs. Migrating to food-rich habitats offers the opportunity of fast growth, larger size at maturity and, consequently, more and bigger eggs. However, these advantages are balanced against the high costs of migration, which decrease longevity. This life-history 'strategy' consists of a high reproductive investment over fewer years. Salmon are extreme examples. They 'boom and bust', growing fast in the ocean, spawning once in fresh water, then dying. Residency is the alternative life-history strategy seen in most river trout populations. It may allow greater longevity but reduced growth, maximum size and fewer eggs. The disadvantages of the latter are offset by the greater longevity allowing repeated spawning, year after year.

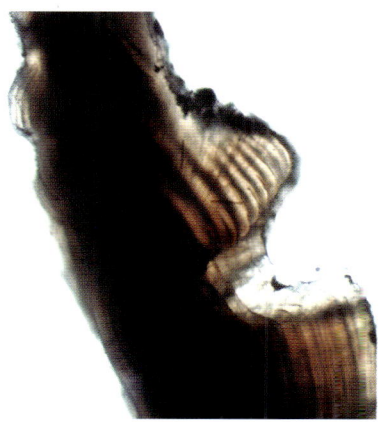

Otolith (earbone), used to determine trout age.

The age of trout can be established from growth rings on their scales and otoliths (earbones). Scales can give reasonable estimates of age for trout up to about five years of age, but then they become unreliable. This happens because the edge of the scale is reabsorbed when trout spawn, which results in erosion of the growth rings laid down in previous years. Otoliths give much more accurate age estimates because these keep laying down growth rings throughout the trout's life and are not reabsorbed at any stage.

The oldest New Zealand trout that I know of, aged from otoliths, were fifteen years. However, brown trout can live much longer than this. For example, two brown trout from a cold lake in Norway were found to be thirty years old. This was a very special circumstance related to slow growth in very cold water.

Age at maturity and frequency of spawning

Most trout begin spawning in their third or fourth year of life, but very fast-growing trout can spawn at age two. Those that first spawn at four years tend to grow bigger because growth slows down once a trout matures.

When plenty of food is available, trout may spawn year after year. However, they may skip spawning in a year when food is scarce. Very old brown trout may stop spawning altogether. This was the conclusion of a study in a North American lake where some huge brown trout were netted from the depths but never appeared in the spawning creeks.

The artful science of trout fishing

Seasonal and size-related movements

When the trout's life cycle is pieced together with an understanding of seasonal and size-related movements, these factors can be used to choose where and when the best fishing might be. Let's start with autumn. This is when mature trout are feeling the urge to spawn, which directs their movements and behaviour. In lakes at this time of year trout will begin congregating off stream mouths and running up into the tributaries. Trout living in rivers may begin moving upstream early, before the end of April. This becomes apparent when big brown trout turn up in pools where there were few good-sized fish during the summer. However, as the main spawning movements of brown trout do not usually begin until May, after the fishing season in most rivers, anglers can not take advantage of this seasonal redistribution of adult trout.

One of the things I like about autumn fishing, especially in lakes, is that the trout are in peak physical condition. This is when you have the best chance of catching a trophy fish, because an extra kilogram of condition can make all the difference.

Autumn can be a time of surprisingly good hatches on some rivers. The first frosts may be accompanied by calm sunny days, ideal for dry-fly fishing, and the sun is still strong enough to warm the water and encourage good hatches.

Winter is for foolhardy or stalwart anglers. This is the time for the annual pilgrimage to the central North Island lake tributaries for fighting rainbows on their upstream journeys to their spawning

Autumn angling close to shore at Lake Alexandrina.

Midwinter fishing can be most enjoyable, particularly with warm afternoon sun on one's back.

grounds. I find that the madding crowds detract from my enjoyment but, if you happen to strike a fresh run of trout, the fishing can be hot.

Some anglers do not realise that rainbows continue spawning until late spring: in fact they are traditionally a spring-spawning fish. You can avoid the early to midwinter crowds on the Lake Taupo tributaries by waiting until closer to spring when there are fewer anglers but still plenty of fish in the rivers. DOC fishery managers are now advertising this fact in order to spread the fishing load on the heavily fished Taupo tributaries.

Try to time your trip to coincide with receding flows following a fresh in the rivers. Floods stimulate ripening fish to run upriver, and you need to be there as the water clears. Just as with salmon fishing, trout take a lure most readily in slightly murky water, and if you can barely see your feet in knee-deep water, you have struck it about right.

Why are trout and salmon easiest to catch on lures when the water is slightly murky? Part of the reason is that more fresh-run fish are about after a flood. Fish that have been in the river a while no doubt see a lot of lures and learn to avoid them, and of course the easy fish have all been caught by then. Drift-dives and trapping in the Tongariro River have shown that during clear conditions, when fishing is slow, there may still be plenty of trout in the pools but they simply are hard to catch. First light is usually the most productive time during these periods.

A drop in temperature combined with a fresh is thought to make the fish more aggressive and more likely to snap at a lure. I also think that in murky conditions fish are more likely to feel at ease in shallower lies, where they are easier to catch. Also, the fish don't get a good look at the lure in murky water. They are less likely to be spooked by the line or hook, and, more importantly, the brief glimpse of movement appears to stimulate them to strike as a reflex action – like a cat chasing a piece of string.

The South Island also offers good winter fishing opportunities for those prepared to brave the cold. The bigger lakes offer winter fishing for brown and rainbow trout, and in some lakes, chinook salmon. Winter fishing is also legal in the lower reaches of some of the larger river systems throughout the South Island.

As spring approaches, brown trout finish spawning and feed around the edges of lakes, packing on condition to replace that lost during spawning. Research has shown that when brown trout leave the spawning tributaries, they disperse along the margins of lakes. Some surprisingly good fishing can be had for these fish in August and September around the margins of lakes that are open to winter fishing. One of my favourite kinds of angling is sight-fishing to trout cruising around lake margins, and even when not fishing I cannot stop myself searching for cruising fish. The Mackenzie Country often enjoys calm weather conditions during winter, ideal for spotting trout. While doing my postgraduate research at Lake Alexandrina I noticed unusually large numbers of brown trout cruising the margins from August onwards, and awaited the opening of the season in November with anticipation. Whether these fish had a sixth sense I cannot say, but by November there was nowhere near the number of browns cruising the lake margins as there had been in the preceding few months.

I often think that spring sees more activity from anglers than it does from the trout. The changeable weather and low water temperatures are still far from optimal for both the trout and their invertebrate foods. For quality fly-fishing I prefer to wait until late November or December. Usually dry-fly fishing is slow until then

Native fish prey. Clockwise from top left: a shoal of inanga, common bully, koaro, common smelt.
Rowan Strickland

– but not always. Good fishing conditions can come early, even in August, in years when settled weather prevails in late winter and spring. In the north, spring and summer are more advanced and spring fishing can be very rewarding.

In spring the larger rivers often are discoloured with snow melt and rain, and spinner and bait are usually the best bets in these conditions. The fly angler should seek out small streams and clear tributaries of the larger river systems, and fish these places with nymphs for brown and rainbow trout 'holding over' after spawning. In fact, while spring fishing generally is a bit slow, this is the best time to fish the smaller tributaries of large river systems before they are fished out (or the flows recede and the streams become too small for large trout). If anglers would show more restraint in taking trout from these waters, good fishing could be stretched out for longer and many more could share the enjoyment of catching the fish. I hope this will improve as catch-and-release wins favour with anglers, and more stringent bag limits are placed on these fragile, seasonal fisheries.

Although invertebrate activity may be somewhat depressed in spring owing to cool water temperatures, small prey fish are active and these provoke the trout into action. Some of the hottest angling action during spring can be expected in the lower reaches of rivers and their estuaries as the whitebait and smelt return from the sea. It is thought that the large freshwater plumes produced by floods attract whitebait, so the best time to find trout feeding on these is just as the river clears, which is when the best whitebait catches are made. The receding floodwaters also provide ideal, slightly murky water conditions for the trout to take lures.

Inanga whitebait stay in the lower reaches of rivers. They provide good feeding for trout throughout the spring and early summer, until their numbers decline. Other species of whitebait, such as koaro, quickly move upstream into small tributaries where they mature, safe from predation by trout.

The mouths of South Island east coast, and some west coast, rivers provide some of the best fishing for sea-run trout, through to early January. Common smelt and Stokell's smelt (also known collectively as silveries) move up into these rivers in prodigious numbers at this time. It is not unusual to see a metre-wide continuous shoal of smelt hugging the gravel banks in the first five hundred metres from the sea. Seagulls, terns, kahawai, trout and immature salmon all gorge themselves on this bounty. Bait anglers use smelt as live bait, bouncing them on weighted spinning gear along the bottom and across the current. Fly anglers, too, have great sport swinging a whitebait or smelt fly (for example, Jack Spratt, Grey Ghost and Hope's Silvery) across the current on a fast-sinking line, especially in the evening on an incoming tide in the steeper rivers with gravel mouths.

You can also expect action as a result of smelt activity during spring along the margins of the central North Island lakes. Smelt in lakes spawn along sandy pumice beaches from spring to early summer, and this coincides with hungry rainbows returning from the spawning tributaries. Small groups of trout may be seen chasing smelt between the shore and the drop-off into deep water. The splashes that they make when attacking smelt are a telltale sign of their presence, and sometimes the direction of their travel. Flies used range from traditional feathered varieties to fully synthetic patterns such as the Silicon Smelt, which is fashioned from silicon rubber. The fly fisher using small smelt imitations can experience really hot action on these fish.

During spring, rainbow trout also offer good fishing in lake tributaries where they hold over from spawning. This applies to larger tributaries of the central North Island lakes and also to those of the Southern Lakes district. Remember, however, that inland lake tributaries usually open later than most other waters (first weekend in November) to allow the fish time to finish spawning.

Many fish are in poor condition at this time and, in my opinion, are wasted if kept for the pot.

Summer is my pick of the angling seasons. Balmy temperatures make for pleasant fishing and the trout and their prey generally are most active, although very high temperatures during the peak of summer can suppress activity. In the lower reaches of rivers down to the mouths, whitebait and smelt continue to sustain feeding frenzies into January. By December most river-resident trout have occupied the habitat where they will remain over the summer growing season. Rainbows that ascend lake tributaries for spawning will continue dropping back into the parent lakes until midsummer.

As spring becomes early summer (late November–December), watch out for evening flights of the brown beetle, the adult of the grass grub. Trout gorge on these, and in many rivers flowing through farmland brown beetles provide the first significant dry-fly fishing of the angling year. They provide decent-sized energy-rich morsels, luring big trout up from deep water and from under cover. As the light fades, otherwise wary big trout become surprisingly bold as they rise for the clumsy beetles buzzing on the water surface. Don't bother arriving on the river until about half an hour before dusk and, as the light fades, expect serious action until about one hour after dark.

As December progresses, water and air temperatures become high enough to encourage aquatic invertebrates to emerge on a regular basis and for terrestrial insects to be on the wing. This means that a lot of surface food is available to trout during the day. Dry-fly fishing now comes into its own. Big brown trout can be seen and heard slurping flies and beetles from the surface around the margins of lakes and under overhanging willows, and they are suckers for dry flies, as are back-country river trout at this time of the year.

Late December sees the appearance of the willow grub, a staple item in the summer diet of trout in rivers with willow-lined banks. The willow grub is the tiny light-yellow larva of a sawfly that is responsible for the red blisters on willow leaves in which it injects its eggs. The larvae grow inside the galls and fall out onto the water surface when they become active on hot summer days. When willow grubs are falling, trout rise freely to them throughout the day on slow, tree-lined sections of lowland rivers. But often they can be difficult to deceive; tying convincing willow grub flies that float is no simple matter.

In January more big terrestrial morsels begin appearing on the water surface. Cicadas can provide top dry-fly action on back-country rivers and lakes from mid-morning until the middle of the

The artful science of trout fishing

afternoon. The green beetle, another favourite of trout, can also be common in late December and January on the the thorny matagouri bushes and manuka. In some years these beetles can literally carpet parts of the surface of lakes. I once saw them so abundant in the lee of a point on Lake Taupo that, at a distance, I mistook the brown and green patches they created for an algal bloom. On closer inspection I found that the beetles were in clusters, trying to climb on each other's backs to get out of the water.

Damselflies are on the wing in large numbers in January, too, and induce characteristic splashing rises from trout in weedy shallows. At this time of year also, a landlocked form of the small native fish koaro (one of the whitebait species) is a key prey for trout in lakes. These little fish begin to shoal in January, and trout, especially rainbows, can be seen leaping and slashing in pursuit of them.

By midsummer trout are becoming more selective and consequently harder to catch, perhaps because they have so much food to choose from and because many have been exposed to

Summer angling – boots and shorts and a crystal-clear West Coast stream.

A buoyant deer-hair 'stimulator' fly – a good choice for prospecting rough water when terrestrial insects such as cicadas become common on back-country rivers in summer.

angling disturbance. High water temperatures also can make trout lethargic, and this brings about their main summer movement, into cooler water. In lakes trout find cold water at depth or off stream mouths. In deep lakes only the surface waters warm up and the trout spend more time in the deeper waters. Deep trolling with wire or lead lines or downriggers (where legal) may be needed to reach these fish.

For the shore angler, stream mouths can be very productive at this time of year, especially in the evening. Lake Rotorua is probably the most famous lake for its stream-mouth fishing in summer. Because the lake is shallow, the trout cannot go deep to avoid warm water so they have only one choice – the cool stream mouths, where they are very accessible to anglers.

Trout in rivers have fewer options. Occasionally, inflowing tributaries may be cooler than the main stream, especially if well shaded or springfed, so the confluence may hold fish. Trout may also be found lying on the bottom of pools during the warmest parts of the day, when they are thermally stressed. This occurs for two reasons. First, if the trout is too warm, its metabolism is overtaxed, its appetite wanes and it stops feeding in favour of seeking cover to rest. Second, in slow-moving pools cooler water sinks to the bottom. Cool groundwater may also flow in from the stream bed. When fish become difficult to find or catch at the height of summer, the best times to catch them are at night, when the water is cooling down, and at dawn, when it is coolest. As the days become longer and warmer with the onset of summer, trout will rise earlier in the morning and go off the feed earlier in the afternoon.

The artful science of trout fishing

KNOWLEDGE OF local seasonal changes in trout movements and feeding behaviour can be used to advantage by the angler. A clear example of this was demonstrated to me on a small Canterbury stream about twenty-five years ago.

During the early part of the fishing season many Canterbury rivers contain migrating whitebait and smelt. The runs are most apparent near to the river mouths and in the lower tidal reaches. October is a good time to fish for the sea-run brown trout that feed on these little fish. Most of the shoals of whitebait and smelt enter the rivers during the highest stage of an incoming tide.

An old angling friend had obviously thought about this quite carefully, then considered how he could catch his share of these trout. His ploy was a simple one. 'The secret to catching these sea-runners,' he said, 'is to use the tides and to get to those fish before anyone else.'

He took me to the lower reaches of his favourite stream. It had a small estuary and a short tidal section – then upstream lay the first pool beyond the reach of the tides. 'This is the place to catch them,' ventured Bill, 'and tomorrow is the day. Full tide tonight is at twelve thirty. A number of trout will come into the river on that tide and get as far as this pool. They'll rest here and be waiting for us at six in the morning. What we have to do is to get here before anyone else.'

In the dawn light, my father, Bill and I stood admiring the promising waters ahead, heartened by the absence of other anglers. The fish sought smelt as food, so that's what we were about to present to them – fresh smelt secured by two small single hooks and weighted by a small cylinder of lead a short distance up the line.

The silvery flanks of a fresh-run trout.

My father went first. Starting at the head of the pool, he pitched the bait into the main flow, slightly upstream, and then waited for it to sink. Once it had reached the river bed he raised his rod tip slightly and took up the slack line. He then had gentle but direct contact with his bait as it drifted along the river bed, swinging in a broad arc. The first drift went uninterrupted, seemingly unnoticed. Dad repeated the cast – still no contact. Following a few more drifts, he shuffled a few metres downstream. He directed his next cast a little closer to the far bank for a longer drift. As his line neared the end of its arc it stopped. Then came the familiar gentle tug-tug.

At this point a novice to this type of fishing would be tempted to strike. That is a mistake. Trout taking drifting fresh bait are usually in no hurry and take after several nibbles. My father waited. Three nibbles, then he struck and a fat silvery trout erupted from the water.

All three of us caught sea-run trout from the pool that morning, success resulting from local knowledge. I believe that some Canterbury salmon anglers use similar logic and pursuit. Likewise, I understand that a run of rainbows can be traced up some Taupo tributaries following a fresh. Some anglers 'leapfrog' their way upstream, hoping to keep abreast of incoming fish.

Throughout the angling year in New Zealand there must be hosts of local seasonal situations that can be, and are, used to advantage by anglers. The key elements in following these are experience, local knowledge and a little native cunning.

CHAPTER THREE

Trophy trout

WHAT CONSTITUTES a trophy trout? In New Zealand the magical ten-pound (four and a half kilograms) mark has traditionally been considered the benchmark for trophy trout. (The 'double-figure' fish has a special significance that makes the use of imperial pounds more appealing in this context than metric kilograms.) However, a smaller fish may qualify as a trophy, depending on the circumstances in which it was caught and on the experience of the angler.

A frequent claim by older anglers is that the fishing is not as good as it used to be, and especially that the trout were much bigger in years gone by. It may come as a surprise to some that this complaint was being made about trout fishing in New Zealand as early as the 1930s. Edward Percival, zoology professor at the University of Canterbury, undertook to study the claimed deterioration of trout fishing in the Oreti River in 1932. He found that, even though the catchment had suffered from deforestation and conversion to farming, the fish were growing as well as before, but that, on average, they were younger. Percival attributed this to increased angling pressure as roading and motorised transport made the waters more accessible. Put simply, anglers had caught many of the old trophy fish and were now catching more of the smaller, younger ones before they had a chance to grow to trophy size. This appears to be a common situation in rivers as they become better known, and most recently it has been witnessed on New Zealand's more remote rivers with the increase in backpacking and the ease of access by helicopter.

High angling pressure can also affect the genetic balance in trout populations. High fishing pressure coupled with a minimum legal size limit theoretically can produce an unnatural selection process in which the faster-growing fish are preferentially killed at an earlier age than slower-growing fish. A study on the intensively fished Au Sable River in Michigan, USA, showed that the predictions of a mathematical model of selective fishing pressure closely matched a decline in the growth rate of brown trout over a twenty-year period. The authors of the study pointed out that there might also be other factors, but selective mortality of faster-growing fish would at least partly explain the decline. The same phenomenon has also been demonstrated in overexploited northern hemisphere commercial sea fisheries.

The premise that selective fishing pressure was the cause of the decline in the size of rainbow trout in the Rotorua lakes led to a selective breeding programme (known as the Big Fish Programme) initiated in the 1980s by Peter Mylechreest, of the former Wildlife Service.

What affects trout growth?

In order to grow big, trout need to grow fast and perhaps also live long. So, to understand why some waters, and some populations, have trophy trout and others don't, we need to understand the factors governing the growth of trout. Growth is not just dependent on how much food is available to trout. Of course food is important; but water temperature is more important still.

Trout are cold-blooded, which means that all of their metabolic and bodily processes are dependent on the temperature of the surrounding water. This includes the rate at which they can digest and metabolise food. In very cold water – say, under 8°C – trout will not grow very fast regardless of how much food is available. Their digestion, appetite and resulting growth are all limited by the cold water. Trout have optimal temperatures for growth. For brown trout feeding on invertebrates it is about 14°C, and for rainbows the optimum is about a degree or so higher and they grow faster at higher temperatures (16–22°C). When brown trout feed on fish prey their thermal optimum for growth is higher, about 17°C. At lower or higher temperatures they grow more slowly.

Over a trout's lifetime, two other factors besides temperature and quantity of food influence growth rate and maximum size. The first is reproduction. Once a trout reaches maturity, up to 50 per cent of its energy intake may be spent on reproduction, and this causes the growth rate to decline sharply. The second is the energy spent on catching prey, known technically as the 'foraging cost'. Consider drift-feeding trout in rivers. The drifting invertebrate prey are mostly small, less than fifteen millimetres in length. To a juvenile trout, each of these represents a decent mouthful, and it only takes a few insects to fill its gut. However, to a large trout, each prey animal gives a smaller return for the effort expended in terms of energy. Large trout feeding on small invertebrates also need to forage for much longer than small trout in order to fill their guts. Consequently, they spend more time swimming to feed and less time resting than small trout. These increasing foraging costs with fish size mean growth rate declines as trout get larger.

The combined effects of reproduction costs and increased foraging costs place a limit on the maximum size that trout can reach in rivers. The graph below shows that here are two ways trout can break through this 'maximum size barrier'. First, they can migrate to food-rich habitats, such as the lower reaches of rivers or the ocean, where they may encounter forage fish prey. Prey fish are larger than invertebrates and richer in energy. If the trout have migrated away from headwaters that were cold enough to slow down their growth rate, they may also now grow faster in the warmer temperatures of the lower river or ocean. However, at lower latitudes (in the north of New Zealand), the ocean and lower river may be warmer than optimal for trout growth, in which case downstream migration is disadvantageous, at least during the warmer months.

Second, trout may attain a larger maximum size by delaying first spawning by a year or two, as already mentioned. Then the energy that would have been spent on reproduction is instead put into growth of body size. The result can be a doubling, or more, of maximum weight. However, this also carries a greater risk that a trout will be eaten by a predator before it has a chance to reproduce.

I have already mentioned the trade-off between growth and longevity. There is also a trade-off between growth and the age at which the fish reaches maturity. There are two life-history options: early spawning, at the expense of large size; and delayed spawning, with attendant larger size and greater egg production. The ultimate measure of the success of these alternative options is the

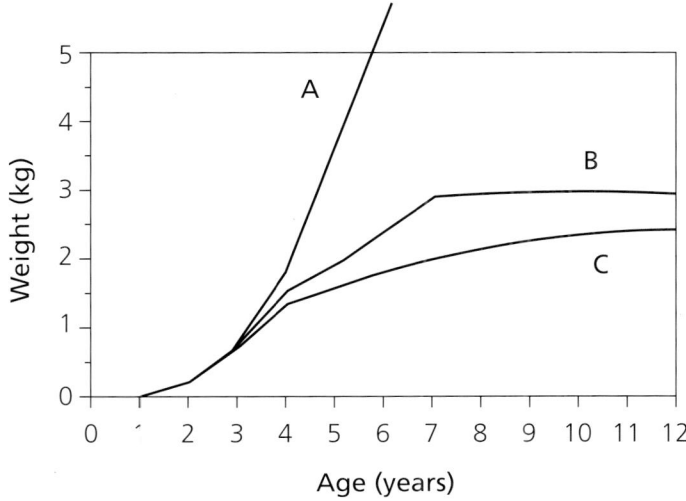

Predicted brown trout growth under various scenarios:
A = No reproduction or foraging costs
B = With reproduction costs
C = With reproduction and drift-foraging costs.

total number of eggs a fish produces in its lifetime. Whichever of the two strategies wins on this measure is the one that will dominate in the population.

Age at first spawning

The age of first spawning in trout can be as early as two years, but generally it is in the third year. Trout that delay spawning until their fourth or even fifth year can grow to a very large size indeed, depending on water temperature, often over the coveted ten-pound mark. The reason for this is that once trout reach maturity most of their spare energy is channelled into reproduction. Trout can devote up to 50 per cent of their energy intake to reproduction – producing eggs, sperm and the physical activity associated with spawning. The graph below shows the effect of delaying maturity by one year for brown trout in a New Zealand back-country river. By not spawning until their fifth year, trout in this river can grow to about 2.4 kilograms, compared with 1.4 kilograms if they spawn in their fourth year of life.

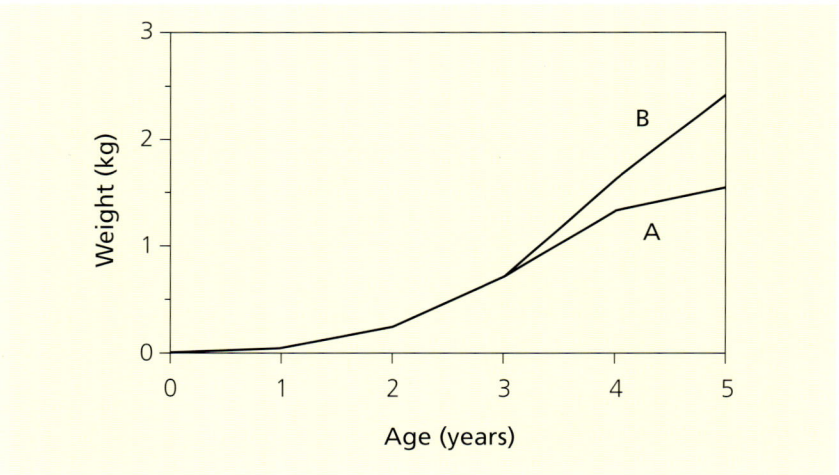

Predicted brown trout growth with reproduction and drift-foraging costs showing the effect of delayed maturity:
A = Trout maturing at age 4; B = Trout maturing at age 5.

Anglers fishing in the Rotorua Lakes district in recent years well know the significance of delayed maturity in producing big rainbow trout. The Big Fish Programme, begun by the Wildlife Service and now being implemented by the Eastern Fish and Game Council, is a selective breeding programme aimed at enhancing the numbers of late-spawning rainbow trout, mainly in Lakes Tarawera, Rotoiti and Okataina. Rainbow trout in the Rotorua lakes grow very rapidly until they spawn, but thereafter they generally grow slowly, if at all. The Big Fish Programme has sought to selectively breed rainbow trout that mature at three years or older, and to increase the proportion of these fish in the gene pool. The programme has received much attention from anglers and appears to be working.

Lake Tarawera had once been famous for producing a lot of trophy rainbows, but by the 1980s these were becoming much rarer. It was found that the trout in the main spawning stream, used as brood stock for the local hatchery, included a relatively high proportion of early-maturing fish, aged two. The selective breeding programme was launched to remedy this situation. Only the largest, and preferably four-year-old trout were used for brood stock. When the programme first started in the early 1980s, 75–85 per cent of the spawning trout matured at three years or older. After twenty years of selective breeding, today 95 per cent of the fish mature at three years or older. The number of double-figure fish caught has increased and the largest fish so far reported is seventeen pounds (7.7 kilograms). However, the success of the programme varies from year to year, depending on annual variations in the productivity of the lake. When productivity is high, the late-maturing fish are big; but when it is low, a late-maturing four-year-old is no bigger than a three-year maturing fish from a high-productivity year. This shows how management intervention can increase the potential of a fishery, but whether that potential is realised still depends on the whim of nature.

Although brown trout do not usually grow as fast as rainbow trout in the early years, they eventually grow larger because they more often continue growing after maturity and live longer. This is the main reason why the largest trophy trout are browns. Browns exceeding ten or even fifteen kilograms have been recorded in New Zealand, but it is very rare indeed to hear of a rainbow exceeding ten kilograms.

Seagoing behaviour

Another reason why the largest trophies have been brown trout is because some of them go to sea and, unlike the rainbow trout in this country, they manage to find their way back to fresh water. Whether or not these seagoing brown trout have formed distinct sea-running stocks in New Zealand is still a matter of debate among scientists, though anglers are more convinced they have. In some rivers in Otago, especially the Pomahaka, each year anglers report runs of large silvery trout believed to be distinct from resident fish and therefore sea-run. The exact nature of these fish, whether strictly sea-run or estuary-dwelling, and whether they are genetically distinct from river residents, is yet to be determined. A general picture that is coming together for the seagoing nature of brown

Trophy rainbow trout are used as breeding stock for the Rotorua Lakes Big Fish Programme. Some of the fish are obtained by trapping one of the spawning streams, and others are donated by anglers. While a little worse for wear after being transported to the hatchery, this prime-conditioned male rainbow will pass on its superior genes to the next generation thanks to the Ngongataha hatchery staff.
Fish & Game NZ – Eastern Region

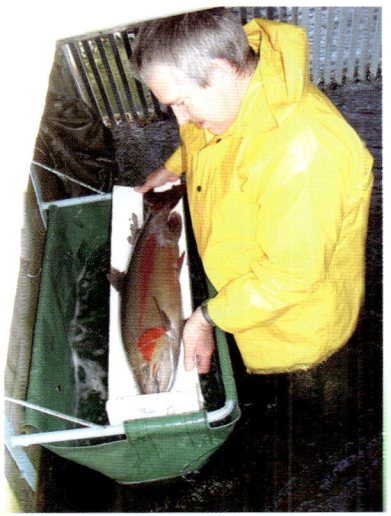

A fish trap on the Te Wairoa Stream plays a key role in Fish and Game's monitoring of rainbow trout in Lake Tarawera. The biggest and best trout are selected and their size and age monitored to gauge the success of the Big Fish Programme.
Mark Sherburn

The artful science of trout fishing

trout throughout the country is that it is highly variable. A proportion of fish, possibly small, may go to sea from any river system at any stage in their life for a variable period of time. Some of them may not go to sea at all but simply feed around the river mouth or estuary. One thing is certain: while at sea or in the estuary they grow extremely fast. Some seagoing or estuarine brown trout reach impressive sizes: fish over eleven kilograms have been taken from the Oreti River in Southland.

Trout and salmon living at higher latitudes are more inclined to go to sea than those at lower latitudes. This is because in colder climes the fish forsake the cold rivers for the relatively warm ocean and its greater food resources. Much of the best sea-run brown trout fishing is to be had in New Zealand's most southern rivers such as the Oreti.

What motivates trout to migrate to sea is hard to ascertain because they can't tell us. However, some form of migration at some stage in the life cycle is a common feature in salmonid populations. It can be thought of as occurring in response to some shortage of a resource necessary for survival. For example, juvenile trout outgrow the small nursery streams they occupy as fry and need to find deeper, faster water with sufficient space, cover and food. Depending upon the availability of these resources, the trout may need to

Accomplished fishing guide Peter Fordham with a big rainbow trout from the upper Rangitikei River, which is renowned for its trophy potential.
Roger Young

migrate to the deeper, lower reaches of rivers, to lakes or even the ocean. Many of the rivers on the east coast of the South Island suffer from periodic summer droughts, and the snow-fed, braided rivers are flood-prone and fairly lean trout habitats. It may be more than coincidental that some of the best sea-run brown trout fisheries in the country occur along this part of the coastline. Perhaps trout from these rivers escape the seasonally unfavourable freshwater habitat by taking refuge in the ocean?

Why don't rainbows in New Zealand do this also? This has long puzzled scientists and Fish and Game managers alike. Perhaps the answer lies in the fact that, in their native range, steelheads (from which our rainbows are descended) make extensive offshore migrations. Oregon, Washington and British Columbian steelhead commonly occur in Alaskan waters and around the Aleutian Islands, and are occasionally caught as far away as Japan. Since these fish are programmed to follow long migration routes, it is thought that they may become lost in the foreign ocean currents off New Zealand. (The same argument has been used to explain why sea-run Atlantic and sockeye salmon have failed to become established in this country, despite intensive stocking efforts.) In contrast, sea-going brown trout in New Zealand appear to stay close to the coast and often move between catchments. They are frequently caught in gill nets set by commercial fishermen along the coast, and tag returns tell of some surprising journeys from one catchment to another. The trout tagged in the Selwyn and caught again five hundred kilometres away in the Matuara has already been mentioned. Another brown trout tagged in the Manganui-a-te-Ao (a tributary of the Whanganui) was subsequently caught in the Kaupokanui River in Taranaki, and had travelled at least 230 kilometres.

Trout fishers enjoy their sport for subtly different reasons. Some like catching a lot of fish; others are satisfied with just one. Many fishermen would rank being in the open spaces as their priority. No matter what an angler enjoys most, I'm sure that all have at one time harboured the hope that the next fish would be the big one.

The association of large trout with estuaries and lakes has been mentioned above. Large fish require much space and food. Lakes and estuaries usually provide both. Less has been written about trophy trout in rivers, and even less is understood.

During my forty-nine years' angling the number of river trophies I've encountered has steadily grown. While I still comprehend little about their behaviour, habits and movements, I have been able to piece together some traits that have been common to those I've seen caught.

Before the 1980s, low angling pressure partly explained why some fish, particularly in remote areas, reached trophy size. But now there are few rivers that are not fished at least once every two weeks. Hence most fish no longer have the same opportunity to live such long lives.

Despite the growing fishing pressure, some rivers still frequently produce very large trout – and some, seemingly similar in character, do not. I have no explanation for this. It just appears so. Those rivers that produce trophy fish, in my observation, have all been major waterways or had close contact with major waterways. Trophy-bearing pools have all been quite substantial and very stable on at least one bank. Generally one bank has been bedrock with the river bed beyond sight under a great depth of water. These pools are the ones that continue to exist every year, despite a sometimes drastically changing river bed both upstream and below. I have noted too that where I've encountered very large trout, fish numbers have been low. Usually the monster was the only fish visible in the pool or, if there was another there, it always kept a distance away. This suggests that these fish command relatively large territories. Within their space, trophy trout rarely remain in one particular place for long periods while feeding. Instead, they range about their pool, not on the surface but at a depth from which they can survey widely above.

Large trout can be very selective feeders. They would not have reached their proportions without this trait. Most often they do not feed from the surface. They are easily scared too – but when they are disturbed I've not seen the mad dash for cover displayed by small fish. What I have noted is more a subtle change, from fluid movement and constant inspection of all around, to a more stilted progress and a gradual shrinking from sight.

An apparent contradiction about the trophy trout I've encountered is that none of them has appeared particularly big when spotted, while all of the fish that give the impression of being huge have proved to be smaller than expected. Trout have to be long, deep and broad across the shoulders to be very heavy. Length can sometimes be estimated, but the other dimensions are not clear until a fish lies on its side on a bank or hoisted proudly in a net.

Really large trout display some common behaviours when hooked. One I caught several seasons ago showed them all in its bid for freedom. I figured it for a two-kilogram fish. It fed in mid-stream, hugging the bed in just over a metre of water. It accepted nymphs left and right but never lifted. The far bank, solid rock, rose ten metres

The fish

above the river. A grove of beech trees clung precariously atop that. Such a tall backdrop allowed good visibility into the pool, while the bank at its base provided a haven for trout when needed. This trout would soon verify that.

Most often when I fish to a trout in about a metre of water I use a weighted nymph below a dry-fly indicator. The situation here was ideal for the rig, particularly as the water flowed fast with a ripply surface reflecting the bouldery bed below. But I remember electing to try a nymph alone, probably because my view of the fish was so clear. The first of many nymphs cast to that fish was a Pheasant Tail. The fish ducked to the side. I waited, then struck. The fast water must have carried my nymph well clear of the fish by the time my strike pulled it skywards. The fish did not notice. I must admit my success in eventually hooking the fish was not entirely deserved. I had struck probably five times before the fish actually took. Yet, in retrospect, the eventual take of the artificial fly was quite distinct, different from the

Potential trophy water with deep, coarse-bedded stable pools that might hold small numbers of large trout.

A well-conditioned jack deserving of trophy status.

interception of naturals. My nymph was taken by a lifting trout, and as the fish took, it rolled slightly.

Then the big-fish character showed. The initial run, upstream and across to the base of the cliff, revealed awesome power. Had I tried to hold the fish even slightly the battle would have ended abruptly with a broken tippet. With line disappearing fast from my reel, I sped headlong into the river, hoisting arms and rod skywards. I had to extract as much line from the water as possible. Often an angler's nylon tippet is broken not by the weight of the fish but by the force of water on excessive lengths of trailing line. Once the fish had reached the depths its tactics changed. It remained right on the bed and against the far bank, and eased first upstream to the head of the pool then turned to nudge its way back downstream towards the tail of the pool. This was a time requiring the utmost patience.

As the fish moved upstream the line became as tight as a bow-string, cleaving the water, vibrating, almost singing. I could feel the fish bumping the river bed, rubbing its jaws. Each return downstream became a relief with less line tension. It was at this time that I tried to ease the fish up from the bottom. For fifteen minutes I failed. Even when I did begin to gain control, any progress was soon lost. But gradually, ever so gradually, the fish began to tire. That estimated two kilograms became two and a half or more. Ten minutes later it was three or four.

The net that I use has a reasonably long handle, which allows me to reach a little further and sometimes land fish more quickly. When the moment came I leaned far out into the river, then eased the tension on the fish so it would drift back tail-first into the net. Then I lifted. The mouth of the net emerged and the fish rose to the surface, but, despite a mighty effort, I could not lift its bulk clear. Instead I dragged it across the surface to the water's edge, then got a closer grip. Up onto the sand came the fish, docile now, gasping for air. A five-kilogram jack, long, deep and very thick.

Earlier I mentioned that large fish do not flee like their smaller offspring when scared. They don't always exhibit the same control when being returned to the river – or at least this one didn't. As soon as it touched the water it leapt violently then disappeared behind an impressive jet of water. I was left to wipe the spray from my Polaroids, contemplating the only fish of the day.

CHAPTER FOUR

Senses

TROUT ARE ESSENTIALLY visual predators. Their eyes are complex and well developed, and they have very large ocular regions in their brain. The eye of a trout has general features in common with ours. Light enters through the pupil (hole in the iris), then passes through a lens that focuses the image on to the retina, the actual light-sensitive surface, at the back of the eyeball. However, there are differences. The human eye focuses different distances by changing the shape of the flattened lens. The trout's lens, however, is permanently round and causes a degree of short-sightedness. The trout eye focuses by moving the lens closer to or further from the retina. It also has a special feature enabling it to focus on near and far objects at the same time. It gains a sort of bifocal vision by reading separate images on separate parts of the retina at the same time. The significance of this is that when a trout is staring intently at the angler's fly only centimetres from its nose it may simultaneously be able to look at the angler.

Trout have a very wide angle of vision. Apart from a small blind spot immediately behind them, trout can scan an arc of almost 180° along each side of their bodies (see page 58). There is a region of overlap seen by both eyes directly in front of the snout, giving binocular vision and thus some depth perception for capturing prey.

Trout also have good visual acuity, which is to say they have sharp eyes. They can see in detail provided they have plenty of time to examine their prey. As evidence of this fact, consider the small size of the invertebrates that trout sometimes eat: often just two to three millimetres long. So keen is its eyesight that a trout will select a size 18 fly after having just rejected a size 16; or a subtle change of fly colour will initiate a take. The time and effort that fly tiers put into their art demonstrates their appreciation of this.

Trout are particularly sensitive to movement – by prey or predator. At a distance, objects without a lot of contrast blend into the background, but as soon as they move they become visible. Trout rely on movement to spot their prey from a distance. If the trout is hungry, the movement initiates an attack response, during which the prey becomes the single focus of the trout's attention.

The artful science of trout fishing

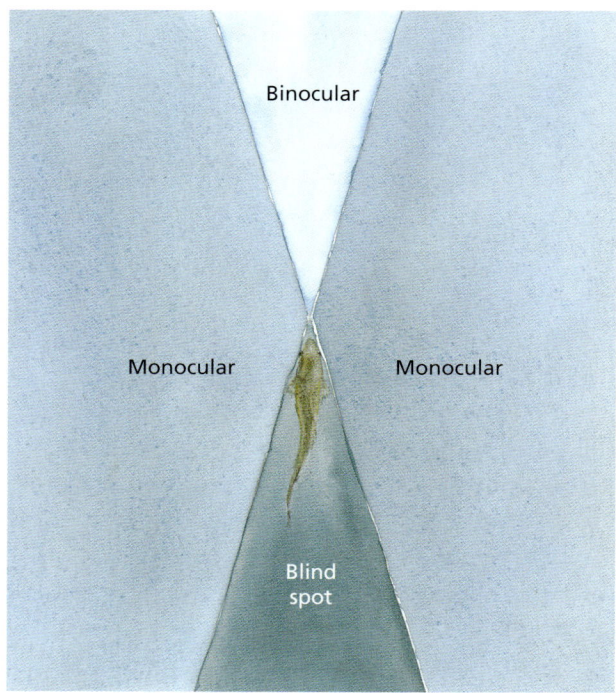

Trout have a very wide field of view, which extends around their bodies almost to their tails.

The window

Much has been written about the trout's 'window' into the world of air, and how the refractive properties of water affect what trout can see above the surface. The window, known technically as the Snell circle, refers to the visual field that the trout has of the terrestrial world above. If the water surface is calm, trout can see into our world – but not throughout the entire hemisphere of their vision. The diffraction of light as it enters the water restricts the visual field to a circle, or cone, extending only 97° from the fish rather than the full 180°. Objects seen near the edge of the Snell circle are greatly distorted. Beyond the circle the trout sees only black and silver; black because incident light reaching the water surface at more than 97° is reflected back into the air, and silver because in some situations the water surface acts as a mirror reflecting light already beneath the surface toward the trout. This mirror is very important because trout can see prey reflected in it, including prey that are obscured from their direct field of view by weed or other cover.

The diffraction of light makes objects appear much closer to the vertical than would be the case if they were viewed directly in air or water Similar examples abound in books on trout angling, and an experienced angler is inclined to skip over them. But a few years ago I had an illuminating experience while drift diving. I was

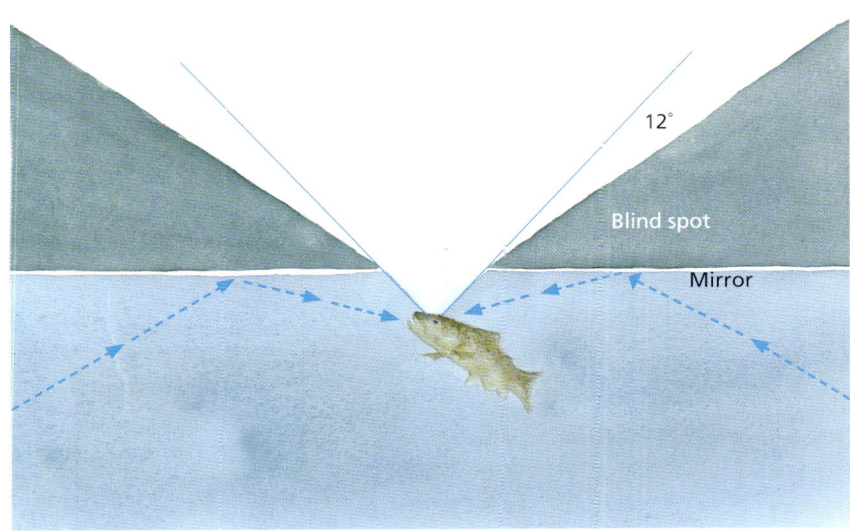

The trout's window of vision above the surface is enhanced by refraction of light (by 12°). Beyond the circumference of the window trout can see underwater prey reflected in the surface mirror.

finning through a long still pool bordered by willows. The glassy water surface provided an ideal opportunity to examine the view of the bank from the trout's perspective. So I took a visual reference on a willow trunk about head height and ten metres away. I carefully sank beneath the surface, turned on my back and looked up into the 'window'. I was not ready for what I saw. The willow tree seemed immediately above me and the lower two metres of the trunk that had served as a visual reference, in place of an angler, was also very prominent and only a few degrees to one side. It is no wonder that trout take so readily to fright when an angler peers over the bank. To the trout, the angler appears to be almost on top of him! A wildly flailing fly rod must be a particularly disturbing spectacle in the same situation. The above lesson emphasises how important it is to keep a very low profile when stalking trout and also to keep the rod low and false casts to a minimum.

On the same dive I was also conscious of the mirror effect. Beyond the Snell circle I could see every boulder and cobble reflected in the silver sheen of the water's surface. It was not difficult to imagine a keen-eyed trout picking up the tell-tale movements of otherwise concealed prey in this giant mirror.

Underwater vision
The first time one dons mask and snorkel and enters the world of trout, it comes as quite a surprise that underwater visibility is surprisingly limited. This is because water, particularly in rivers, has in suspension many particles that scatter and absorb light. To

Drift divers counting trout. It is often surprising how limited the underwater visibility is even when the water appears clear from the river bank.
Cawthron Institute

Good undercut-log cover for trout – a typical hiding place in which drift divers find big trout.
Darryl Torckler

the angler on the bank, a river might appear 'gin clear' with every stone on the bottom visible, yet under water it may be impossible to see objects more than five metres away, and in many rivers the underwater visibility is much less. The fact that trout are somewhat short-sighted now makes sense: long-range vision is unnecessary under water.

The scattering of light under water is significant with respect to light and shade. Brown trout in particular like to sit under banks and debris near the river bottom, and the obvious reason is that they are hiding, but there may be more to it than that. In bright sunshine, underwater vision can be severely impaired by light scattering. On dive surveys to count trout, it is common practice to search the sunlit water from the shade of a bank. Once out of the shade in the sunlight, the intense scattering of light can essentially blind the diver. Trout may be even more blinded in these conditions because their pupils are not adjustable like ours and they can not control the amount of light entering their eyes. But a trout lurking in the shade of the bank has the best of both worlds. It can see prey and predators in the sunlit water beyond the bank, but remain unseen by them.

These light and shade effects are worth keeping in mind when presenting a fly or lure to trout. A trout sitting in sunlit water cannot see into nearby water that is shaded, so is unlikely to see a fly presented there. Similarly, it cannot see well on the side facing the sun.

Another important issue is the difference between calm and rough surface conditions. In calm conditions, particularly in lakes, trout can be especially difficult to catch. But if a breeze springs up and roughens the water surface, the fish may suddenly come on the take. I have often wondered why this should be so. Some angling commentators point to the fact that in calm conditions the trout can see all too clearly what is going on above the surface and are easily scared by movement, rod flash, and by the fly line or its shadow. One suggestion is that the fly line breaks the surface mirror as it falls on the surface, thus startling the fish. I have no doubt all of these ideas have merit, but I would like to add another insight, again stimulated from underwater observations. In calm conditions trout may see the fly or spinner too clearly and recognise it for the deception that it is. However, when the water surface is roughened something interesting happens under water. Suddenly, dappled patterns of light appear to be dancing, breaking up the outline of objects and generally creating a confusing effect. I suspect that in these conditions trout don't get nearly as good a look at their prey as they do in calm conditions. The dancing light would have the effect of making small fish and other prey disappear then reappear, and may cause the trout to strike out of reflex.

Colour vision
There is no doubt that trout have colour vision. Scientists have found that trout possess both types of light-receptive cells (rods and cones) in their retinas. These are the same types of light-sensitive cells that we have. The density of rod cells governs the intensity of light that can be detected, while the cone cells are for colour vision.

What colours do trout prefer? Research presenting rainbow trout with dyed trout eggs has shown that they have keen colour discrimination and distinct preferences for particular colours in particular environmental settings. The order of colour preference in daylight was blue, red, black, orange, brown, yellow and green when viewed against a pale greenish-blue background. This order largely was related to contrast with the background colour. Particular colour combinations such as yellow and black, and yellow and blue, were even more highly preferred. At low light intensities the order of preference was yellow, red, blue and black. Red is a popular colour for trout flies and lures, and this is borne out to

The artful science of trout fishing

some extent by the above results. It stands to reason that trout, and other salmonids, must respond keenly to red because it so commonly occurs as a body coloration in these fishes, particularly around spawning time.

The aspects of colour vision so far mentioned mainly apply to shallow water. There are special considerations when it comes to deep lakes. With increasing depth, the longer wavelengths of light – red light – are absorbed by water. Blue and green light are absorbed the least. The more turbid the water, the more the light is absorbed. Even in very clear water most of the red light is gone at depths of six to nine metres. This has important implications for what colour of lure to use. At depth, a red lure appears black to the trout. A green or blue lure retains its colour but is difficult to see because it blends in with the blue/green of the surrounding water.

It is worth noting that orange and yellow, which have wavelengths at the middle of the spectrum, can be seen to depths of nine metres and more. These colours, therefore, may be better choices than red for a lure fished in deep water, or at dusk and dawn, especially when matched with contrasting colours.

In really deep water, colour becomes less significant because the light intensity is so low. In the dim light at depth (and, in shallower water, at dusk and dawn), the silhouette of the prey against the surface lighting is what the trout detects. Brown trout can see better than rainbows in dim light conditions and in turbid water. In fact, of all the salmonids, brown trout are thought to have the best vision at night. This helps explain why 'lunker' browns are caught so often at night, and maybe why brown trout (but hardly ever rainbows) survive happily in the turbid lower reaches of some rivers.

Camouflage

Another aspect of light is its effect on colour changes in trout. Both brown and rainbow trout are counter-shaded (dark on top and light underneath) so they can blend in with the bottom when viewed from above and with the pale, silver surface when viewed from below. Brown trout in particular can impressively match the shading and pattern of their background, and change their shading in a matter of minutes. This can be demonstrated by placing a trout in a white bucket: after a few minutes it turns very pale to match the background, but place a lid on the bucket and the trout soon turns dark. Pigment cells in the skin, called chromatophores, are responsible for these colour changes. There are a variety of chromatophores distributed in different places on the trout's body, and each has different coloured pigments. These cells can disperse

Brown trout are masters of camouflage. This one blends almost seamlessly with the river bottom, and the dappled, dancing light further serves to break up its outline.

Darryl Torckler

and aggregate the pigment. Dispersing the pigment colours the surrounding skin, while aggregation of the pigment causes the colour to fade.

The action of the chromatophores is under both nervous and hormonal control. The nervous system is responsible for rapid changes in shading, and to a lesser extent in colour. The eyes detect the surrounding light conditions, and messages are relayed via the nervous system to the chromatophores, to disperse or to aggregate the pigment. The fact that blind trout always are darkly coloured demonstrates that light acting through the sense of sight controls the shading response. Hormones control longer and more pronounced changes in colour. Trout gradually acquire the hues of their surroundings by the action of hormones affecting the type and quantity of pigments in their chromatophores. In this manner trout can take on a limited range of colours to match their background. For brown trout, these tend to be various shades of gold, brown and green. I recall catching a couple of Lake Brunner browns that were particularly difficult to spot as they glided in peat-stained water over weed beds on the edge of a kahikatea swamp. When landed, these fish had a weird golden-green coloration, the like of which I had never come across before.

BEHAVIOUR WHEN APPROACHING trout is as important as the fishing method used because, whatever the procedure, pursuit is futile once a trout has been scared. This is less of an issue for spin fishers, wet-fly, lure and bait fishers because they generally fish long casts and deep water.

Dry-fly and shallow-water nymph exponents, however, must be most discreet. On river banks and lake shores they should avail themselves of all possible cover. Obstacles in front of an angler are best, but a body close to rear cover (assuming that movement is minimal) may be well concealed too. Fishing rods should be held low when not in use, and the angler should keep a low profile. Anglers who fish in close to their quarry should wear clothing that blends with the surroundings – army-style camouflage clothing is suitable for most situations.

If a trout lies to the right of the sun, an angler should cast a fly or nymph to the trout's right, avoiding shadow crossing the fish. Shadows are longer early and late in the day.

Many fly fishers contend that the way in which a fly is presented is just as important as the type being used. This means that an angler not only must place the fly on the water very gently, but must also think carefully about where to place it. When considering light

The artful science of trout fishing

A suitably attired angler wearing dull-coloured clothing. A hat shades his eyes, and his body is protected from sun and sandflies.

in this respect an angler should note that when a trout views a fly floating between itself and the sun, it is less able to see colour or detail beyond shape. A fly placed on the opposite side, though, will exhibit even subtle tones and much texture.

There are endless ways in which anglers unwittingly reveal themselves to trout. It would be impossible to identify them all, but the following list may alert some readers and provoke thought in others.

- Use dull-coloured and matt-finished rods and avoid highly reflective reels (dull green and black are favoured).
- Avoid flashing silvery watches and watch straps, and note that most fly and lure boxes are shiny.
- Be aware that a trout deep in the water can see wider above than a trout close to the surface.
- Always wear a hat that shades your face.
- Be conscious of how visible your clothing is: white, yellow and red should be avoided. Remember that the clearer and more placid the water, the more easily a fish can see you and the more discerning it will be.
- Avoid moving bank-side vegetation.
- Probably the most important tip of all is move slowly. It is movement on the bank more than anything else that will warn trout of your presence.

TROUT ARE SENSITIVE to two types of sound: normal sound waves and very low-frequency vibrations. One type can be heard, while the other is felt. Sound travels extremely well in water, five times faster and further than in air. Trout probably don't hear normal above-surface sound very well, because 99.9 per cent is reflected off the water surface. However, above-surface sound is transmitted easily through solid objects in contact with the water, such as the bank or the bottom of a boat.

Trout hear normal sound by means of their inner ear, or membranous labyrinth, which is also an organ of equilibrium. This is a system of fluid-filled canals and chambers in the trout's skull immediately below the brain. Suspended inside the chambers are three pairs of otoliths, which are calcareous concretions. Sound vibrations cause the otoliths to move, the movement is detected on fine sensory hairs projecting out from the chamber walls, and these send nerve impulses to the auditory part of the brain. The position of the otoliths in the chambers also tells the fish which way up it is.

Trout sense low-frequency vibrations by means of their lateral line system. The lateral line can easily be seen running along the middle of each side of the trout's body. It houses a series of pores and sensory structures that detect pressure changes such as are caused by the swimming movement of the fish and pressure from nearby objects such as rocks, the water surface and other fish. It is thought that fish maintain their position in schools by detecting the pressure wakes of the other fish around them. The distress vibrations made by injured fish are also detected by the lateral line and bring about an immediate attack response from predatory fish, including trout.

I cringe when I hear noisy anglers in boats particularly in aluminium dinghies. One thing that underwater and stream-tank observations of trout have taught me is that sharp, loud noises bring about an immediate flight response in trout. For example, juvenile trout can be surprisingly undeterred by a diver's presence, but clap two rocks together under water and the whole school darts off in panic. Given this fact, clumsy practices such as dropping fishing gear and oars in the bottom of boats and hurling anchors overboard with a resounding splash should be avoided at all costs. In boisterous rivers, noises made by anglers probably are not so significant

A bouldery stream where a careless angler could easily knock stones together and alarm fish.

in relation to the background noise of turbulent water and moving stones. Nevertheless, it is good practice to avoid heavy footfalls and dislodging rocks while wading, particularly in quieter waters.

My friends and I like to stalk trout in a leisurely manner by drifting around a lake edge in an inflatable boat and casting from the platform it provides. On one such occasion a broad swamp fringed the West Coast lake that we were fishing and, as we drifted past this edge, we discovered a deep narrow channel draining into the lake. The channel was just wide enough for the boat to negotiate. We eased forward by pulling on overhanging vegetation, and saw four or five trout diving under vegetated banks ahead. Their presence kept us forging on, hoping to find fishable waters. Eventually the channel, dug many years ago, opened to a wider, more natural stream. I jumped ashore. While the bank was clear enough for me to stalk along, a profusion of flax and matagouri overhanging a deep muddy bed suggested that if we did find a trout the boat remained the most hopeful place to cast from.

I crept ahead, with the craft twenty metres downstream. Navigable water was short. I soon approached the first shallows, an inviting, ripply run. If a trout resided in the pool immediately downstream, this was where it would feed. So I signalled for the boat to remain well downstream. The caution proved justified. A large black-backed, dark-flanked trout, matching the tea-coloured waters, lay against the near bank. I watched for a short time. Although the fish did not feed, it appeared alert – poised off the bed and in the flow. I was sure it would take. I was also convinced that few fishermen would have tempted it in the past.

Downstream and well away, the boat rested. 'Come up slowly,' I called. 'There's one here, but you'll need to be much closer to cast.' I turned to watch the fish again. As I did so, a dull clunk came from the boat, as an oar dropped onto the wooden floor. The trout responded instantly. I didn't see it disappear, it moved too quickly. All I observed was a billowing cloud of mud where it had been. Facing the boat once more, I frowned. 'Who dropped the paddle?' 'Not me!' chorused three voices, only too aware of what had happened.

I am aware that many anglers move about in their boats on lakes and still catch trout. Similarly, a trolling boat's noise is considerable, yet fish are caught. Trout are clearly alarmed by some sounds and not by others. I suspect that proximity to shallow water and banks may be important.

Anglers should be aware of other sources of sound that trout may perceive. Spin fishers must be wary of the splash caused by their lure or bait when casting. If the lure lands too close to a fish, it may cause alarm. Fly fishers should be wary each time their line touches the water when casting. A heavily dropped nymph is often detected too. Sometimes this attracts the fish, but more often it achieves the opposite.

Trout detect chemicals in water via the senses of smell and taste. To fish, taste and smell really are just two sides of the same coin. Taste involves detecting chemicals in high concentrations close to the fish. Smell involves detecting low concentrations of chemicals over much greater distances, some associated with food, others with danger and others with orientation.

Trout have a limited sense of taste compared with some other types of fish. Catfish, for example, have taste receptors over much of their body surface. Nevertheless, trout do have the ability to discriminate between pleasant and unpleasant tastes. Some invertebrates are known to be unpleasant to trout and are avoided. These include stink bugs, some other bugs (Hemiptera) and even some species of water boatman.

Although trout are primarily visual feeders, they also have a highly developed sense of smell. Their nostrils (on top of the snout) have two openings to enable the free flow of water over the chemo-receptor cells. These cells are set in a much-folded membrane to maximise the surface area available for sensing chemicals. This very efficient design indicates that trout (and other salmonids) have a well-developed sense of smell. Further evidence for this comes from the remarkable homing ability of both salmon and trout. It is not their sole means of navigation, but when it is time to spawn, salmon and trout rely greatly on smell to find their way, often over thousands of kilometres, to the stream of their birth. Some scientists think that the migrating fish cue in on subtle chemical differences between the stream of their birth and the hundreds of other tributaries they may pass on their journey from the sea. Others suggest that migrating salmon and trout are able to smell the chemical signals released by non-migratory members of their population remaining in the natal stream.

Perhaps more relevant to the angler is the use of smell by trout for detecting food and avoiding danger. Many fish, including trout and salmon, are remarkably sensitive to very faint prey and enemy odours. For example, sockeye salmon are known to be able to detect extract of shrimp at a concentration of only one part in a hundred million parts of water. The chemicals that elicit both feeding and fright responses are amino acids, the building blocks of proteins. An amino acid that is known to cause an alarm response in salmonids is L-serine, and this is present in water that has come into contact with the skin of bears, seals and humans.

A former colleague of mine, Don Jellyman, recounted an interesting observation of trout apparently detecting divers by smell during a drift-dive survey on the Oreti River in Southland. One of the field crew was waiting for the divers to drift down to the end of a survey reach, and began watching some big brown trout feeding in a pool. The fish were observed feeding for some time when suddenly they headed for cover. A few minutes later the divers drifted into view. Most experienced back-country river anglers and guides are keenly aware that trout are disturbed by the scent of anglers upstream. They avoid fishing in a downstream direction and, when they have to do this, they go to great lengths to avoid wading.

The nature of a waterway and how frequently it is fished may have some bearing on the importance of smell in a trout's defence. Streams and lakes in intensively farmed rural areas receive daily chemical inputs from animals in the water, run-off from paddocks, from vehicles and so on. Logically, the odour of an angler in such places will be insignificant. Some streams and lake inlets are visited daily by many anglers who spend hours wading upstream or casting out into the lake from chest-deep water. Their frequent presence, providing a familiar odour, seems to render the signal unimportant. However, where forests replace farmland and rivers run clear and chemical-free, faint odours are quite foreign and therefore immediately significant.

Opening day, on the first weekend of October, is one of the busiest on New Zealand rivers. I always try to choose places that others avoid: where there are few fish and a long walk is involved with as many inhospitable barriers as possible. Usually they are places with sparkling streams. On opening weekend two years ago, Tony Allan and I braved innumerable barriers to escape other anglers. Our chosen stream flowed down the most boulder-strewn bed imaginable. Its banks clothed in second growth sported a mixture of blackberry, supplejack, gorse and bush lawyer. We had to negotiate both river bed and scrub.

Our early-morning goal was to head upstream without fishing, to put distance between possible intruders and us before beginning to stalk our prey. It is easy to conceive plans in Christchurch on a Wednesday night, but with a pack hooked in supplejack and lawyer wrapped around one's neck, one certainly should question the wisdom of

In clear back-country rivers human odour can be a strong enough foreign stimulus to scare trout.

following them up. At ten o'clock we were doing just that. Half an hour later we surrendered the upstream struggle and headed for the nearest pool.

The river bed, being constantly buffeted by floodwaters, was not a stable one. Good pools were few with a great distance between. We greeted each stretch of holding water enthusiastically. The first pool that we approached flowed along the base of a lofty cliff – not a face of solid rock but the remains of an ancient river bed. Water oozed and dripped from the porous structure. Huge boulders and loose rocks lay exposed, ready to tumble down. We were pleased to be on the far bank. Our approach towards the tail of the pool was very cautious, and justifiably so, because there against the near bank hovered not one but two fine trout. Both fed freely. We stepped back a little to prepare our rods far from sight. We'd worked too hard to make foolish errors now.

As we extracted our angling paraphernalia from vests and packs, we continually looked back towards the fish – to verify their presence perhaps, or just to observe? Both of our heads were up at one time.

I'm not sure who saw him first. I know our feelings were the same. About two hundred metres upstream, on the other side of the river, a hunter had emerged from the bush. 'I'll bet the bastard crosses the river to avoid that cliff,' said Tony. He hadn't seen us, and certainly hadn't heard Tony, because into the torrent he plunged. We stood, hands on hips, in dismay.

Our attention now turned to the fish. They fed on. We knew they would for a while. We were out of sight. The hunter was far from view. But the smell of his sweaty legs approached fast. When big trout see an angler they frequently move toward cover quite sedately. But I've noted that fish scared by sound or smell appear much more alarmed. These two were. About two minutes after the hunter had entered the water, the fish dived upstream as one, not to be seen again.

Secure on our side of the river, the hunter eventually saw us and approached for a chat. We hid our disappointment, thinking about more fish further upstream. 'How far down the river have you come?' I asked, knowing that crossings would have been frequent. 'From the bridge,' he replied. Tony and I exchanged forlorn glances. The bridge was about ten kilometres upstream!

There are many situations where anglers should think carefully about their scent in a river. For example, it is common, particularly in remote areas, for anglers to fish in pairs or groups. This works well especially when the group remains as one. But when the party splits up and individuals begin 'leapfrogging' each other upriver, the danger of scent from upstream anglers scaring the fish below becomes very real. Spin fishers often work downstream, covering considerable distances. For these anglers it may prove wise to avoid river crossings or excessive wading.

PART TWO

The habitat

Although New Zealand is a relatively small country, it boasts a remarkable variety of trout waters: from tiny tarns to huge lakes; from creeks to large rivers. Each river is unique and conditions vary from pool to pool.

Few rivers have ideal conditions for trout along most of their length. Those that do, such as the Mataura and Motueka, have high fish counts (per kilometre). Most rivers, however, have some waters harbouring healthy fish numbers, with varying distances between where the waters may hold few fish or be completely barren.

Rivers and streams with a varied distribution of trout are the norm in the South Island high country. East of the Main Divide the barren reaches can be much longer and more extensive than the areas where trout hold regularly. Despite this, I return annually, with friends, to one particular river. The section that we fish involves about a twenty-kilometre return walk for the day, and over a four-year period in the 1990s the fish seen from the bank were twelve (1998), twenty (1997), seventeen (1996) and sixteen (1995). Although the numbers of fish were quite low, their quality was significant and the river surroundings are magnificent.

On this section of the river (as in many places) the fish are predominantly found in the same places – not just in particular pools but in the same feeding lies within those pools. In 1994 my brother Ho landed a fine hen fish from a pool about halfway up the ten-kilometre reach. The fish was memorable because of its very dark (almost black) colour. A year later the same fish (still as black as previously) was caught again and we named the spot Black Lady Pool. In 1996 our black friend lay on station and, again accepting a passing fly, was brought to the net. She was long and broad across the shoulders but lacked a belly. Over the three years she should have grown to top four kilograms but weighed about three each time.

From 1994 to 1996 Black Lady Pool, with one long bouldery shore, yielded several fish each year in addition to the matriarch. This reflected the clear attraction of this section of river, which contrasted markedly with the fish-less kilometre downstream and the long walk upstream to the next reliably productive pool.

When we searched the pool expectantly in 1997 the Black Lady could not be found. While we were saddened by her absence, we were thrilled with her replacement – a fish estimated at six kilograms. The monster was played for about twenty minutes before it took control and sped off downstream towards the next deep water.

Sadly, when we returned to the river in 1998, evidence of El Niño-induced floods was everywhere. Where formerly deep green

Good trout water – clear, cool and well oxygenated. This deep stable pool has plenty of cover for fish.

pools once awaited us there were now mounds of loose gravel strewn with uprooted beech trees. In places the river course had altered, and everywhere the pools were shallower and choked with sediment. It stands to reason that when floods rearrange a river, change its course and fill in pools, there should also be new pools created. But experience tells me that this is not so. The big floods merely destroy and fill. It is during the two or three more normal years following that holes develop and mature.

Even from a distance we could see that Black Lady Pool had changed. It was now shorter, straighter and much shallower. Worst of all, there was only one small fish there. We 'introduced ourselves' then moved on, disappointed that we were not delayed as long as in previous years.

The fish counts mentioned above show that the 1998 sightings were significantly lower than during previous years, and our experience in Black Lady Pool mirrored this. The difference presumably related to changes in habitat, the quality of which had been diminished by floods. This also explains the predictable distribution of trout throughout the ten kilometres of river. The places where fish were regularly found had stable banks, beds of coarse material and deep water nearby – environments providing both food and shelter.

CHAPTER FIVE

General habitat features

THERE IS A BROAD SET of environmental conditions that must be met before a river or lake can support a population of trout. The first, obviously, is that there must be sufficient water, and anglers who fish New Zealand's drought-prone east coast rivers will no doubt relate to this comment. More will be said later about the physical habitat requirements of trout in terms of water depth and velocity.

The water must be of reasonable quality. Water quality means many things. Chemical pollution springs readily to the minds of most anglers, but despite what we hear of pollution in the news media, chemical poisoning of fish is not common in this country. Low dissolved oxygen concentration is a far more common problem. It is associated with organic pollution from sewage, freezing works, dairy factories and pig-farm and cowshed wastes – common discharges throughout New Zealand. However, since the passing of the Resource Management Act in 1991 these sources of pollution have been better controlled than previously. Trout have a high metabolic rate as fish go, and require high dissolved oxygen levels, at least three milligrams per litre (mg/l) of water. Trout will avoid water with less than 5 mg/l if they can. For brown trout, the optimum dissolved oxygen level is at least 9 mg/l below a water temperature of 10°C, and at least 12 mg/l above 10°C. This is higher than for rainbow trout (at least 7 mg/l below 15°C, and at least 9 mg/l above 15°C), and may explain why, in summer, browns become lethargic in the warm northern waters of New Zealand and are not regarded as good fighters.

Three main factors determine how much dissolved oxygen water can carry: temperature, biological oxygen demand (BOD) and chemical oxygen demand. These latter terms refer to how oxygen is used up by microscopic animals and bacteria, and by some chemical reactions in water.

As temperature increases, the oxygen saturation level of water decreases but the oxygen requirements of trout increase. At 1°C the solubility of oxygen is about 14 mg/l, but at 25°C the solubility falls to about 8.4 mg/l. The solubility of oxygen also decreases with altitude: there is a 2 mg/l drop in solubility with every thousand-metre increase in altitude.

Dissolved oxygen can fall to low concentrations near the bottom of lakes (below the thermocline) and in the lower, slow-moving reaches of some rivers, where the absence of riffles and other broken water means there is little aeration taking place. This effect is further compounded in rivers and lakes with high nutrient levels and organic loading. Waterways like this are said to be eutrophic, and their high nutrient levels stimulate algae to grow. By day, the alage produce oxygen, but at night, photosynthesis stops and algae actually use up oxygen (respiration). Microbes that break down organic pollution also use up oxygen – the more organic material, the higher the oxygen demand. The combined oxygen demands of algae, bacteria and other microbes, particularly at night, can deplete oxygen below the level required by trout to survive – especially when the water is warm.

More important to the angler, however, are the sublethal effects that reduced oxygen brings about in trout, as these influence where and how easily the trout will be caught. During warm-summer low flows in rivers, trout can sometimes be found closer to the base of riffles and rapids – possibly because the water is better aerated there, but also, as we will see later, to maximise their drift-feeding rate. In lakes, low oxygen in the deep water may drive trout to the upper levels, concentrating them and influencing where the angler should present the lure. If a trout is confined to water with low oxygen, it can be expected to be lethargic and little interested in feeding.

The fact that oxygen levels affect behaviour and distribution of trout is of little practical use to anglers because we do not carr.y tools to measure it. Temperature is much more relevant and easier to measure. Small thermometers are cheap, easy to carry and can sometimes help you figure out where trout may be found and why they are behaving in a particular manner. Temperature is a key variable affecting aspects of trout physiology, behaviour, distribution and catchability. Research in North America has shown that above 19°C the catch rate declines below levels considered satisfactory by trout anglers. Studies on the temperature preferences and tolerances of trout help explain why this is so.

Brown and rainbow trout can survive over similar ranges of water temperature. Brown trout stop feeding and growing when the temperature exceeds 19°C, while rainbows may continue to feed up to 20–22°C.

Short-term exposure (a few hours) to water temperatures

higher than about 25°C will usually kill trout, unless they can find cool-water refuges. Long-term exposure to lesser temperatures can reduce their survival too, even temperatures that are otherwise suitable for feeding and growth. Mortality increases as water temperature rises above the optimum for growth (14–17°C for brown trout, 16–18°C for rainbow trout). A North American study found that although rainbow trout continued to grow as temperature rose above the growth optimum, the contribution that this made to the population biomass (total weight of all fish) was balanced by losses of fish due to increased mortality once seasonal temperature reached 21–23°C. At this point net population production was zero. A comparable temperature for brown trout is probably 19°C. Stress, increased disease risk and greater activity of fish predators are reasons for the increased mortality with increasing 'sublethal' temperatures.

An angler measuring the temperature of the water, a key element in stream ecology.

As discussed earlier, brown trout require cooler water at the egg stage than do rainbow trout, which may explain the limited northern distribution of brown trout in New Zealand. Their eggs die above 11°C, whereas rainbow trout eggs can survive up to 15°C. In New Zealand, rivers with winter temperatures greater than 10°C hold very few or no brown trout.

Sometimes juvenile rainbow trout seem to prefer temperatures a few degrees higher than do adults. During midsummer young rainbows can be found in surprisingly warm shallow margins of lakes and rivers in water at 20–25°C.

If trout have a choice, as in a lake, they will avoid water above 18°C. However, sometimes trout will endure higher than optimal temperatures near the lake surface, even approaching the lethal limit, if that is what they must do to feed. Then they return to the cooler depths to digest their meal.

Provided the above conditions are met, the main habitat conditions that trout need are akin to those required by most animals, including ourselves:
- space in which to live
- food
- shelter or cover.

The angler armed with knowledge of these three key habitat features can recognise good trout water and the spots likely to yield best success.

What constitutes these three key features of trout habitat, and how they relate to New Zealand conditions, is the subject of the next two chapters.

CHAPTER SIX

Running water

MOST NEW ZEALAND RIVERS are unstable, owing to our unpredictable and variable climate. The numbers of trout in most of our stony-bed rivers sourced by run-off (freestone rivers) appear to be strongly influenced by frequent flood events. Floods can cause the loss of most of a year's new fish, resulting in what is called a weak year-class. Sometimes virtually no new fish are produced for a year or more in succession, and this is called recruitment failure. A study on the Kakanui River, North Otago, found about an eighteen-fold variation in juvenile brown trout numbers between good and bad years, probably caused by floods during the late incubation and early fry stages (August–November). These floods had an average return period of four years. Periodic year-class failures because of floods can profoundly affect the age structure of river trout populations, producing gaps in age-classes and interspersed periods of poor and good fishing years. Much larger floods later in the season (March) had little to no effect on juvenile or adult trout in the Kakanui River. This is a typical pattern; floods during the summer and autumn are less damaging. Juveniles

Poor trout habitat, with unstable banks and bed offering no cover, and a lack of deep water.

cope reasonably well with them and adult brown trout are the most resistant, but this still varies with the size of the flood. In good trout rivers, normal channel-forming floods, which have an average return period of about two years, have little effect on the trout. Severe, less frequent floods, such as those with return periods of twenty to a hundred years, are the ones that do the most damage.

In March 1986 a big storm hit the east coast of the South Island and caused severe flooding in most of the foothill-draining trout rivers. A Ministry of Agriculture and Fisheries (MAF) drift-dive study of the effects of these floods on seven rivers in South Canterbury and North Otago found 90–100 per cent of small brown trout were lost, but only 26–57 per cent of the big fish. Rainbow trout disappeared completely from two of the rivers. These floods had expected return periods of nineteen to five hundred years. Variable and severe high flows may be the reason why many of our headwater river fisheries have a predominance of large trout, and few juveniles.

MAF drift-dive counts have shown that the best trout rivers are those that have stable flow, such as spring- or lake-fed rivers. Lakes buffer the effect of storm and flood, thereby protecting juvenile trout from harsh flows. Lake outlets tend to have plentiful food because the stable river levels ensure that their beds are not scoured out or dried up, as occurs regularly in flood- and drought-prone rivers. Moreover, the plankton in lake waters provides food for filter-feeding invertebrates, which are common on river beds near lake outlets, again owing to the stable flow. These productive conditions mean that more trout can be supported in the first few kilometres downstream from a lake.

A stable flow seems to be particularly important for rainbow trout habitat. In New Zealand rainbow trout are most prevalent in rivers that have lakes in their catchments or that drain pumice catchments – specifically those of the central North Island rainbow fisheries. A feature of pumice geology, perhaps not appreciated by anglers, is a sponge-like ability to absorb heavy rainfall and release it slowly. This greatly stabilises river flows.

There are good river rainbow trout populations that are exceptions to the above rule. One that has enticed anglers and intrigued researchers is in the Pelorus and Rai Rivers, in Marlborough. There are good numbers of brown and rainbow trout, yet there are no lakes in the catchment and the rivers are not particularly stable. Perhaps the shallow head of Pelorus Sound, into which the Pelorus River drains, acts in the same manner as a lake, providing a benign environment for trout that may be washed, or migrate, downstream during floods. The gradient and morphology of the rivers may also

This stream, with stable banks and bed, and some deep water, provides trout with excellent habitat.

play a part in this mystery. The Rai and lower Pelorus have low-gradient, meandering channels. Large floods usually overflow the channel and can dissipate their energy on the landscape, rather than on the channel and the trout.

Gradient

Steep rivers or steep sections of river are unsuitable for trout. Research has shown that in New Zealand rivers trout abundance decreases with increasing river gradient and altitude. Trout are most abundant where the gradient is 3 metres per kilometre (m/km) or less, and above 5 m/km trout numbers become very low. These guidelines may be put to good use when examining topographical maps before a visit to a new area. Simply work out the increase in altitude from the contour lines over a measured length of river, and divide the change in altitude by the distance to calculate the gradient.

The decline in trout numbers with increasing gradient may partly be related to the greater energy of floods in steeper rivers. Physical habitat also plays a part – rivers with easy gradients usually have deeper and slower water more suitable for trout.

The artful science of trout fishing

For a variety of reasons, trout generally are most abundant in the lower reaches of rivers, especially where there is plenty of cover, and least abundant in the headwaters. Not that fishing will always be best in the lower reaches of rivers, for other factors also influence the ease with which trout may be caught and the enjoyment of angling. Even though trout may not be abundant in headwaters, they often are extremely visible to the angler and can provide quality angling in a scenic environment.

Channel shape
The cross-sectional shape of the river channel directly influences how suitable the habitat will be for trout. The channel shape defines not only the general physical habitat available for trout but also the way it will respond to changes in flow.

The best overall conditions are moderately U-shaped cross-sectional profiles where the water fills the channel most of the time. Such channels provide extensive areas of suitable depths and water velocities for trout, and changes in flow do not bring about large changes in habitat unless the flow drops to very low levels. Large, deeply entrenched channels usually provide poor habitat conditions for both trout and their invertebrate foods because the water may be too deep and fast.

In flood flows there are forces strong enough to reshape the cross-sectional channel profile. Rivers with large flood flows but relatively small flow most of the time have shallow cross-sectional profiles. They provide poor trout habitat because they are spread over wide, oversize channels where the water is too shallow most of the time and especially at low flows.

Unconfined, unstable channels such as these in the Rakaia River catchment offer poor trout habitat.

The habitat

The best channel profiles for trout tend to be seen in lake-outlet and spring-fed rivers. The highest trout densities recorded by drift diving in New Zealand have been in large lake-outlet rivers, most notably the Gowan (draining Lake Rotoroa), the upper Buller (draining Lake Rotoiti), the upper Hurunui (draining Lake Sumner) and the Clutha just below Lake Wanaka. Lake- and spring-fed rivers have less variation between flood, median and low flows, compared with runoff (or freestone) rivers. Because flood flows are moderated, the channel is not scoured to the extent that it becomes oversized in relation to the river. Consequently, lake-outlet and spring-fed rivers tend to have U-shaped channels that are always well filled with water. Provided that the river is big enough to begin with, there will be plenty of living space for trout, even at low flows, and stable water levels to encourage a constantly high density of aquatic invertebrates for trout to eat.

The upper Gowan River flows from Lake Rotoroa in a confined, stable channel.

What the river looks like at low flow is important

The average annual low flow is a critical factor dictating how many trout a river can support. Anglers new to a river can easily be deceived by its appearance if they first see it soon after a fresh, or early in the season when flows are higher than normal. A river that at first sight appears to have plenty of flow with inviting swift runs and deep green pools may, in late summer, degenerate to a thin veneer of water over shallows and still, transparent pools with no nooks or crannies for trout to hide in.

Water depth is critical for trout in small, shallow rivers. Look for areas where the river runs through gorges and the narrower channel provides deeper water: often these may be the only places

The same river at moderate and low flow. The latter dictates the carrying capacity for trout.
John Hayes

where you will find large trout. Gorges can be easily found by studying a topographical map of the area and looking for spots where the contour lines are close together on either side of the river's course. Otherwise, look for sections where the river frequently changes direction. You can expect to find a pool at every bend, where the river meets a hard bank at right angles to the flow and is forced to dig downward during floods. Some of those pools may be deep enough to hold large trout.

Land use and bank-side vegetation

A low-to-moderate amount of agricultural development in a river's catchment can enhance the productivity of the river and improve conditions for trout. Overseas research has shown that enrichment from fertiliser application can stimulate algal and aquatic invertebrate production in rivers that are naturally low in nutrients and increase trout and salmon abundance. However, over much of New Zealand the degree of agricultural development far exceeds that which is beneficial to trout. Research has shown that New Zealand rivers or sections of rivers that have more than 30 per cent of their catchments developed to improved pasture have less diverse, and smaller, aquatic invertebrates, and only a third the trout numbers of less developed catchments. The reasons are complex and may include the following. River beds become silted and general water clarity declines owing to accelerated erosion. Wetland drainage and compaction of soils means flows are less stable, owing to higher flood highs and lower lows. Clearing of trees and other shade along the river banks means water temperatures are higher and more variable. There is more growth of periphyton (sludgy growth of algae, fungi and bacteria coating the bottom), which smothers the aquatic invertebrates preferred by trout. Large invertebrates such as mayflies and stoneflies, in particular, decline in number. Stream channels become wider and shallower, and bank-side cover is lost through stock grazing and trampling.

It is widely recognised that bank-side (riparian) vegetation is an important habitat feature for trout. However, it is not just a simple matter of providing, or protecting, trees along the banks. In the past, acclimatisation societies in conjunction with angling clubs have attempted to enhance trout streams with bank-side planting. But sometimes such good intentions can backfire. The type of plants must be matched to the size of the river and it is important to control the vigour of the vegetation. If the tree or scrub canopy grows right over the stream channel, too little light penetrates for algae to grow on the river bed, thus aquatic invertebrates have nothing to eat and trout numbers (especially the smaller trout) will decline.

Too much woody vegetation, especially willows, can choke smaller streams. Planting large trees, even natives, can cause small stream channels to widen because they shade out the grasses that would otherwise bind the stream banks.

In small streams, exotic grasses, native tussock, carex, flax and small shrubs are the best choice for riparian cover. Trees can lead to the problems mentioned above. In larger rivers with more erosive power, moderate densities of trees and scrub provide the best riparian cover. Willows, if managed properly, bind the banks well with their fibrous roots and provide plenty of snags for trout to hide among.

Management of bank-side vegetation for trout habitat in New Zealand raises an awkward paradox for Fish and Game managers. Members of angling clubs often are keen to assist with habitat enhancement. Some clubs have their own enhancement programmes that they undertake with their Fish and Game council's blessing. One of the most productive habitat enhancement activities in which angling clubs could partake is the management of riparian vegetation – making plantings where cover is inadequate for trout and controlling vegetation were it threatens to become excessive to maintain optimum trout habitat and access for anglers.

Left: *A stream grazed right to its banks, which are badly eroded.*

Above: *Well-vegetated and stable stream banks.*

However, these activities, even when sanctioned officially by Fish and Game councils, risk falling foul of regional and district councils charged with flood control. The relative merits of trees for riparian trout habitat versus their role in flood protection, and whether they can be managed for both simultaneously in this country, is an unresolved issue that needs addressing.

Food and space are both important

Features including gradient, channel shape and flow regime act together to determine the quality and quantity of physical habitat for trout and their aquatic food, which in turn can determine the abundance of trout. The two general features required in a trout river are physical habitat for the trout to live in and food for them to eat. In fact, research has shown that the two flow-related features that have most influence on the numbers of adult brown trout in New Zealand rivers are the amount of habitat for adult trout at the average annual low flow, and the amount of habitat for benthic invertebrates at median flow.

What constitutes trout habitat and benthic invertebrate habitat? Ask a group of anglers on the river bank what they think good habitat is and their opinions probably would differ — no doubt coloured by experience. Fisheries scientists have defined suitable habitat for trout and their invertebrate food in numerical terms to avoid the confusion that arises with subjective assessments of trout habitat made by different people. This sort of information is commonly needed when decisions are made for allocating part of a river's flow for hydro-power generation or irrigation.

Habitat requirements of trout food

The main food of trout in the more swiftly flowing middle and upper sections of rivers is benthic invertebrates, mainly aquatic insects, most of which live on the river bed and usually in riffles and runs. Benthic invertebrates are also found in pools, but most of the types that trout eat are not nearly as abundant there. (Snails are an exception, which may become abundant in the slower waters of rivers during long periods of stable flow.) Most of them prefer fairly coarse bed materials, from coarse gravels (17–64 millimetres in diameter), cobbles (65–256 mm), to boulders (more than 256 mm). Fine substrates such as fine gravel, sand and mud support few of the invertebrates that trout feed upon (except in some stable margins and backwaters where plant and algal growth can establish). Because benthic invertebrates occur in riffles and runs, the water in which they generally are found is shallow to moderately deep (0.2–1.2 metres) and moderately fast (0.3–1.2 metres per second).

A river bed with much coarse material providing good habitat for aquatic invertebrates and feeding lies for trout.

Although much has been written about the selective feeding behaviour of trout, as a general rule they will take any prey they can catch, within a size range they can handle. Some invertebrates, and most fish prey, are too large for trout fry to catch and eat. However, it does not take long for trout to reach a size sufficient to handle most of the aquatic invertebrates found in a river. Availability is the key factor dictating whether or not an invertebrate prey species is being eaten by trout at a particular place and time. Any species will be eaten that, by their behaviour and obvious presence, make themselves available to trout – and especially those which routinely drift in the water column or on the surface. Drifting aquatic invertebrates are mostly immature stages of insects that later metamorphose into winged adults. The main groups are mayflies, stoneflies, caddisflies and midges (chironomids). Stoneflies are cold-water insects most common in headwaters and back-country rivers, especially where the catchment has plenty of native bush cover. Midges are more abundant in the middle and lower reaches of rivers because, unlike stoneflies and mayflies, they are able to cope with heavy growths of periphyton and silt on the river bed which often occur as a consequence of agricultural enrichment and erosion.

Several types of mayfly including *Deleatidium*, the most common genus in New Zealand, graze algae from stone surfaces. However, they prefer only a thin layer of algae, especially diatoms, which usually form a brown coating on stones. Grazing mayflies are like rabbits, which do best on short grass and decline in numbers when growth becomes too rank.

Some invertebrates are routinely exposed on stone surfaces

Trout invertebrate prey. Clockwise from top left: nymphs of Deleatidium sp. (mayfly), Nesameletus sp. (swimming mayfly), Sigara sp. (water boatman), Olinga sp. (cased caddisfly), Stenoperla prasina (green stonefly).
Peter Hamill

and are slow and cumbersome enough for trout to browse directly off the river bed. These include some of the cased caddisflies and snails, while mayflies generally are too alert and quick for trout to pick off the surface of stones.

The average size of invertebrates generally declines downstream. This is mainly because the larger stoneflies and mayflies prefer the cleaner, colder upper reaches of most New Zealand rivers, while smaller midges prefer the enriched lower reaches.

In the slow-flowing lower reaches of many trout rivers, brown trout take advantage of the abundance of small fish. Many of New Zealand's native fishes are sea-migratory during part of their life cycle: the five whitebait species (of which inanga is the most common), several bully species, smelt and eels. Several of these are fairly weak swimmers and do not penetrate very far upstream. Consequently, the abundance of native fish usually declines fairly rapidly upstream from the river mouth.

Brown trout prey most heavily on native fish, particularly whitebait and smelt, in the tidal reaches of rivers. In places where the outgoing tide runs fast, whitebait and smelt hug the slower edges of the river. In such places, the trout will use any projections, snags and other 'velocity refuges' to shelter from the current and ambush prey as it swims past. Whitebait and particularly smelt are not always confined to the river margins: often in tidal reaches they will migrate in mid-channel with the push of the incoming tide. Then the brown trout will hug the bottom to shelter from the current and attack from below.

Further upstream, bullies become the main small fish prey for trout. Bullies mainly prefer the shallow margins of rivers, and it is here in the slower edge-water, especially of pools, where trout hunt them down. Trout rarely hunt bullies in fast water because of the higher energy demands of swimming in the full force of the current. Also, because bullies come out from beneath cover at dusk, trout hunt them mainly at night.

Depth, velocity and bed material preferred by trout

I have made measurements of the habitat used by drift-feeding brown trout in New Zealand rivers. Adult brown trout (over forty centimetres) prefer water greater than about half a metre deep, and especially depths of a metre or more. Average water column velocities where these fish feed in medium-sized, moderate-gradient rivers are between 0.3 and 0.6 metres per second. These are the conditions in which adult brown trout generally are encountered by fly anglers sight-fishing in most New Zealand rivers, except of course in those parts of rivers with slow or no current such as lowland reaches and backwaters.

Water velocity varies through the water column, but an average water column velocity of 0.3–0.6 metres per second in metre-deep water equates to about 0.3–0.70 m/s at the surface. Scientists use special current meters to measure water velocity, but it is possible to get a reasonable estimate by recording the time taken for a stick to travel a set distance.

Trout try to find shelter from the full force of the current when drift feeding – usually behind or in front of a boulder. Other objects used for this purpose include bedrock projections, large cobbles and logs. When nothing else is available, even a depression in the river bed will do. Usually trout will sit behind boulders that are fully submerged, but if a boulder protrudes through the water surface, they usually ride the pressure wave generated in front of it. Most velocity refuges used for drift feeding are close to the bottom of the river, where friction with the bed slows the water down and cobbles and boulders break up the flow. It is here – on the bottom – where trout spend most of their time.

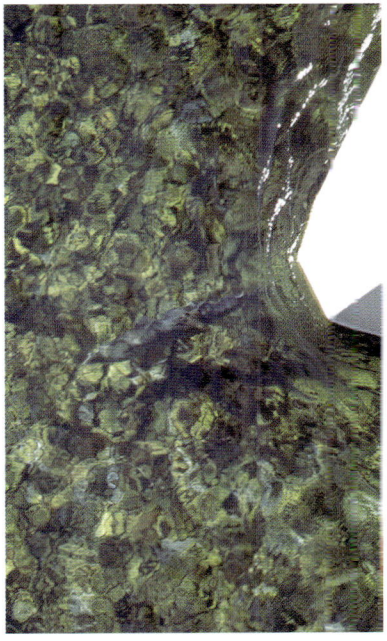

Fish on station, awaiting drifting food. Trout frequently sit behind or ahead of obstacles such as a large boulder (above) or a bridge pile (below).

The artful science of trout fishing

Casting to a fish feeding downstream of a large bedrock.

By taking advantage of velocity refuges in this manner, trout are able to feed in faster water than they could otherwise manage if exposed to the full force of the current all of the time. This behaviour makes a lot a sense when you consider that the quantity of drifting invertebrates over a given time period is directly proportional to the water velocity.

When trout feed from a velocity refuge into the faster surrounding water, they are making use of zones over which the velocity rapidly increases (velocity shears). Mostly these are in the vertical direction, with the trout rising up from the river bed rather than moving horizontally, although they also make use of horizontal velocity shears such as those formed in the eyes of pools or by bank extensions.

This angler has tempted a trout from its lie behind a bank extension.

The habitat

The depth and velocity conditions preferred by adult brown trout for drift-feeding occur most often in moderate- to fast-flowing, deep, boulder-lined runs. Not surprisingly, then, boulder runs usually hold good numbers of large trout — a fact that drift-dive surveys have confirmed. Another productive habitat is pocket water: fast, shallower runs with large boulders. The trout can be found in the deeper pockets interspersed among the boulders, which provide plenty of refuges from the current and vertical velocity shears for drift feeding.

In smaller rivers, or as flow recedes, depth becomes the main factor determining the suitability of habitat for adult trout. When runs become too shallow to hold adult trout (at least in rivers where adults are larger than about forty centimetres) the fish are confined to pools. As a consequence, small rivers, or those with low summer flow, have a lower carrying capacity for adult trout (unless they are stunted) than rivers that are large enough to provide deep-run habitat.

Where water velocity permits in pools, slow runs and backwaters, trout will browse invertebrates off the river bed, but these must first be in sufficient number and exposed on the bottom — usually in the slower, more productive lower reaches of rivers. The energy constraints of swimming in strong currents preclude this form of feeding in the faster-flowing parts of rivers. Trout feed

Success in a bouldery run with many feeding lies.

Exploring pocket water.

on the slow-moving cased caddis and snails by browsing off the river bed (or off aquatic weeds). Rivers that have large slow pools and long periods of stable flow are rather like lakes in terms of the habitats and feeding opportunities they offer trout. There may be abundant snails on the surfaces of stones and aquatic weeds, and the trout also target small fish and swimming invertebrates such as water boatmen.

Most other aquatic invertebrates here are tiny or, owing to their behaviour, unavailable; for example, midge larvae and aquatic worms. Therefore small prey fish such as bullies, smelt and inanga (adult whitebait) provide a particularly important food link for trout populations. They eat the tiny invertebrates, then the trout eat them.

I have often seen anglers, especially those new to the sport or visiting from overseas, methodically fishing riffles. This generally is a waste of time unless you want to catch small or juvenile trout. Usually only the heads and tails of riffles, where the water depth is sufficient to hold adult trout, are worth fishing. Riffles are the preferred habitat of juvenile trout, safe from harassment by larger trout and right where most of the benthic invertebrate food is produced.

Juvenile brown trout prefer water about 0.3–1 metre deep (the smaller the fish, the shallower the water in which it can live) with mean water column velocities in the range 0.1–0.5 metres per second. Juvenile trout most prefer water flowing at about 0.2–0.3 m/s. At first consideration, riffles might seem too fast for little trout, but the shallow riffle margins, where friction with the bottom slows the water down, provide plenty of spots within this velocity range, and generally there are plenty of velocity refuges for the little fish behind rocks.

During the autumn, new season's brood and yearling fish may move into pools, where they form schools and are sometimes seen by anglers. Trout generally move into deeper water as they grow, but this autumn movement is not entirely related to that. Similar movement by juvenile trout has been reported in North America and is thought to be a seasonal behaviour related to coping with the rigours of winter – possibly with the combined effects of low temperature (which reduces the swimming ability of trout) and floods. As a general rule, both juvenile and adult trout are found in slower water during the winter than at other times of the year.

A related behaviour displayed by new season's and yearling trout is winter hiding. As water temperatures drop below about 13°C little trout begin to hide beneath rocks on the river bed, and at temperatures below about 9°C most juveniles are hiding. Winter hiding habitat, such as loosely embedded cobbles and boulders, and submerged tree snags, log jams and branches, can be a population-

The habitat

The junction of a tributary stream and a river creates a favourite dining spot for trout.

limiting factor in some rivers. This has been clearly demonstrated by research in North America, and there is no reason why the principle should not also apply in New Zealand. Sedimentation resulting in cobble and boulder habitat becoming embedded is a serious threat to the amount of winter hiding habitat for juvenile trout. Trout avoid fine gravel and sand, as there are few aquatic benthic invertebrates and no cover for hiding or for sheltering from the current.

Less physical habitat information has been gathered for rainbow than for brown trout in New Zealand, but research overseas, and anglers' observations here, suggests that rainbows prefer slightly faster water. Where the two species occur together, often rainbows are found in the faster, more turbulent water. Brown trout certainly associate more with the river bed than do rainbows. They will usually be found tucked in behind or in front of rocks. Rainbows, on the other hand, are quite happy to feed up off the bottom in the bellies of pools, and less likely to stick to a single feeding location than brown trout.

There are many skills involved in stalking trout, starting with concealment and the ability to spot the fish themselves in a variety of water and weather conditions. But equally important is the skill of 'reading' the water: locating sections of a river or lake where fish are most likely to feed. This usually precedes looking for the fish themselves.

The obvious 'hot spots' are easy to locate — where a tributary stream enters a lake or main river, for example, or the eye of a pool or adrift of a huge mid-stream boulder. But much smaller hidden deep pockets or submerged obstructions delineating shear zones are more difficult to locate.

As John has mentioned, there are two types of velocity shear zones that trout use when selecting a feeding position – horizontal and vertical. The former is the easier to locate by reading water, so I will discuss it first.

There are two clues to locating and identifying a horizontal shear zone. First, and most obvious, is the physical obstruction to flow that causes the shear, and then the line or lines on the water's surface showing that a shear exists below.

The flow obstructions are either bank extensions or midstream barriers. In each case the larger and more solid the hindrance to flow, the more clearly defined are the shear lines.

The most common shear zone caused by a bank extension is at the eye of a pool, where the river usually becomes wider after its rush down through the confines of a rapid or riffle. Often the river curves here too, accentuating the width of the eye. Downstream from the eye there will be a distinct line of current change. On the river side of the line the flow will be fast; on the bank side the flow will be considerably slower. It takes a little practice and imagination to locate this horizontal shear zone (especially where the bank extension allows some through-flow, as in a cobble or boulder bar), but there are distinct lines running with and parallel to the flow.

Horizontal shear zones are also caused by midstream obstructions. The most obvious obstructions are those that protrude from the water. These produce very distinct lines of current change on the water's surface, lines that do not run parallel downstream from the rock barrier but spread gradually instead. Shear zones caused by protruding obstructions extend long distances downstream, while those caused by submerged rocks are much shorter. In this situation, surface clues about the refuge below are more subtle – there may be a surface 'boil' above the obstruction and a flatter water surface downstream – the boundaries of the less rippled waters showing where the shear zones exist below.

Rocks are by far the most common obstruction to a river's flow, but other barriers also exist; for example, bridge piles have a similar effect to a protruding rock. Viewed from above, the lines of current change can be seen clearly, while the finer river-bed material directly downstream of the pile hints at the lack of current there. The downstream extent of the flow obstruction can also be observed clearly from above, and from the upstream side of the bridge the pressure wave ahead of a pile can also be seen.

The physical clues to the presence of a vertical shear zone are more subtle. In particular, the downstream current lines are absent. Vertical shears exist wherever there is a submerged obstruction to a river's flow or where there is a dip or depression in a stream bed. These can be identified in a number of ways. First, where a river

The habitat

A horizontal sheer zone at the head of a pool, highlighted by low-angled sun.

bed is made up of very coarse material (rocks, boulders, logs, collapsed banks, etc.), numerous vertical shears will exist. If the water is deep over the coarse bed, there will be few clues about the trout lies below. However, if the water is shallow (a metre or less), the presence of more sizeable shear zones below may be hinted at by a flatter, more glassy water surface.

Often these surface clues can be more easily seen from a distance. As a stalking angler I regularly look for water surface variations well ahead as I work upstream. Another subtle variation I seek is the richness of the water colour (when rivers are clear). Most of the streams that I fish have an attractive green hue to their waters. The shade of green usually darkens as water depth increases. This can be very useful in identifying vertical shear zones, particularly

The ridge where shallow water drops off into deeper water forms an obvious vertical sheer zone.

95

in shallower pocket water or where drop-offs exist. Again, vertical shears and deeper pockets can be identified from a distance – in this case by noting the areas where the waters show a richer, deeper colour, and where boulders and other underwater obstructions stand out from the surrounding river bed.

IN ADDITION TO VELOCITY REFUGES, trout also require security refuges: places they can flee to when frightened. Usually this is a pool two and a half to three metres or more deep, or overhanging banks and vegetation, undercut boulders or submerged trees and root clusters. These latter types of cover are very important in smaller rivers where deep water is not often available. Another form of security refuge is the overhead protection of surface turbulence and white water, obscuring the view from above. Rainbow trout particularly like this form of cover. A security refuge will usually include two or more forms of cover together, such as large boulders or tree snags on the floor of a deep pool with a turbulent or whitewater section where the water rushes in at the head. It is rare to find a large trout further than about thirty metres from a security refuge consisting of at least one of the above forms of cover.

In the slow lower reaches of some rivers, water weeds can provide security cover, especially for smaller trout.

The above forms of cover are less important in turbid rivers where trout are hidden from predators, including anglers, by the murky water all around.

THE TERRITORIAL BEHAVIOUR of trout has been well documented and is frequently observed by anglers. Those who repeatedly fish a particular reach of a river not only become familiar with the most favoured feeding territories along 'their' section of river, but also can recognise the individual fish that reside there.

Obviously a feeding place must be rich in food to be attractive, but it must also be energy-efficient for the fish. I can visualise hundreds of such places on hosts of rivers – places where week after week, year after year, trout are found in residence – that are favoured by discerning fish.

One particular feeding lie on the Maruia River seems to have a unique attraction for feeding fish. Rarely have I visited the spot and not found a trout there. Fish that claim the lie seem to be quite possessive about it.

The niche is a textbook velocity refuge. A huge, ancient log

Snags and overhanging vegetation can provide useful cover for trout.

buried by a metre or so of gravel extends from its bank-side grave, out across the river bed for a short distance. The short arm of the tree pushes much of the bank-side flow away from the shore, creating in its lee a quiet haven – the kind that brown trout adore. A stable, stony bed upstream provides ample insect habitat and the midstream waters run deep if a run for cover is needed.

I can remember very clearly the first fish that I caught there – not because it was especially big (although two kilograms is good enough), but because of the events that followed the initial capture. It was in mid-December. Green beetles were dropping onto the river in abundance and the trout were taking their share greedily. The fish rode high in a little more than a metre of water, adrift of the log. I punched a beetle up into an annoying breeze and, after a couple of short drops, managed to curl one just ahead of the fish. Up it came in an instant and snatched impatiently at the beetle. I tightened almost as quickly and fortunately the hook took hold. Immediately the fish made for the safety of midstream, then, with the assistance of stronger flow, it extended its advantage, taking more and more of my line. I struggled in pursuit, stumbling over slimy boulders and negotiating untidy heaps of flood debris. Within minutes we approached the tail of the pool, but the fish plunged

The artful science of trout fishing

into the rapid that drained the pool and raced on even faster towards the next deep water. The fish and a huge belly of fly line were too much for my delicate tippet. It broke and the fish was free – still fleeing far from its former home. 'I wonder how big it was?' I mused, as one inevitably does in defeat.

As I made my way back upstream I became more aware of how far the fish had strayed from its home. The downstream pool where the fish now presumably lay was three hundred metres from the log. I approached the ancient tree again. To my delight, another fish had taken up station. I offered it another beetle and this time I managed to hold the fish on a shorter line and land it. A one-and-a-half-kilogram hen, clean and fat – a delight to hold before returning it to the river.

Three days later, I again worked the same reach of the river. A likely-looking fish hovered in the same spot, sheltering from nearby boisterous flow. Its behaviour, sitting up off the bed, signalled its intentions, and I obliged by tossing a fat beetle into its feeding lane. Up came the nose and it took the fly. I battled the fish for some time, keeping my line as short as possible, and ten minutes later it succumbed. As I lifted its head from my net, I noticed a short length of nylon emerging from the trout's mouth. On opening the

The pressure wave ahead of a large protruding rock provides a stable feeding lie. The bedrocks, also visible, offer promising lies on their lee side.

hooked jaw I found not one beetle imitation but two – the one just taken, and my fly lost three days prior! I enjoyed the moment but later marvelled at the fish's very strong desire to reoccupy the territory it had been separated from.

Many years have passed since I first found the log and the feeding lie that it created. It is still there. The river has changed little and almost every time I stalk that bank I find a resident fish. I'd like to say that I catch one on every visit, but that isn't so. However, the significant fact is the constant attraction of the lie to trout. There is obviously plenty of food passing by. The midstream depths offer security, while the log, firmly embedded in stones, deflects most of the current. The log is covered by a metre or more of water during high spring flows, while after long dry spells water flows around, rather than over, the obstruction – but there is always some flow and a pocket downstream. When I imagine the lie I picture everything that a trout could desire in its feeding territory – an ideal trout dining area!

CHAPTER SEVEN

Still waters

IN RUNNING WATER, food generally comes to the trout carried by the current or it swims past. Consequently, local habitat conditions (microhabitat) are very important for trout living in rivers. Microhabitat provides favourable conditions in which to intercept prey, while also providing cover and other essential features for survival. In lakes, microhabitat is usually less important because deep water is readily available for cover and the food does not come to the trout – rather, it must find where the food is. Much more than in rivers, food distribution in lakes dictates where trout will be found. This is also affected by seasonal physical changes in lakes, driven primarily by water temperature

Thermal and oxygen stratification

In order to understand where the food is produced in lakes, and where the trout may be found, it is helpful to know some basic facts about different types of lakes and changes with the season.

Lakes are dynamic environments in which temperature and oxygen conditions vary seasonally and have a dominant influence on trout and their prey.

Increasing solar radiation in spring and summer causes surface waters of temperate lakes to warm up. Because the warm surface water is less dense than colder bottom water, it tends to remain at the surface. This surface layer (epilimnion) becomes thicker and warmer and eventually isolates the cold deeper waters (hypolimnion) from the atmosphere. Wind mixes and aerates the surface layer but this mixing does not extend down into the hypolimnion.

The zone between the surface and deep layers is called the metalimnion (or intermediate thermal stratum) and includes a zone of rapid temperature change called the thermocline. During summer the exchange of nutrients and oxygen between the epilimnion and hypolimnion takes place by diffusion in the metalimnion – a much slower process of nutrient exchange than is possible by water circulation (or mixing).

During summer, oxygen levels in the hypolimnion may become

depleted because the deep waters are isolated from the atmosphere, and biological and chemical processes use up the oxygen. If the productivity of the lake is sufficient, and the size of the hypolimnion is small in relation to the entire lake volume, oxygen depletion of the deep hypolimnion may be severe enough to force trout to stay in the surface waters.

In midsummer, trout distribution may be further restricted by surface water temperatures exceeding their thermal tolerance. In New Zealand, brown and rainbow trout have been found to go deeper when surface water temperature exceeds 19–20°C. In the Rotorua lakes during summer, medium to large trout (more than thirty-five centimetres long) are confined mainly to water deeper than ten metres (in the metalimnion), owing to excessively warm surface waters.

When both oxygen depletion of the hypolimnion and excessive surface water temperatures occur simultaneously, trout experience a 'habitat squeeze', being confined to the metalimnion, which in extreme situations may be only a few metres thick. These conditions generally occur only in shallow, productive lakes at lower latitudes (in the upper half of the North Island). However, fish may avoid high surface-water temperatures in midsummer at least as far south as the Waitaki catchment in the South Island.

Movement of trout into deep water over summer is well known by anglers who fish the central North Island lakes. In the deeper lakes, rainbows may be taken by surface harling mainly in the spring, but over summer, and even into late autumn, the deep water is best.

Water quality and productivity

The concentration of nutrients in a lake has a strong influence on other water-quality features such as oxygenation, clarity and colour, and overall productivity – although the morphology (shape) of the lake is important too. Lakes are classified by biologists according to their primary productivity (how much plant food they produce to form the base of the food chain), and this is largely governed by nutrient concentrations.

Oligotrophic lakes have low primary productivity, are usually deep and cold, and are reasonably well oxygenated at all depths throughout the year. They provide good habitat conditions and food for trout, although their fish-carrying capacity may be limited. Examples of oligotrophic lakes include Taupo, Tarawera, Te Anau and Wakatipu.

Eutrophic lakes have high primary productivity. Generally they are comparatively small, shallow, and warm in the summer. They also are characterised by algal blooms, particularly of blue-green algae, which proliferate when water layers of different temperature form. Blue-green algae are undesirable in trout lakes because they are unpalatable to most of the zooplankton – thus the energy they trap from the sun cannot be passed on through the food chain to trout. Moreover, when algae rot after a bloom they generate a high biological oxygen demand that strips the hypolimnion of its oxygen. Such habitat conditions are far from ideal and, although trout grow rapidly in some eutrophic lakes, populations can suffer from periodic fish kills, owing to heat stress and deoxygenation. Examples of eutrophic lakes include Horowhenua (Levin), Tutira (Hawke's Bay) and Ellesmere (Canterbury).

Mesotrophic lakes are the most productive for trout. Oxygen and temperature conditions generally are favourable and their greater productivity over oligotrophic lakes results in faster growth and greater carrying capacity. Examples of mesotrophic lakes are Aniwhenua and Rotoiti in the North Island, and Alexandrina and Heron in the South Island.

The trophic classification system discussed above does not always neatly fit lakes with good or bad trout fisheries. This is because the classification system attempts to fit lakes into categories of productivity when, in fact, productivity varies along a continuum. Lake Rotorua is an example of a eutrophic lake that supports a good trout population. However, during summer the trout come under temperature and oxygen stress and seek out cool stream mouths because the lake is too shallow to provide a deep-water thermal refuge. Paradoxically, this situation improves what otherwise can be dull summer fishing in Rotorua by concentrating trout off stream mouths, making them available for shore anglers.

One interesting side issue is the effect of eutrophication on the palatability of trout. Trout from eutrophic and even mesotrophic lakes and rivers sometimes taste muddy or musty. In my experience even smoking does not disguise the unpleasant flavour (although I am very sensitive to the muddy taste). A good example is Lake Aniwhenua in the Bay of Plenty. Trout I have tasted from Aniwhenua have been particularly muddy – which is even more reason to practice catch-and-release in this lake, which is becoming so well known for producing trophy fish. The flavour is due to volatile chemicals produced by some blue-green algae and microorganisms called actinomycetes, and accumulated through the food chain.

Where the food is produced

Most food for trout in lakes is produced on the lake bed and associated weed beds (the littoral zone) or in the water column (the limnetic or pelagic zone). The littoral zone is the zone of rooted vegetation, and the limnetic zone is open water down to the depth at which light is insufficient to support plant life (algae or phytoplankton). Deep lakes have a further zone – the profundal zone, which extends from the lower boundary of the limnetic zone down to the bottom. Plants cannot grow in the profundal zone because there is insufficient light. This zone (and the lake sediments) is inhabited by decomposer organisms, which derive their sustenance from dead plankton and other organic material that sinks from above.

Littoral food resources for trout include bullies, aquatic insects, snails and koura (freshwater crayfish) associated with weed beds and rocks on the lake bed. The plants upon which these littoral prey communities rely are the weed beds and the periphyton (attached algae) growing on the weeds and rocks. Limnetic food resources for trout include forage fish (mainly larval and juvenile smelt, galaxiids and bullies) and water fleas, or *Daphnia*, a group of planktonic crustaceans. The larval prey fish feed on planktonic animals (including water fleas), which in turn all rely on phytoplankton (microscopic algae) in the water column as the primary producers in the limnetic zone.

An angler fishing the littoral zone of a lake.

When limnetic forage fish are present, they can cycle food production from the limnetic zone into the littoral zone. Over winter and spring, larval bullies feed on zooplankton in the limnetic zone, where they are important food for one- and two-year-old trout. In late summer, post-larval bullies move into the shallow littoral to settle on the bottom and begin the benthic stage of their life cycle. At the same time, post-larval galaxiids (whitebait stage), and in some lakes post-larval smelt, also move into the shallow littoral, where they can be seen shoaling along the shoreline or over the drop-off into deeper water. This is a bountiful time for large trout, especially browns, patrolling the shallow littoral. In smelt lakes during spring, adult smelt concentrate in the shallow littoral to spawn along sandy beaches. This movement of baitfish provides the best surface and shore fishing for rainbow trout.

Lake morphology is important

Depending on the morphology (shape) of the lake, trout may derive most of their food from the littoral zone or from the limnetic zone, or from both. The ideal trout lake provides a large littoral foraging area extending deep into the lake, while also having a significant part of its volume generating limnetic food and providing a deepwater retreat for trout during the heat of summer. This balance of littoral and limnetic habitat is particularly important for supporting mixed-species stocks such as brown and rainbow trout, and perhaps also chinook salmon. The balance of deep and shallow water enables the different species to exploit their various habitat preferences. For example, brown trout make heavy use of the shallow littoral zone near the shore.

When most of the food produced is plankton, as in deep lakes with narrow littoral margins, it is vital that the food chain should include plankton-feeding forage fish, so that the lake's productivity can be channelled into the production of trout. In New Zealand, smelt have proven to be the best forage fish for this purpose, especially in the North Island. Galaxiids and larval bullies are also useful forage fish but cannot sustain trout predation year-round to the extent that smelt can.

Long, narrow lakes have a far greater length of shoreline in proportion to their surface area than circular lakes, and therefore provide more littoral habitat. Gently sloping shorelines at the ends of a narrow lake, as in most such glacial lakes in New Zealand, further enhance the area of littoral habitat.

The extent to which light can penetrate (the bottom boundary of the photic zone) limits the depth to which phytoplankton and weed beds can grow. The productive zone of a lake is confined to the surface waters down to the maximum depth of light penetration, so it follows that the carrying capacity for trout is related mainly to surface area rather than volume. It follows too that the extent of the littoral zone is also extremely important. Providing that temperature and oxygen requirements of trout are satisfied, the most productive lakes for trout are those that are no deeper than the photic zone over their entire surface area – giving maximum area for both littoral and limnetic production.

However, temperature and oxygen vary seasonally and greatly influence the vertical and horizontal distribution of trout and what proportion of these zones they can exploit. The best lakes are those in which trout have access to all or most of the littoral habitat for foraging year round.

Distribution of trout in relation to habitat, size and species

So far we have dwelt on features that, although useful for understanding how lakes function and indirectly affect trout, are somewhat removed from what the angler is immediately interested in when on a lake – figuring out where the trout are!

In addition to anglers' experience, several studies of trout in New Zealand lakes have provided information to make some generalisations about their distribution. To tackle this subject it helps to divide lakes into two categories: those where smelt predominate, and those with mainly a littoral invertebrate food chain. New Zealand research that we can draw upon includes:

- a four-year study of rainbow trout in Lake Taupo, our best example of a lake with a predominantly smelt food chain
- studies of brown and rainbow trout in Lake Alexandrina, where littoral invertebrates predominate
- a study of trout in Lake Waikaremoana, with a mixed smelt and littoral invertebrate food chain.

From these we can draw together the common threads to come up with some principles that may apply to New Zealand lakes generally.

In Alexandrina and Waikaremoana, the shallow littoral is occupied by large adult brown and rainbow trout (forty-five to seventy centimetres), and young-of-the-year of both species. When brown trout are present in sufficient numbers, they dominate the shallow littoral zone and displace adult rainbows to the weed beds further offshore. The littoral zone extends to about eighteen metres in Lake Waikaremoana and about ten metres in Lake Alexandrina. At night, adult rainbows move inshore to share the shallow littoral with brown trout – probably because aggressive interactions between the species are not possible in the dark. When brown trout are absent, adult rainbow trout will use the shallow littoral during the day.

In mid- to late summer, when surface water temperatures exceed 19°C in Lake Waikaremoana, large brown trout divide their time between cruising the shallows feeding, and periods of fifteen to twenty minutes to cool down in cooler waters offshore. In Lake Alexandrina, warm surface water on summer days also affects trout in the shallow littoral, forcing them offshore or to into the cooler waters of springs and stream mouths.

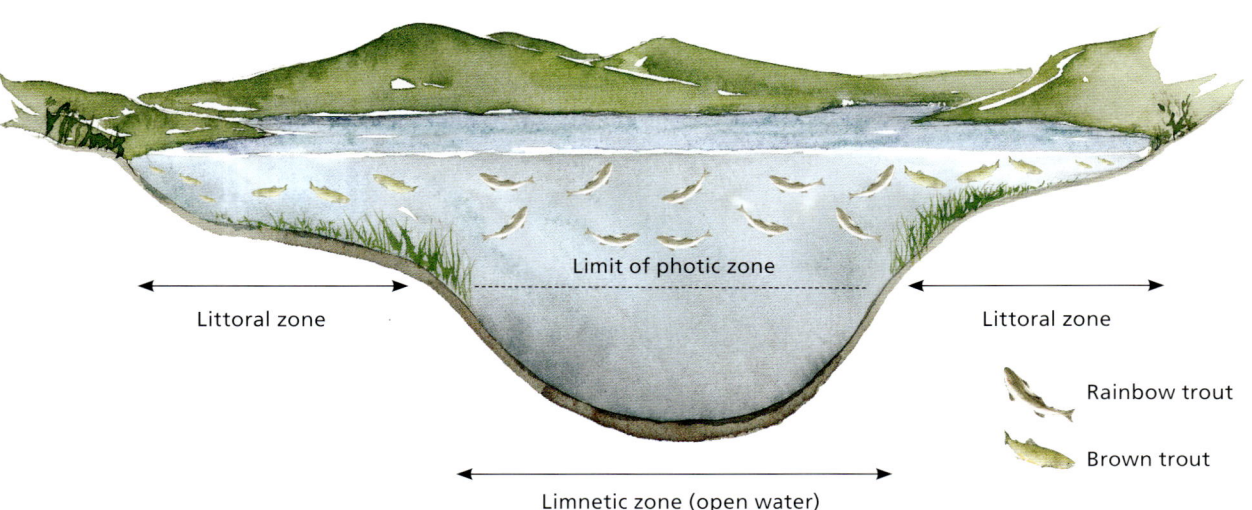

Distribution of trout in lakes by species and size class.

The habitat

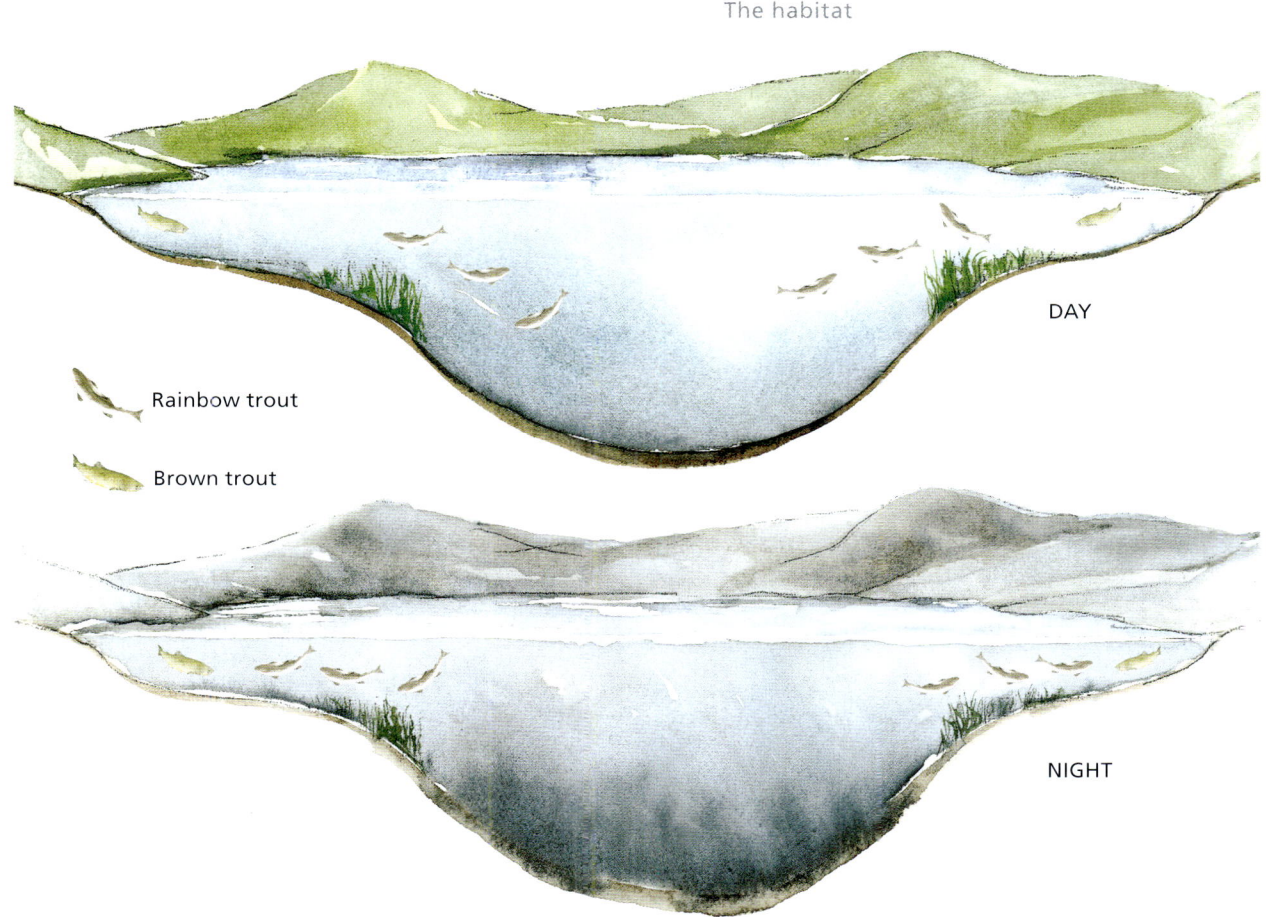

*Change in species distribution in lakes between day and night.
By day large brown trout dominate the shallow littoral zone.
At night territoriality breaks down and large rainbows can invade the littoral.*

Adult brown and rainbow trout in Alexandrina and Waikaremoana share the shallow littoral with young-of-the-year of both species. Small trout take advantage of the cover provided by rocks and vegetation around the shoreline. They do not present a competitive threat to the adult trout because they take much smaller prey.

The size of a lake and variations in the shoreline substrate also affect the productivity of its littoral zone, and this in turn affects the distribution of trout. In Lake Taupo, the pumice-sand substrate and large waves create an unstable shallow littoral zone with sparse weed growth and a very poor invertebrate community. This means there is little to attract trout into the shallows – except when smelt move into the sandy beaches to spawn in spring/early summer. Most of the time large adult rainbows are further offshore – still within the littoral zone, but occupying deeper water down to about twenty metres. This zone extends as much as two kilometres offshore, but still is only about seven per cent of the lake's area.

Lake Alexandrina in autumn.

By contrast, Alexandrina has a rocky shoreline, little wave action and a stable water level, and so has a very productive shallow littoral invertebrate community, where large trout feed year-round. Waikaremoana is between these extremes: it has a rocky shoreline that supports more productive food communities than Taupo, but also has reasonably large waves, and unstable water levels owing to hydroelectric power generation. These two factors lower the productivity compared with Alexandrina. Another factor in Waikaremoana is the presence of smelt, which attract trout offshore and introduce a complicating influence on the food chain and seasonal distribution of trout.

In Waikaremoana, juvenile trout spend two to four months growing in the shallow littoral and then move out to the limnetic zone, where they spend most of their immature life. Many of these fish move back into the littoral zone after reaching sexual maturity, at about forty centimetres or more.

In Alexandrina, fewer trout live in the limnetic zone. Rainbows mainly occupy the littoral zone, including the shallow littoral, and spend only a small proportion of their time in the limnetic zone.

Young-of-the-year trout concentrate in the shallow littoral and share this habitat with large adult brown and rainbow trout – similar to the pattern in Waikaremoana. The shallow littoral is in fact the favoured habitat of Alexandrina's larger browns and rainbows. Intermediate-sized trout (twenty-two to forty centimetres) occur more in the deeper littoral (over the weed beds) in this lake. Few adult trout use the limnetic zone in Alexandrina: most of the fish here are yearling rainbows, which use the limnetic zone during spring and winter, then move into the shallow littoral over summer.

Less is known about the distribution of yearling browns in lakes. It is thought that they stay closer to shoreline cover, for longer than rainbow yearlings, in keeping with the strong association that brown trout have with the substrate.

Trout also undergo vertical movements, both seasonally and daily. Overseas research shows that lake trout move into deep water over winter. Daily vertical feeding movements of trout in lakes are also well known. In the limnetic zone, zooplankton migrate to the surface waters at dusk to feed on phytoplankton, which are concentrated in the surface waters. Small fish follow their zooplankton prey, and the trout in turn are keyed into their movements. Another reason why trout move up into the surface waters of lakes at dusk is simply to see their prey better as the light fades.

Lake Waikaremoana.

The artful science of trout fishing

Information on seasonal depth movements of trout in New Zealand lakes is sparse. Research on Taupo has shown that rainbow trout use all depths, especially in winter and spring, but concentrate during the day in deeper water. In daylight, most Taupo rainbows are at eighty to a hundred metres during winter. In summer, most are below the thermocline (thirty metres) and are concentrated at ninety to a hundred and twenty metres in summer (see below).

So what does all this mean for the angler? First, if a lake has a productive shallow littoral zone, with diverse substrate, stable water level and limited wave action, this is where the largest trout are likely to be. Second, the limnetic (open-water) zone is the best place to fish in smelt lakes if you are simply interested in catching fish regardless of size. Third, few legal-sized trout occupy the open

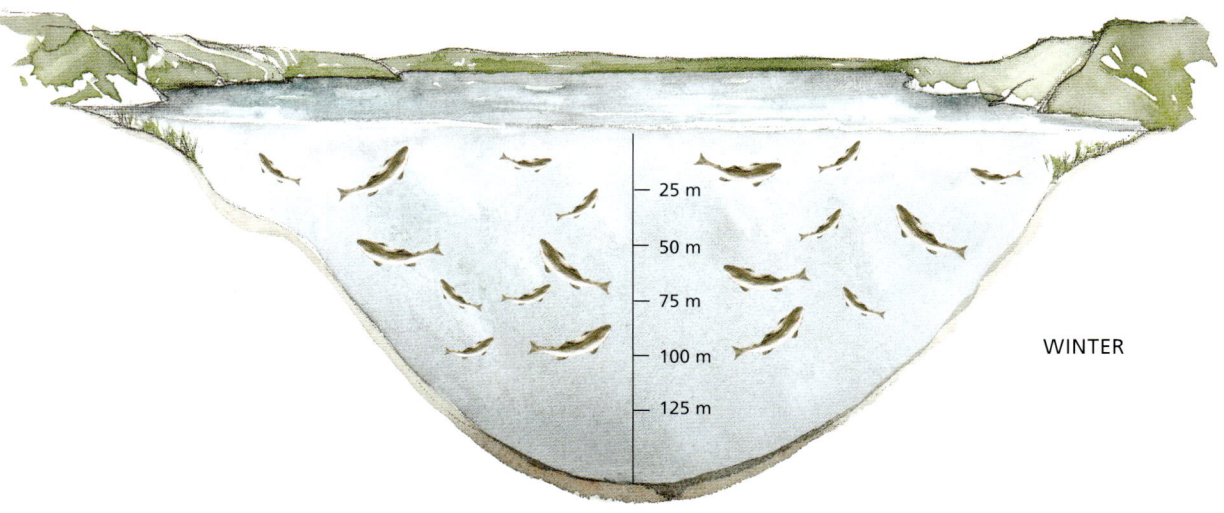

Winter and summer depth distribution of trout in Lake Taupo.

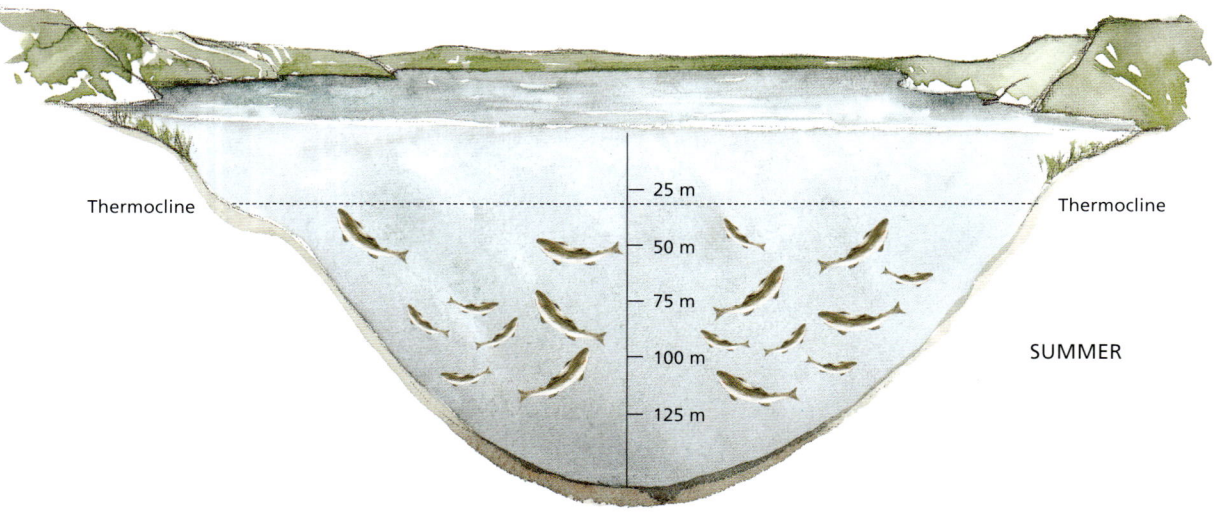

waters in lakes that lack smelt, so the littoral zone – including deep weed beds – is better, with the largest trout inhabiting the shallow littoral.

However, this does not mean that adult trout are never encountered in the limnetic zone. A recent study of radio-tagged trout in Lake Coleridge during mid- to late summer revealed that some adult rainbows wandered between the littoral and limnetic zones, spending much of their time near the surface offshore. These fish were feeding primarily on terrestrial insects and had no need to stay within the confines of the littoral zone because the lake's entire surface was a potential banquet table. In the same study, yearling rainbows in the limnetic zone were found to be feeding mainly on larval bullies at about ten metres depth.

Adult brown trout have also been radio tagged in Lake Coleridge. In contrast to rainbows (but in keeping with the results of other studies), these browns spent most of their time in the littoral zone near the shoreline.

Distribution of trout in relation to the distribution of food

Comparing trout diet between Taupo, Waikaremoana and Alexandrina highlights the differences in the relative importance of littoral versus limnetic productivity, and explains why the trout are distributed they way they are in the respective lakes.

In Lake Taupo, smelt comprise by far the bulk of the diet of rainbow trout. Because smelt are pelagic fish, living mainly offshore in midwater, that is where the trout spend most of their time. Smelt densities are usually low in the shallow littoral, except in late spring, when adult smelt move inshore to spawn. Spawning smelt are vulnerable to trout predation, and after spawning, in their weakened condition, they are particularly easy prey. Also, because the spawning smelt are the biggest fish, they provide better energy return for effort of capture than smaller smelt.

The size of smelt may limit the average size of trout in Lake Taupo (and also in the Rotorua lakes), and be responsible for changes in the diet of larger trout. For best energy-efficiency, predatory fish feeding on pelagic forage fish prefer prey at least 10 per cent of their own length. Most smelt eaten by trout in Lake Taupo are about four centimetres, and few grow more than five centimetres. The growth of rainbow trout in Taupo slows down after the fish reach about fifty centimetres in length – roughly coinciding with the 10 per cent rule above. Among the Rotorua lakes, those that grow the largest smelt also grow the largest trout. This is thought to be linked with the energetics of feeding on actively swimming prey, which are more difficult to catch than invertebrates on the bottom.

The artful science of trout fishing

As trout grow, the energy return for effort in capturing active prey like smelt diminishes and eventually limits maximum size. This is because the energy cost of swimming (and chasing prey) increases exponentially with the size of trout.

Lake Taupo produced much larger trout during the early days of its fishery. During the 1890s, rainbows up to twenty-seven pounds (twelve kilograms) were taken and double-figure fish were routine. At that time the lake had a prolific population of koaro, which the trout apparently found easy prey. As the koaro population became severely depleted, trout size and condition deteriorated, causing consternation among anglers and the fishery managers. The solution was to introduce common smelt to the lake: the trout recovered condition but never again attained the large size that they did when koaro were abundant.

Koaro live longer and grow larger than smelt, so, in addition to a huge seasonal biomass of whitebait, large numbers of adult koaro also would have been available for trout to prey on in Lake Taupo. Therefore, in the early years Taupo fish were less limited by the energetic constraints of feeding on small forage fish, unlike nowadays when smelt are their main food.

When rainbow trout in Lake Taupo reach about forty-five centimetres, they change their habits to include more littoral prey in their diet — presumably associated with the decreasing energetic return from smelt. For example, smelt make up 78 per cent of the diet of juvenile trout, dropping to 64 per cent when they are legal-sized trout. Larger trout eat even fewer smelt. Green beetles and midges comprise much of the remaining portion of the diet of both juveniles and older fish, but snails are also important for the older trout. Rainbow trout in the Rotorua lakes also have been found to rely less on smelt and more on littoral prey as they grow larger. Smelt comprise up to 99 per cent of the diet of juvenile rainbows in the Rotorua lakes, declining to 58–80 per cent of the diet of trout larger than forty-five centimetres. Other prey of these larger trout include koura (4–35 per cent), bullies (6–15 per cent) and insects (less than 7 per cent). In turbid waters, trout feed more on littoral forage fish like bullies — presumably because they find these easier than smelt to catch when visibility is poor.

As discussed earlier, trout make more use of the littoral zone in Waikaremoana than in Taupo because the former has a more productive shallow littoral zone. However, both these lakes contain smelt, so trout live in the limnetic zones of both for a considerable proportion of their lives. Smelt provide a reliable food source in the limnetic zone, and they are available for a longer period of the year than either larval bullies or water fleas. In Waikaremoana, this

The habitat

means that it is worthwhile for trout to grow in the limnetic zone past the yearling stage, until they reach sexual maturity at about forty centimetres. As trout approach this length they move inshore to feed on larger littoral foods such as dragonfly larvae, koura, bullies and even frogs.

When smelt are not present the limnetic zone is much less attractive to trout, and the littoral zone is where they find most of their food. Apart from smelt, the main limnetic prey include larval bullies, whitebait, chironomid midges (mainly pupae emerging from the lake bed and rising to the surface, and adults) and water fleas. However, unlike smelt, these are only seasonal.

In Alexandrina, the only fish to make any real use of the limnetic zone are rainbow trout – and then only seasonally, during spring and winter. The trout must move into the littoral zone at an earlier age than in smelt lakes because prey are not available year-round in the limnetic zone. Snails are the staple year-round littoral prey for trout in this lake. Three species are eaten: the tiny but very abundant *Potamopyrgus* (six millimetres), through the middle-sized,

Beautiful Lake Alexandrina offers sport for anglers stalking the shore or fishing from a boat.

soft-shelled and easily digestible *Physa* (twelve millimetres), to the large air-breathing pond snail *Limnea stagnalis* (forty millimetres). Only the larger trout eat this last species, which can often be seen floating at the water surface as it takes in air.

The other important prey for trout in Alexandrina are forage fish, including galaxiids (koaro whitebait) and bullies. Koaro and post-larval bullies are important in mid- to late summer (January–March), when they make up a quarter of the diet. At this time the post-larval bullies move to the shallow littoral and settle on the bottom. Adult bullies are important prey in winter, when they form 89 per cent of the diet.

Other prey are seasonally important; for example, emerging pupae of midges and caddisflies, in spring to early summer. Emerging chironomid pupae comprise 58 per cent (by number) of the diet of trout in Alexandrina in October to November. Dragonfly larvae are favoured in late spring to early summer (December–January) as they leave the cover of weed beds and crawl out on to the shoreline and its vegetation to metamorphose into adults. Damselflies are also targeted in late spring to early summer, when the trout eat both the narrow, wriggling larvae and the adults. Usually it is the younger, more active trout that feed on adult damselflies – catching them with spectacular leaps and slashing rises.

This is also a time when many terrestrial insects (including green beetles) are on the lake surface. Anglers can be guaranteed to encounter rising trout, especially large browns, around the shore of Alexandrina and other South Island lakes. Research has shown that terrestrial insects comprise up to 20 per cent of the diet of rainbow trout in summer, and suggests that brown trout feed less from the surface than do rainbows. However, shore anglers encounter brown trout more often than rainbows feeding from the surface of lakes – especially during early summer. Later in the summer, warm surface waters can restrict trout to bottom foraging.

Over summer, the larger trout in the Rotorua lakes feed more on bullies, koura and other prey on the lake bed than at other times of the year – possibly because the warm surface waters limit their access to smelt in the surface waters.

In quest of a cruising trout

Lakes offer varied fishing opportunities – perhaps more so than rivers. For many anglers, Les and myself included, stalking trout is the ultimate angling experience. New Zealand is internationally renowned for its many rivers that lend themselves to stalking big trout in clear waters. Perhaps less well known are the many clear lakes that also offer stalking opportunities. Living in Nelson,

The habitat

I can choose among a wealth of rivers not too far from home that offer opportunities for stalking trout. However, the region is not so blessed with quality lake fisheries. A trait of human nature is to covet what we can not have. Perhaps it is for this reason that I find myself so often reminiscing about, and pining for, clear lakes in which to stalk trout. A lake neither too large nor too small, with trees along its margins to offer shade for an angler to rest on a hot summer's day and to give cover for big cruising brown trout, comes to mind; not unlike Lake Alexandrina, now too far from home, where, in the past, I have spent so many memorable fishing days.

On one such day, with no hint of breeze to stir its calm, Alexandrina returned a perfect reflection of grey mountains and the azure sky. Voices of black swan, scaup, and crested grebe were carried far across the water by the still air. The warm light of an early-morning sun sparkled on the water under overhanging willows, and the aromas of the Mackenzie Country filled the air: dust, tussock, the sweet flower of the matagouri bush, and merino sheep. A consummate day for spotting big browns cruising the lakeshore.

Over half an hour had passed since I had left the hut and a brisk walk on dusty sheep trails along the willow-lined shore of the lake

A trout cruising a lake edge in search of food.

The artful science of trout fishing

had led me nearly to my goal. In pursuit of one particular trout I had passed by several likely spots along the way, giving them only a cursory glance. I was anxious to keep moving in case this day's potential was lost by a wind stirring, or by another angler seeking the same piece of shoreline.

Five days earlier I had trodden the same path. I had heard the fish first, a faint 'slurp' under thick willows up ahead, and stopped beside a big white lichen-covered boulder on the side of the hill overlooking a twenty-metre gap in the willows, which ran in an unbroken line for hundreds of metres either side. I strained to see over the matagouri bushes scattered along the clearing below me. In a window free of glare, I could see through the water surface for a few metres along the mossy bank before the willow margin up ahead. I waited, five minutes, ten minutes, fifteen minutes, which seemed like an hour. Fighting impatience to move to a new position, I waited another five minutes. I saw the bulge of the rise first, then the slurp five metres away, but still under the edge of the willows. Thirty seconds later a very large brown trout materialised in the window. It turned toward the bank, very slowly rose up and broke the surface with the by-now-familiar slurp. My heartbeat kicked up a few levels as I took an adrenaline hit. I hunched down a little in case the trout could see me and waited for it to pass by. It clearly was not comfortable in the open, because it only swam a third of the way across the clearing before turning out to the edge of the drop-off and cruising back the way it had come – to the safety of the willows.

As soon as the trout was out of sight I scrambled down the bank among the matagouri and flicked a size 12 Love's Lure dry fly out about three metres from the water's edge. I then eased back and crouched under the cover of a big matagouri bush, draping the fly line carefully over the grass and resting the rod tip on the ground to avoid scaring the trout when it returned. There I waited, my focus shifting alternately from the fly riding high on the water surface, to the edge of shade from which I expected the trout to appear.

Five minutes went by, then ten. I shuffled about to ease the cramp in my legs. Then I heard a slurp from thirty metres away, and another a little later, closer at twenty metres, and yet another only ten metres under the willows. This is it, I thought: any minute now . . . In anticipation I judged the distance of the rises out from the bank as being only two metres, so I carefully drew the fly in towards the bank a little. I waited . . . and waited . . . another ten minutes went by, and with them my hopes. Reluctantly, I conceded that the trout had turned and cruised back under the willows again, avoiding the clearing, and my trap.

Another fifteen minutes of waiting exhausted my patience, so I

The habitat

A lake-shore stalker whose pronounced lean foward suggests that a trout is cruising in the vicinity.

retrieved my line and carefully stalked a few metres back from the bank under the willows. The problem I faced was shade and glare: I just could not see clearly enough to spot the trout without it seeing me. Changing tack, I climbed up a convenient willow and along a bough leaning out over the water. From this position I could see through the water directly underneath and for a few metres either side. No sign of the trout. I slowly moved my rod into position and dapped the fly on the surface directly below, taking care to pull the leader knot clear of the tip ring and avoid a disaster in the event of hooking the trout. I resigned myself to another interminable period of waiting.

It was the suddenness of the trout's appearance that unsettled me – and its size. I was just getting comfortable in my new position when a broad-backed, heavily spotted female brown trout of at least four kilograms appeared below my fly and engulfed it. My reaction was instinctive instead of calculated. I struck upward, to the extent that the overhanging branches allowed – in hindsight, too early before the trout had turned down with the fly. The line tightened momentarily, the trout gave a heavy swirl and dashed for the deep water over the drop-off, leaving my line tangled loosely among the willow branches beside me. I felt the hollow emptiness of opportunity lost.

Soon afterwards, the wind came up and put an end to any further chances with other fish that might have lessened the disappointment of losing my big fish. On the homeward journey I hesitated, hopeful, at the big boulder overlooking the clearing, ruefully playing over in my head the course of my failed stalk. The image of the trout's broad back, big head, and its eye turning, focused on my fly in the instant of the rise, was still fresh in my memory. In resignation I turned and trudged away, reassuring myself that I would return as soon as the weather allowed.

Now, five days later, I was back on a perfect Saturday morning with everything in my favour: the weather and first-hand knowledge of the big trout's feeding beat. If she would, just for a moment, forgo the safety of those willows and cruise out into the open of that clearing, I felt sure I could catch her. And now yet another thing was in my favour: the warm weather over the past week had encouraged green beetles to stir among the matagouri. I could see them peppered on the water's surface. Opening my fly box, I selected a fair imitation of this favourite of cruising trout, tied it to a four-pound tippet, and doused it in fly floatant.

With anticipation building, I quickened my pace. As I rounded a bend within three hundred metres of the clearing my heart sank as two anglers strolled along the track toward me, both intently looking down toward the lake edge. The elder of the two was in front, a gaunt figure with a grey beard, the other younger – possibly the son? As the distance between us closed, our eyes met and uncomfortable, but polite, greetings were exchanged.

'Having any luck?' I asked.

'Yep, the young fella got one half an hour ago,' the greybeard replied. 'It was a real beauty, a nine-pound hen. We left her in our boat in the shade away back there, so we can't show you now.'

'Heard her rising under the willows and ambushed her in the open,' the young one said eagerly. 'I got her in the next clearing in the willows, the one with the big boulder with a white patch on the top.'

They must have noticed – my entire body sagged. 'What fly are you using?' I choked.

'Green beetle,' they replied in unison. 'You must have seen them – there are heaps on the water.'

PART THREE

Feeding behaviours and fishing strategies

The artful science of trout fishing

As the following chapters will show, trout are extremely efficient and adaptable feeders. A trout guarding a river-edge territory may drift feed for a period, then stray into an area of still water and immediately adopt a bottom-feeding, cruising strategy. The same fish will respond immediately to a surface hatch, or forage along grassy banks covered by discoloured waters during a fresh.

The physical conditions of a river or lake are continually changing, and the life in these waters responds too. Trout are an integral part of this, continually modifying their behaviour. However, one thing that does not change for many dominant fish is the general feeding territory, particularly in less populated high-country rivers. Big fish achieve their size by feeding efficiently. Fundamental to this is selecting a favourable territory and occupying it for a long period of time – sometimes for months, even several years.

I have frequently noticed that some fish can be found in the same feeding lie throughout a season, and then in the same spot for several years thereafter. To be reacquainted with such trout, especially ones weighing four kilograms or more, is an exciting prospect and vindicates the practice of catch-and-release.

Several encounters with one particular Canterbury monster illustrate the strong territorial ties that some fish hold. I first caught this fish in early summer a few seasons ago. The river jostled along energetically, still boosted by spring snowmelt. Because the current was strong, my stalking was focused close to the bank, especially where the undercuts were pronounced. I was very cautious when approaching an attractive looking lie – ahead a mass of large boulders kept the bed stable, while below the rocks the bed deepened to a fine pocket, part of which remained concealed beneath the bank.

I stood focused on the pocket for some time. It was one of those places that had to hold a fish. And it did! My first sighting was nothing more than a glimpse. A shape drifted sideways into view, then returned into hiding. I stood only six metres away, but because the fish lay out of view I had no hesitation in casting from close by. My nymph pitched into the river first and a dry-fly indicator landed lightly above, then drifted towards me. On this occasion the indicator proved unnecessary: the rise of the fish from the bottom was obvious, as was the opening and closing of its huge jaws. From the moment that the hook was set, the immense energy of a fish in prime condition prevailed. In an instant the big trout sped into midstream, then cavorted about on the surface. My contribution to the battle was minimal – a firm grip on my rod, generous offerings of line when the fish demanded it and an appreciative audience as it wore itself out.

A back-country river holding large territorial trout, such as the one stubbornly resisting this angler.

Once the trout lay secure in my net and the line tension was released, the hook fell free. This allowed me to return the trout to the water quickly, but not before I noted that its right-side maxillary (jaw) was deformed – a minor blemish on a fat young four-kilogram jack.

In mid-April of that season I landed the same fish (verified by the broken maxillary) for a second time. On this occasion it was feeding on the outer edge of its pocket, several metres from the bank, enjoying an autumn mayfly hatch until I interrupted the feast with a tiny imitation. The fish demonstrated its disapproval of my intrusion, as it had done a few months before, but eventually relented to grim determination and a little luck.

The third landing of the same trout occurred in late spring two years later. This time it refused several flies before succumbing. I doubt that it remembered our previous encounters – I imagine that its selectivity related to the low flow and clarity of the water. However, it fed in the same lie, still had its broken maxillary – and, excitingly, had grown to about four and a half kilograms. After congratulating it on this achievement, and encouraging it to do even better during the next year, I released the fish for the third time.

CHAPTER EIGHT

Feeding behaviour in rivers and fishing strategies

Trout have flexible feeding-behaviour patterns that enable them to exploit a variety of habitats in rivers, from swift headwaters, to meandering lower reaches and backwaters, to turbid tidal reaches. Broadly speaking, trout feeding behaviour in rivers can be categorised into drift feeding, benthic (bottom) browsing and ambush feeding. A fourth, minor, foraging strategy is still-water-column feeding.

Drift feeding

Drift feeding is the predominant foraging behaviour of trout in flowing water. At any time the density of aquatic invertebrates drifting in the water column represents only about 1.5–2 per cent of those on the stream bed. However, most aquatic invertebrates live in relatively fast, shallow water, while trout are found in deeper, slower water.

Drifting is the process by which invertebrates from shallow riffles and runs are transported to the deeper water where trout live. Rather than expending a lot of energy fighting the current to feed in fast water, trout hold position in moderate currents and let the invertebrates come to them. The river can be thought of as a giant conveyor belt carrying the food to the waiting trout.

Incidentally, the 1.5–2 per cent of drift in the water column is roughly equivalent to the average surplus production of benthic invertebrates in most trout rivers. This means that by feeding on the drift, trout do not normally overexploit their invertebrate food supply.

Benthic invertebrates in trout rivers typically number about 1,600 per square metre of coarse gravel or cobble riffle, and weigh perhaps fifteen grams. With 1.5–2 per cent surplus production, each square metre of river bed should generate twenty to thirty animals to the drift. This represents about 200,000–300,000 invertebrates per hectare, weighing 0.85–1.28 kilograms. A riffle a hundred metres long and ten metres wide would produce each day a harvestable surplus of about 50,000–89,000 drifting invertebrates, weighing 590–890

Underwater photo from video footage of a drift-feeding trout.
Cawthron Institute

The artful science of trout fishing

grams. This amounts to 700–1,000 kilograms per hectare of river bed, sufficient to support about seventy to a hundred kilograms of trout. This is within the typical range of fish production reported for trout rivers around the world.

In moderate to swift water, drift-feeding trout improve their energy return for effort by sheltering from the full force of the current in velocity refuges, such as behind a rock or bank extension, from which they swim out to intercept invertebrates in the faster water. Sometimes they hold station in front of boulders, taking advantage of the pressure wave. In slow water, or when a hatch produces a temporary abundance of food, trout may forage in the full force of the current, often near the surface, and weave about in the current as they intercept one insect after another.

It can be seen from the following example that drift feeding is an energetically profitable strategy. My research team studied invertebrate drift in the Maruia, a typical back-country river in the South Island. We found average drift densities over summer of about 3.8

An angler drifting a fly down with the flow to a sighted fish.

insects per cubic metre of water — equivalent to about 1,500 insects per hour passing through the foraging area of a fifty-centimetre or larger adult trout. However, many of these insects are too small for trout this size to bother with. If we look only at insects larger than six millimetres, about the minimum prey size for trout larger than fifty centimetres, then we are left with about 0.48 insects per cubic metre, or 915 per hour passing through the trout's foraging area. This is about 13,725 insects over a day in the middle of summer (say, fifteen hours of daylight). So there is indeed a very large number of prey available to trout in a good back-country river.

Of course, the trout will not attempt to eat all of the potential prey. Some insects will drift by undetected, especially if the water is discoloured, and a proportion of the smaller insects will be ignored in favour of the larger ones. An Alaskan colleague and I found that, during daylight, adult drift-feeding trout (fifty to sixty centimetres) in a New Zealand back-country river were 55 per cent efficient at intercepting invertebrates passing through their foraging area. This foraging-efficiency estimate was for invertebrates in the size range that adult trout ought to be able to see and attempt to eat.

At dusk, drift densities are even higher. Trout may be exposed to a superabundance of food, although only for a short time before darkness shrinks the foraging area to a small fraction of that during daylight. When the trout are exposed to high drift rates, as at dusk, most are able to fill their guts relatively quickly. They then need to seek out safe, low-velocity resting positions and digest their food. Small trout are more quickly satiated than large trout, owing to their small gut capacity, so they spend more of their time hiding and resting. However, this only applies if the diet is restricted to benthic and drifting invertebrates. If larger prey such as fish or koura are abundant, large trout can more quickly fill their bellies and may only come on the feed for short periods each day, such as at dawn and dusk.

Drift-feeding brown trout are masters of energy conservation. In addition to using velocity shelters, they use their large pectoral fins to gain lift off the river bed when intercepting invertebrates. This hydrodynamic lift, or Benouli effect, allows the trout to be lifted off the bottom with minimal effort. Browns also employ their pectoral fins to hold station in fast currents with minimal energy expenditure. By twisting the pectoral fins down at the leading edge, the trout can use the force of the current to sit tightly on the stream bed.

To offset the energetic cost of making feeding forays into a fast current, trout prefer large food items. Generally, adult trout don't bother with insects less than three millimetres long, and even insects less than six millimetres are rarely eaten. A six-millimetre insect corresponds to a size 18 fly. Diet studies have shown that trout strongly

A trout's large pectoral fins are used to generate lift during feeding.

prefer the larger prey items, up to thirty millimetres, if available. This does not necessarily mean that the angler is better off presenting large artificial flies to the trout, because the larger the artificial, the more likely the trout is to shy, especially in smooth water.

When trout feed on small insects they do so in slow currents where swimming costs are lower. In midsummer on willow-lined lowland rivers, trout may be found feeding almost exclusively on willow grubs – the four- to six-millimetre larvae of a tiny sawfly that produce the red blisters on willow leaves. The abundance of willow grubs and the slow current make feeding without the aid of a velocity refuge energetically profitable.

In back-country rivers, where gradients and water velocities are higher and the trout are large, big flies are more effective. In fact, back-country trout often will ignore flies smaller than size 14. Because these fish feed in fast currents, they do not have the time to carefully inspect food items rushing by, so they usually are not spooked by large dry flies. Sometimes very large dry flies elicit adrenaline-pumping responses from back-country river trout. In these rivers, big trout can be enticed to move up to three metres across a current or up from the bottom to intercept a bushy size 8 deer-hair dry fly.

Research on drift-feeding salmonids has shown that the distance they will move to intercept a drifting invertebrate (the foraging radius) depends on how far away the fish can see the prey (prey-detection distance, or reaction distance), and the water velocity. The prey-detection distance is primarily determined by the size of the prey, but also by the size of the fish itself. Larger fish have bigger eyes that can detect objects further away because more light falls on the retina.

At first there is a rapid increase in the maximum prey detection distance as a trout grows from the fry stage to about nine centimetres and ten grams. Thereafter the increase in prey detection distance becomes less with increasing size, finally flattening off at about sixteen centimetres and fifty grams. For trout worth catching, prey size is the main factor influencing the prey-detection distance. The latter is proportional to prey length – the larger the prey, the further away trout can see it.

Once the prey is detected and the trout starts moving sideways or upward to intercept it, water velocity determines whether or not the fish can capture the prey before it is swept past. This means that, for a given water velocity, the prey-detection distance must be close enough to allow the trout enough time to intercept the prey. The larger the prey, the greater the detection distance, and so the greater the foraging radius.

A few years ago I made a computer model that used these principles to predict the foraging radius of drift-feeding trout and how much food they could get from the drift (see page 128). The model was part of a larger computer program that predicted how fast drift-feeding trout should grow, related to water temperature and invertebrate drift density.

If you watch trout drift feeding in New Zealand back-country rivers, you will see that they rarely move more than a metre to intercept drifting prey. When I began testing the computer model it was predicting that large trout (over fifty centimetres) ought to move three metres or more for large invertebrates (over twenty millimetres). Big trout will move these sorts of distances to take large, bushy, attractor-pattern dry flies – so why don't they for naturals? This puzzle was solved once I looked at the range of sizes of invertebrates drifting down our rivers. Most of them are small: less than ten millimetres long. The computer model predicted that the foraging radius of a fifty- to sixty-centimetre trout feeding on ten-millimetre prey should be about a metre. The predicted foraging radius increases in roughly one-metre steps for every ten-millimetre increase in prey length, but prey of twenty millimetres or more are uncommon. During the time that most anglers watch a feeding trout, preparing to try to catch it – say, ten minutes or so – there is only a low chance that a large invertebrate will drift through the trout's foraging area. Consequently, most of the time trout appear to make relatively short feeding forays.

The trout's prey-detection distance is also very dependent on the water clarity. One of the reasons why trout in New Zealand's back-country rivers grow so large is that the water clarity gives them a large foraging radius. This means they can make the most of the large invertebrates, even though these are infrequent. The trout's prey-detection distance and resulting foraging radius decrease very rapidly as water becomes turbid, because the foraging area is proportional to the square of the foraging radius. In other words, a small reduction in water clarity of a very clear river will bring about a comparatively large reduction in the foraging area of trout. At the other end of the scale, in already turbid rivers, a similar proportional reduction in water clarity produces a much smaller relative reduction in foraging area. Over time, even a relatively small reduction in the foraging radius can seriously reduce the trout's food intake.

Unfortunately, many of New Zealand's lowland rivers now run turbid for much of the year, owing to accelerated erosion caused by agriculture and related processing industries. These rivers include some formerly great trout fisheries. The impact on the aquatic insects and trout has only recently begun to be realised among New Zealand fishery scientists and managers.

Occasionally trout will move a long way to intercept a large

The artful science of trout fishing

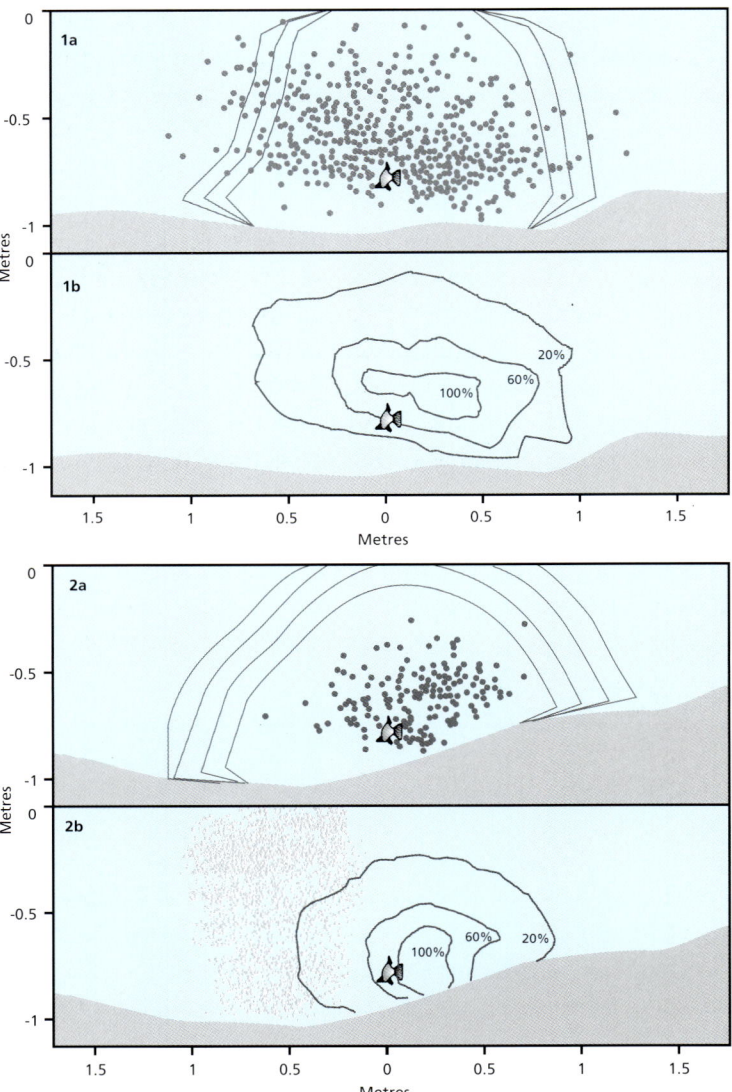

Figures comparing the foraging areas of drift-feeding brown trout predicted by computer models with actual prey interceptions recorded by stereo underwater video cameras. Figures 1a and 2a show the actual prey interceptions (dots) and the predicted foraging boundaries for different prey size classes (stepping up in millimetre increments from six millimetres). Figures 1b and 2b show foraging efficiency contours, estimated by comparing actual foraging rates with predicted foraging rates based on estimates of the invertebrate drift rate (determined from drift sampling and measurements of water velocity in the foraging area).
The trout rarely move more than a metre sideways to intercept drifting prey because most drifting aquatic insects are too small for them to be seen and intercepted at greater distances before they are swept past the fish.
Figure 2b shows the effect of a bubble plume, at the head of a plunge-pool, reducing the foraging efficiency on the left side of a trout. Bubbles, bright sunlight and drifting debris (sticks and leaves) can confuse drift-feeding trout, causing them to narrow their attention span and to concentrate on that part of their visual field in which they can see most clearly.
From Hughes et al. 2003

Feeding behaviours and fishing strategies

nymph or dry fly. A moving lure can provoke an attack at even greater distance. However, it pays to attempt to place the fly within about a metre of the fish because, as mentioned above, trout make most of their feeding forays within that distance from their focal points. And, of course, the smaller the fly, the closer you have to present it to the fish.

When nymph fishing, it is very important to get the fly down to the fish, within the strike zone. Anglers inexperienced with back-country river fishing in New Zealand often underestimate the depth at which the trout are lying, and use nymphs with too little weight. In fast, deep runs and in deep pools a really heavy 'bomb' is often necessary. One option is to use a large nymph (size 10 or larger) incorporating plenty of lead. However, educated trout may refuse such a large offering – except perhaps in fast water when they can't get a good look at it. Another option is to use a large, heavy nymph plus a small nymph on a dropper (short trace). Other options include lead shot or lead putty, or even tungsten beads in nymphs, which are even denser than lead and sink very fast, but are expensive.

HUMAN MEMORY is an intriguing thing. There is no doubt that it deteriorates with age and people can be quite selective in what they can recall. Some of us can remember names and faces; others retain trivia quite remarkably. My selective memory seems to focus on days spent fishing, and the events of each day.

About twenty years ago I fished at the mouth of the Roaring Lion River, close to where it enters a lake formed when the Karamea River was dammed by earthquake activity. My day's remembered highlight was the hooking of one particular fish. At the time I was fishing with Eric Sawers, who was just beginning to learn to cast a fly. We had positioned ourselves downstream of a feeding fish with the intention that Eric should try for it. Uncertain about the length of line to use, he suggested that I work the right amount of line out first, then he would take charge of the rod and cast.

Where we stood the river ran reasonably free of obstructions. It flowed relatively placidly. I lifted a short line into the air, and then worked the rod back and forth, increasing the line length. Sometimes when doing this I like to drop the fly on to the water, well clear of a fish that has been targeted. By laying out the line an angler can see very clearly whether the 'in air' estimation has been accurate. On this occasion I elected to put the fly down in order to be sure that Eric would have a good chance of tempting his fish.

I recall being conscious of not wanting to attract the trout's attention with a heavy false drop, so I aimed for a spot about five or six metres away. And that's where it landed. Instantly the fish responded and raced towards the fly. Eric's fish? No! It was now Les's fish! To whip the fly clear of the water would undoubtedly cause alarm. I can recall clearly the determination that this fish showed: a relentless pursuit for a remarkably long distance. I felt very guilty as I passed the rod to Eric for him to complete the landing. I knew that he would have been more satisfied had he set the hook.

On another occasion I remember landing a fine jack fish that weighed around three and a half kilograms. This trout fed close to shore near the tail of a deep pool. Because the water was deep and the flow quite slow, I dropped the fly about two metres to the fish's side – far enough away to be less likely to scare it. From the moment the fly fell, the trout was in pursuit. This was a big fish. It displayed no haste. Instead, it turned sedately and weaved gradually downstream. I became increasingly anxious at the fish's lethargy. I could see a belly of line developing and being caught in an accelerating tail of the pool flow, then the fly began to drag on the water's surface. At this point I expected the fish to slow even more and abandon its chase. However, the opposite occurred. As the fly increased its downstream speed, the fish went faster. I watched in amazement as the trout seized the fly just before it tumbled into the next pool. The pursuit ended many metres from the fish's feeding position.

Both these incidents occurred on remote rivers, and both times I am certain that the fish had been subjected to little or no angling pressure. I have observed a similar pattern of behaviour often enough to suggest that fish that encounter few anglers are more likely to range wider for food than those disturbed frequently.

Another factor I believe affects the distance that trout will move to take food is the nature of a stream's flow. Where a fish holds in a lie sheltering from nearby fast current, the trout is less likely to venture far. There are two explanations for this. First, such a fish would not need to move far because the flow is fast and should deliver a lot of drifting food. Second, for the fish to venture far would use too much energy.

Conversely, in slow-flowing reaches or still waters like backwaters or lake edges, trout not only use little energy in ranging further, but the flatter nature of the surface (when the wind doesn't blow) enables the fish to sight food from further away. These fish do move further to take an insect than their fast-water cousins, but because their vision is unimpaired, they must be sought with greater caution.

Two other factors that affect the distance fish may move to take food are the nature of the food offered and the water clarity.

Obviously, trout can see further in very clear water, and they use this to advantage. I've seen it demonstrated very often in the pristine waters of many Fiordland streams.

In summer, when large terrestrial insects such as cicadas and beetles fall into rivers, trout will move remarkable distances to take their fill. Similarly, they will range widely during a prolific hatch of aquatic insects. They can afford to because the food intake can be large – the energy balance is clearly in the trout's favour.

A very clear river in which trout enjoy excellent visibility.

S TUDIES OF TROUT FEEDING have repeatedly shown that they prefer larger prey. However, on the river we are often faced by trout appearing to do the opposite. Many readers will recall infuriatingly selective trout ignoring their flies for tiny midges or other minuscule naturals – or taking mayflies to the exclusion of anything else, including everything in the fly box. How can this paradox be explained?

First, although trout show a degree of selectivity, they are still basically opportunistic and eat a great variety of prey, varying in proportion by season, time of day, place, and between individual fish. So there is always the hope that a selective trout may be caught later, or that another fish around the next bend in the river will be more obliging.

Selective feeding is more common among trout in lowland

The artful science of trout fishing

A fine brown trout taking a natural surface fly.

rivers, especially when they are taking abundant small prey. The more abundant any one prey is, and the longer trout have been exposed to it, the more they tend to specialise on it. This does not mean that they will entirely ignore a novel prey item passing through their foraging area, but they will take proportionately less of it than the more common prey. Trout are thought to develop a 'search image' that enables them to more efficiently see and more quickly capture their prey. Theoretically, this increases their total prey intake, even when it means they overlook some other prey.

Trout take time to habituate to new prey. In one study it took five to twenty-five minutes, during which time 25–250 prey drifted by, before any of a new prey were taken by trout, and at least six days for selective-feeding behaviour to fully develop. It is therefore not surprising that trout often ignore an artificial fly. It is tempting to conclude that these observations imply that trout might eventually respond to an artificial fly, provided the angler has the patience to continue casting. I have heard the odd story where persistence has paid off. However, in my experience the more the trout is presented with a fly that it has refused, the more likely it is to spook. Unless each presentation is faultless, the angler runs the risk with each cast that the trout will sense something is out of place.

Studies of optimal foraging behaviour have shown that fish are more likely to be selective when food is abundant. When prey densities are low, trout select large and small prey equally often, as they have to make the most of all prey. But at high prey densities they select large prey, thereby maximising their energy intake and minimising their activity costs. Something similar is presumably going on when trout key into one prey of average size, such as mayflies.

It needs to be appreciated that when trout are searching the water column they are faced with distinguishing real prey items from a host of other objects – sticks, leaves and other debris, and foam and bubbles on and within the water. A search image for the prey that is most abundant at any one time enables them to do this efficiently. That trout learn to distinguish between real prey and flotsam drifting by is demonstrated by the fact that recently emerged fry will sample just about everything within their visual range that is small enough to fit in their mouths. Within a few weeks, however, they become much more discriminating and only rarely mouth drifting debris. When a lot of debris is drifting down a river, trout may also reduce their foraging radius, as scientists have found for Arctic grayling.

Another factor that may give the impression of selective feeding is that the artificial fly simply may not be a convincing deception.

This point is particularly relevant in situations where trout have become 'educated' through fishing pressure, though that may not be the sole cause of this behaviour. Seasonal changes in flow and water temperature may also make the trout more difficult to catch. In back-country rivers around Nelson during midsummer and later, trout often spook at the sight of an artificial nymph. Sometimes they are less likely to be spooked by a dry fly, presumably because they do not get such a clear look at objects on the surface. Through bitter experience I have found that in these situations it is best to present a dry fly first. If this is refused, then try a nymph, but it is not wise to present the same nymph if the fish has had a good look at it on the first pass and refused it.

One way to beat wary or selective trout is to concentrate your fishing effort on fast water where the trout have little time to inspect the fly. In summer, big trout often feed in the fast water right at the heads of runs and pools, nosing into the riffles and rapids. They can be difficult to see, but they can be consistently taken on nymphs and dry flies when trout in slower waters are difficult to catch because they have plenty of time to inspect the fly or see the angler and line.

Two cruising trout approach a dry fly.

One of the fish has taken the fly while the other begins to flee.

The artful science of trout fishing

ONE WAY TO DECEIVE selective trout is to make flies so cleverly, so convincingly, that they 'match the hatch' and are taken by trout along with available naturals. The selectivity exhibited by trout feeding on mayflies is legendary. The endeavours by some creative fly tiers to match natural mayflies cross the boundary from pragmatic approximations of the real thing into works of art. Matching the hatch can also be necessary for catching trout that are selectively sipping willow grubs – trout that, for a while, ignore passing mayflies and other seemingly inviting insects.

In midsummer, willow grubs can fall onto a stream in abundance. I've often watched trout feeding on them, particularly along a slow-flowing, willow-infested stretch of a Nelson stream. While it is a particularly challenging place to fish, with little room to cast and flat water on which to drop fly and line, it is also a most inviting spot. I am attracted by the challenge that the difficulties present, but equally enjoy seeing the fish so clearly and so close as they range about on the surface of the pool, sipping tiny grubs from the surface film.

The last time I visited the stream there were three fat fish feeding boldly and widely. For several minutes I hugged a broad willow bough that sloped out above an undercut bank over deep water. The fish searched widely for their prey – under the willows of the opposite shore, midstream and even right under my hiding place. To an enthusiastic angler the sight of a surface-feeding trout no more than a rod's length away is bettered only by a fish rising to a fly with nylon attached!

I slipped back onto the bank to prepare for at least one deception. Convinced that the nearby fish were feeding on willow grubs, I searched through my fly box for a dainty imitation. For several minutes I rummaged through the multitude of windowed compartments, which seemed to hold every conceivable pattern except a willow grub.

Trout feeding on willow grubs want willow grubs. I knew this, but with none to offer, I clung to the faint chance that one of these fish might accept a small mayfly dun instead. For more than an hour I pursued this hope. My fly passed over each fish several times. It did get inspected at least, inducing brief excitement as the distance between fish and fly narrowed, but the fish fed on, single-mindedly.

I searched my fly box once more and discovered a range of tiny midge pupae. Those tied with black or reddish bodies did not catch my eye, but those with a green body offered possibilities. Their small size was about right, as was the colour. I found four. One had a more generous body and shorter thorax. With scissors and knife I trimmed its tail and then the thorax. While the length of the green body was

Feeding behaviours and fishing strategies

less than ideal and an undesirable length of hook showed where the thorax had been, it was the best I could manage. I attached it to my tippet and waited for a chance to drop it close to a fish.

During the next hour each of the three trout got a look at my grub. The first was frightened off. The second rose to it but threw the hook. The third demonstrated its wariness by inspecting the fly several times before taking it, encouraged to do so, apparently, by an ambitiously close cast adding some movement to the fly. Finally a fish came to my net, one of three that would apparently take only tiny yellow grubs or objects closely resembling them.

Aquatic insect drift increases at dusk and is highest at night, when more large insects also enter the drift. This behaviour is thought to be related to predator avoidance, because trout and other fish prefer large prey. The increase in numbers of large drifting insects at dusk draws large trout out from daytime hiding places – more so in lowland rivers, where they sometimes lie under cover or in deep pools during the day.

In rivers where trout are out feeding during the day, including most back-country rivers, the trout will be found drift feeding in runs and in the heads and eyes of pools. The eye is usually near the head of the pool where the fast water forms an eddy on the side opposite to the main flow of the current. This is a zone of current transition from fast to slow, where the trout can tuck into a suitable feeding velocity and be close to the source of incoming drift. During dusk, and sometimes into the night, trout may move to the smooth tails of pools and margins, especially when there is an evening hatch. The slower current, smooth surface and shallower water presumably give the fish better access to insects on the surface. Trout also become bolder under the cover of failing light. They no longer feel exposed in shallow water and are much less easily disturbed by the angler. Trout more readily accept large dry flies in the evening – partly because they become bolder, but mainly because large flies are more easily seen. A rule of thumb is to use larger flies as the light fails.

Trout change their feeding behaviour with the seasons too. Early in the season they mainly eat aquatic invertebrates, so nymph fishing is consistently most productive – although even then some trout can be tempted to take a dry fly. There are a lot of large late larval stages of aquatic insects in our rivers in spring – so large artificial nymphs generally are worth trying. Rivers are often discoloured at this time of year, which is another reason why large flies (and spinners) work well then. As summer progresses, trout rise

A spent-spinner dry-fly pattern.

more freely because aquatic insect hatches and terrestrial insects become more common. Also, an increase in water temperature (provided it does not get too warm) speeds up their metabolism, requiring them to eat more.

Good mayfly hatches occur on many rivers as autumn approaches. In April, frosty weather provides still conditions for fly fishing and by early afternoon, if the water temperature has risen sufficiently, mayflies may begin emerging. However, by this time of the year many anglers have hung up their waders, leaving the rivers deserted for those whose appetites have not been satiated by the angling excesses of summer.

Each year I look forward to late November and early December, when brown beetles emerge for their mating flights. These beetles are the adults of the grass grub, a pest that feeds on the roots of pasture grasses, and may be the bane of farmers but are a godsend for trout and anglers.

An evening on the upper Matuara comes to mind. It began with my sitting on a grassy bank, watching a deep pool overhung by willows on the far side. The glassy surface was occasionally broken by a delicate rise for a mayfly, but I resisted the temptation to begin fishing, not wanting to disturb the pool prematurely. As the light faded, a buzzing sound began from the field behind me. Looking back across the paddock at ground level, I could see hundreds of brown beetles silhouetted against the setting sun, clumsily beginning their mating flights. Five minutes later the first serious rises began – becoming more bold and frequent as the trout began to gorge. Three fish were rising in the deep water near the far bank. I crept down to the water's edge, being careful not to be seen against the sky. I cast a size 12 deer-hair beetle imitation a metre above the last rise, but the trout had moved closer to the far bank, where it noisily sucked down a natural beetle. My next cast brought success. I counted to two as the rings spread from the rise, then lifted the rod tip solidly. A strong first run into the submerged branches of a fallen willow on the far bank threatened to end the fight prematurely as I grimly held a tight line. However, the trout turned, raced for the tail of the pool and jumped. The next time it headed for the branches I was ready and turned it more easily. The stubborn trout was soon brought to the net and returned to the water.

Time was precious as the light continued to fade. Impatiently I false cast to dry the fly and cast to another trout. It rose to the fly, but I muffed the strike. The pool was now disturbed so I quickly forded the river and headed downstream to a slow run where I had seen fish earlier in the day. Here I was in a better position to see rises by looking across the water surface into the setting sun. The light was very dim; brown beetles were swarming over the paddock behind me, bumbling into my head and crawling down my neck. Six large trout were boldly rising through the length of the run. I cast to the nearest, which immediately took the fly. In the dim light I misjudged the strike and the size of the fish and was promptly broken off.

I wasted time selecting and tying on a new fly, and the torchlight temporarily ruined my night vision. I listened intently for the sound of a rising trout, my eyes straining in the darkness. Two fish were rising near the far bank, so I cast in their general direction. I heard a fish rise, but was it to my fly? I tentatively raised the rod and a solid tug broke me off for the second time! Muttering a few choice words, I attached yet another deer-hair beetle to the leader and was back in business.

A loud slurping rise indicated a large fish only a couple of metres downstream of my position. I flopped, rather than cast, the fly in the general direction, mended loose line, waited three seconds for the drift, and vaguely discerned a rise. This time the line held and I was into another strong fish. I fought it quickly, impatient to cast to another. Within five minutes a fat two-kilogram trout was brought to the net and released. Over the next twenty minutes I landed two more of similar size before darkness brought a stop to the rise. That night on the Mataura was brown-beetle fishing at its best.

Freshes can also provide promising fishing opportunities because they affect drifting invertebrates and trout feeding behaviour. Drift rates increase initially when rivers rise with a fresh, but are often lower than normal following a flood, owing to insects being scoured from the river bed and the greater dilution with higher flow. Good fishing can be experienced in the brief period during the rising stage of a flood before a river becomes too dirty to fish. At that time good sport can be had with very large nymphs (size 6–8 or larger), Woolly Buggers or streamer flies.

O N MOST OCCASIONS when rivers are rising what is happening within the stream goes unobserved. Rivers usually rise while it is raining, a time when most anglers retreat to more comfortable surroundings and miss any action. Also, when a river begins to rise, the period of time before it becomes discoloured is quite short. However, there have been occasions when I have remained streamside in inclement weather – usually when I have been enjoying a week or more 'in the bush' and therefore am more strongly committed to fishing. My most vivid memories are of days fishing in northwest Nelson in the early summer, when trout behaviour is clearly focused on feeding and distractions related to spawning are either in the distant past or months ahead.

What I have noted during that short time while a stream is rising and just before it discolours is that many fish become quite active. I remember one day when Graeme Marshall and I fished a tributary of a major waterway. We had left the hut in between the showers of a frontal system that was passing over us. The stream was getting quite full, covering areas that were previously dry, and we managed to cover just one pool before the inevitable colour arrived. During that brief period we were surprised at the number of fish we saw congregating in the eye of the pool. We hooked two in succession (in a place where we would normally find only one) and saw several others.

Another time I worked my way up the Karamea River while it was quickly rising. I clearly recall the sight of a number of large fish that ranged about on the surface in the main body of the pool. A steep, bush-covered bank prevented me from casting to them so I am not certain whether they were feeding, but the manner of their movement suggested this. What I did observe with certainty (and have since on many occasions) was the increase in debris being carried by the still-clear waters — leaves and twigs in particular. Presumably these had been washed from trees and other vegetation during rain, or picked up from newly covered shores. The volume of trout food would obviously also be increased in the same manner.

By observing the increased drift being carried by rising waters, Brian Smith and I were once saved the difficulties associated with being caught on the wrong side of a high-country river. We had crossed it knee-deep on a sunny morning after having listened to some good showers on the roof of our shelter several hours earlier, then we began stalking upstream, enjoying the bright conditions. We had been fishing for more than an hour and were a considerable distance from the ford when we noticed many more leaves on the water's surface. Although the river was still clear, it was suddenly apparent that its level was rising fast.

We retreated with great haste, running where we could and risking breaking our rods as we weaved through thick beech forest. We linked arms and negotiated the now waist-deep water, then watched in amazement as the river changed from green to brown and from friend to monster in minutes. If there had not been a dramatic increase in drifting debris carried by clear but rising waters, we would have noticed the change too late to cross safely.

Trout not only feed on the more abundant aquatic drift on the rising stage of a fresh, they also move into the inundated river margins seeking food. Many terrestrial species such as worms and grubs get devoured in swollen waters, especially when the fury of a flood has passed. After the worst floods this feast may help to sustain them through leaner times ahead if former feeding beds have been scoured away.

Angling with nymph, wet fly and dry fly is tailored to the pursuit of drift-feeding trout. This is not to say that other methods will not work. Because trout are opportunists, even those that spend most of their time drift feeding will readily attack a feathered lure or spinner if it is presented in an enticing manner. However, it is nymph and dry-fly fishing that arguably offer the greatest reward to the angler. Fly fishing can be a rich and absorbing hobby, and even become a consuming passion involving a lifetime of learning about trout and their insect prey.

Much is made in the angling literature about which flies to use, and when. A casual browse of the myriads of fly patterns on display at any tackle store gives the impression that trout are very discerning and fickle, and that these mysteries need to be mastered before one can hope for success. Fortunately this simply is not so. The variety of fly patterns available has more to do with insects being so diverse and numerous, and the imagination of fly tiers, than with fastidious eating habits of trout. In practice, half a dozen flies, in different sizes, are sufficient to enjoy a good measure of angling success.

The key to successful fly fishing, and to any form of trout fishing for that matter, is realising that much of any river holds no fish, and in most rivers the bigger trout occupy only a small fraction of the available water. It is essential that you learn to 'read' the water and concentrate your fishing effort on the most productive spots.

Most North American anglers that I have taken fishing on New Zealand back-country rivers have difficulty adjusting their fishing style to suit our rivers. They usually start out by methodically fishing the river, spending a lot of time casting and covering the water with the fly. This approach meets with little success, as most New Zealand rivers, especially back-country and wilderness ones, have relatively few trout. However, they make up for it in size.

As a generalisation, North Americans are used to fishing rivers with high numbers of small (fifteen to forty-five centimetres) trout. These can be found in fairly shallow water such as riffles and shallow runs, as well as in pools. When methodically fishing runs and riffles in rivers that hold high densities of these fish, an angler may catch several trout in a few hundred metres of river. Similar river fisheries exist in New Zealand, mainly low-gradient spring creeks, but they are the exception rather than the norm. Most rivers in this

The artful science of trout fishing

country carry larger trout than is the case in North America, and these require deep-water habitats, which can be quite limited in many of our rivers. For this reason, fishing indiscriminately will not usually produce fish. In most New Zealand rivers – and especially when big trout are sought – it pays to be fussy about the water you fish. For consistent success you need to be prepared to walk considerable distances to find the best spots.

First, consider whether the habitat is suitable for the trout, and then whether the depth and flow of the river will suit your gear and method. In special circumstances, if the fish are abundant and small, it can be rewarding fishing riffles and shallow runs. These spots can be good places for beginners to fly fishing. The shallow

Drifting a fly at the head of a pool.

'Joggly' runs are ideal to blind fish with nymph or dry fly.

water suits the gear and the broken surface of the water means the trout will be less easily spooked by a clumsy approach. However, in most situations the trout will not be abundant and those encountered will often be large.

It usually pays to concentrate your fishing effort on deeper water – deep runs (glides) and pools. For the fly fisher, these can be difficult to fish efficiently unless the trout are rising on the surface or visible to the angler. Casting blind over these smooth water surfaces carries a high risk of spooking the trout and it can be difficult to get a fly deep enough for long enough to reach the trout on the bottom of a pool.

When fishing for brown trout, the most productive spots in a pool are the head and the tail-out. The tail-out is usually only worth fishing if fish or rises can be seen or if there is a deep, fast-flowing slot where a blind cast is less likely to spook the fish. The head of the pool is usually the most productive spot, except when the trout are rising to a fly hatch, when they often concentrate in the shallow tail-out of the pool.

The edge of the fast water, either in the eye of the pool or just at the lip where the water is flowing over from the upstream riffle or run, is where brown trout find the best feeding locations. Big rainbow trout can be found in deep water in the main body of pools as well as at the head. Fly fishers should look carefully in these locations when attempting to spot trout. They also produce well to a blind drift with a dry fly or heavy nymph. Usually the water surface is turbulent or broken, and the trout can be only in a limited

The artful science of trout fishing

area, which allows the casts to be focused and reduces the chance of 'lining' the fish (scaring it by the fly line landing on top of it).

The above discussion applies to resident, feeding trout. When fishing for rainbows on their spawning migration, as in the Taupo tributaries, it is essential to be able to sink a fly deep in the pools, because this is where most of the trout hold. This subject is covered later in this chapter.

Getting back to resident trout, the very best spots for nymph and dry-fly fishing are in slightly broken water of moderate depth, where shallow water gives way to deep water. A fishing buddy of mine looks for what he terms 'joggly' runs and knows from experience that these hold the best chance of catching a fish by blind fishing a nymph or dry fly. The greater the proportion of the day that is spent fishing productive water, the more chance there is of catching trout. As long as the legs are up to it, it is better to pass by a mediocre reach in favour of a better spot around the next bend.

The spin or bait angler is better equipped than the fly angler to fish deep pools and big, wide, smooth runs. It is easier to fish a lure deep with spinning gear, and wide featureless reaches of a river can be covered more quickly and efficiently. One drawback, however, is that in very clear water the trout may shy off the spinner or simply follow it to the bank. If this is the case, very realistic lures such as Rapalas may do the trick, otherwise try fishing in the evening when the trout are likely to feed more freely and attack the lure boldly in the waning light.

Smooth, glassy pools such as this are very difficult to fish.

Feeding behaviours and fishing strategies

Sight fishing

One of the most rewarding kinds of angling is sight fishing for large trout in rivers. New Zealand is renowned for clear back-country rivers holding large trout, which provide plenty of sight-fishing opportunities. Spotting trout, however, does not come naturally to many anglers. Many often struggle to spot trout, even when an experienced angler or guide has located the fish for them.

The best way to learn to spot trout is practice, and there are a few essentials to bear in mind. First, the conditions must be good for seeing the fish. The water needs to be clear and the weather relatively calm so as not to ruffle the water surface too much. If you are fishing in open country away from bush, you need the sun to be out, otherwise the glare on the surface will prevent you from seeing into the water. Polaroid sunglasses are almost essential to reduce the glare, but on cloudy days even these may not eliminate it. However, if you are looking into the river with a backdrop of bush or steep hillslope, you can still enjoy good spotting conditions on overcast and cloudy days, and even in light rain. Heavily bushed rivers, therefore, allow trout spotting over a wide range of weather conditions.

Another essential in seeing trout is to concentrate your effort on likely spots. With experience, you learn not to bother looking in detail over the entire river. Trout may occasionally be encountered in shallow runs well away from deep water or cover, but this is the exception rather than the rule. It pays to scan such places quickly, then move on to more likely spots. Look intently where there is a lot of structure – boulders, logs and tree roots – and where the depth is variable – deep slots in runs and at the head of pools. Boulder edges of deep runs, which have a good layer of brown periphyton (slime), provide prime feeding lies, and the heads and tails of pools are other hot spots. The eyes of pools are worth special attention. These are found near the head of pools where the water may swirl around in a back eddy. Eyes occur on the inside of bends opposite the side with the fastest current. Trout usually will be stationed on the edge of the current on the far side of the eddy.

After some experience with spotting trout, you will find that fish begin to stand out. Look for long, dark grey smudges that seem out of place in the rounded broken pattern of the river bed. Be conscious of movement too. Once you spot anything out of the ordinary, it may pay to look slightly away from the object and view it on the edge of your focus point: this helps you detect movement more easily and can make vague objects stand out more against the background. Watch for the white flash as the trout's mouth opens when it takes prey or yawns (which happens quite often).

An angler beside the eye of a pool, a favoured place for big brown trout to feed.

Another useful trick is to make use of 'windows' of smooth water travelling with the current in turbulent water. These give a momentary glimpse of detail through the water column down to the river bottom.

Anglers sight fishing New Zealand rivers usually see large trout. Small fish are more difficult to spot. Also, our rivers are unusual compared with those in most other countries because they tend to support large fish in the headwaters, where most sight fishing is done. In contrast, headwaters of North American and European rivers are nursery grounds, so trout generally get smaller as you go upstream.

Once a trout is located and is cast to, it pays to be aware of what constitutes normal behaviour. An unsuspecting trout will make regular feeding forays to intercept drifting insects. Often it will be continuously weaving about in the current. With experience you can tell when the trout becomes suspicious, as when it sees the angler or line or detects something not quite right about the artificial fly. A tell-tale sign is the trout going 'off the feed' – reducing the frequency of its feeding forays or stopping completely. This often coincides with the trout dropping down through the water column and settling on the bottom. When this occurs you should stop casting and wait to see if the trout comes back on the feed. If your patience is rewarded, use a different fly pattern and very carefully recommence casting.

A common mistake is excessive false casting. The fly line in the air easily spooks back-country river trout, especially in the low, clear water conditions of mid- and late summer.

The following steps should be taken in presenting the fly to a trout in clear water. Carefully move into a position, out of sight and usually downstream from the trout, that will provide a drag-free drift over the fish once the cast is made. Make the first cast away from the trout across the river from your position to estimate the required line length. Then cast to the trout, making as few false casts as possible, and preferably only one or none. For an even more stealthy presentation, use side casts to keep the line low. Avoid dropping the leader directly over the trout: it is best to loop the leader to one side, and allow it to curl around, with the fly falling in front of the fish. If the sun is shining, cast to the opposite side of the trout so that it is not spooked by the shadow of the leader.

For more complete descriptions of sight fishing and how to spot trout and read the water, see *Stalking Trout: A serious fisherman's guide* (Hill & Marshall, 1985) and *Reading Trout Streams: An Orvis guide* (Rosenbauer, 1988).

Opposite: *A sight fishing sequence.*

Top: *A trout has been sighted feeding near the surface downstream from the log, and the angler has cast his fly just ahead of the fish.*

Bottom left: *The trout has taken the fly and the angler has set the hook.*

Bottom right: *The fish is drawn towards the net.*

The artful science of trout fishing

WHEN SIGHT FISHING for trout, I usually search initially for lies – likely feeding stations – and *then* for the fish. In my experience, anglers who are best at spotting trout are those who have the greatest and most natural talent for recognising feeding niches.

Visual clues help identify prime drift-feeding lies. The nature of river bed material is most important. Fine material (sand, silt and small gravel) does not make good habitat for trout food, or good shelter for the fish. Coarse material (large stones, rocks and boulders) in the right water depth is better. As John has mentioned, algal growth on coarse bed material is another hint that the habitat may be suitable for trout. Some areas in rivers have distinct algal growth (especially along the margins), and some areas appear scoured clean. The more stable zones should be searched for feeding lies, especially where the bed material is coarse.

John has also mentioned that trout are likely to lie in places where there is variable depth. These can sometimes be spotted by noting subtle changes in water colour. For example, in many New Zealand streams the deepest pools have an intense green colour that becomes paler as the water shallows. On broad areas of pocket water the most likely lies can be identified from a distance, being those areas with subtly stronger colour. Surface characteristics of

A river with much coarse bed material and many possible feeding lies.

An angler about to net a trout hooked in prime sight fishing water.

the water also reveal the location of trout lies; for example, flatter water hints at the presence of a velocity refuge below.

In *Stalking Trout*, Graeme Marshall and I described the identifying features of several types of prime feeding lies. A significant feature of most lies is the presence of 'a line of current change' – defined as a 'shear zone' in the present book. These are both horizontal and vertical. The most obvious horizontal shear zones exist downstream of boulders that emerge from the water, or in the eye of a pool. Vertical shear zones are less obvious, but they exist downstream of any submerged obstruction and are therefore abundant where a river bed is composed of coarse material, large cobbles and boulders. The secret to finding the majority of feeding fish is to identify the best places with vertical shears.

The artful science of trout fishing

SOMETIMES TROUT CAN BE SEEN browsing aquatic invertebrates off the river bed. Usually they do this where they can lazily mooch along the bottom without having to fight strong currents. Often they will be seen cruising backwaters or slow margins, feeding on the bottom. For trout to feed consistently in this manner there must be ample invertebrates exposed and available on the river bed. Slow, stable, often weedy rivers such as spring creeks provide such conditions. Snails often are the most abundant prey for benthic-browsing trout, but caddis larvae also commonly are eaten.

In some rivers, trout may be found browsing off the river bed in faster water, usually feeding on net-spinning caddis larvae (for example, *Aoteapsyche*). Generally these locations are restricted to bedrock shelves and large boulders that provide a stable substrate on which the larvae anchor their nets. Caddis larvae are often very abundant where there is a lot of bedrock, or where flows and substrates are stable, such as in lake outlets and spring creeks. They are also more common in shaded parts of rivers, where the lack of bright sunlight prevents periphyton growing on the river bed and clogging the larvae's nets.

Still-water-column feeding

Trout often combine benthic browsing with still-water-column feeding. In still or very slowly flowing water, trout are on the lookout for invertebrates suspended or swimming in the water column. Water boatmen are common prey when fish are feeding in this manner — usually in backwaters and the still margins of slow-flowing reaches. Damselfly nymphs also are taken in this manner by trout feeding over weed beds. Such habitats can be considered as the river equivalent of lakes, in terms of the feeding opportunities that they offer to trout.

When cruising trout are searching for insects in the water column, they particularly respond to movement by the prey. A useful angling ploy in these situations is the 'induced take'. This technique applies to wet fly or nymph and consists of casting well ahead of the cruising trout, or laying a fly in its path, and twitching it to attract attention. Usually, just a ten-centimetre pull is sufficient to bring about an immediate reaction: the trout will lunge forward to intercept the fly, or at least give it a close inspection. At this point avoid moving the fly again, because this risks spooking the trout. If the fly is refused following a charge by the trout, change to a different pattern and repeat the procedure if the fish is still feeding.

A few years ago I was sitting on a rock beside a Canadian lake, fruitlessly flogging a spinner, when I happened to see a damselfly nymph swimming along – not on the bottom but right up in the water column. Five minutes passed and other nymph swam by, then another. What struck me most about these nymphs was the exaggerated wriggling movements they made. This movement can be simulated using articulated damselfly imitations retrieved with short pulls of the line and twitches of the rod tip.

Trout browsing in food-rich areas generally are opportunists, taking whatever food appears (and appeals) as they cruise. However, there are occasions when fish apparently have specific food in mind. One such caught my attention on the lower reaches of a Fiordland stream.

When first spotted this trout was cruising along the bed of a deep backwater, plucking snails from the stones and lifting occasionally to intercept a passing water boatman. The fish's meandering suddenly ceased as it headed towards the flowing waters nearby. The reason was soon obvious. Mayflies were emerging in abundance. The onset of the hatch was impressive: suddenly there were duns being swept downstream in thousands.

Fishing the river end of a backwater.

The fish I had been watching was on course to get its share. It made its way quite deliberately to the mouth of the backwater and took up station beyond where I could cast effectively.

The width of the backwater now separated us and all I could do was watch. The fish hovered just beneath the surface and sipped continuously – drifting left and right, allowing nothing to pass. But while the hatch continued I noted with interest a number of flies drifting into the backwater, being pushed in by side eddies and accumulating en masse, seemingly disinterested in taking to the air immediately.

I watched for some time – twenty frustrating minutes perhaps – then, almost as suddenly as it had begun, the hatch ceased. The fantails that had been feeding with 'my' trout returned to the bush and the fish became more rigid. The change took only a few minutes.

When I thought about it afterwards, what happened next might have been rehearsed. The fish stayed on station for a short while, then, still close to the surface, returned to the backwater. As it began picking off the remnants of the hatch – the mayflies pushed into the backwater – I realised that this would continue until the surface food had gone, and then the water boatmen and snails below probably would be targeted once more. I never did find out because the small mayfly imitation that I had attached to my line earlier was soon whistling towards the approaching fish . . .

CRUISING TROUT in still or slow water require a stealthy approach. In clear water the smooth surface gives the trout a good view of approaching danger. Cruising trout are usually in shallow water, often a considerable distance from the security of deep water, making them very spooky. This is often the situation when cruisers are located in river backwaters.

Use bushes and other cover to hide from the fish. Avoid casting directly at cruising trout, as this often spooks them. Instead, anticipate the path the fish is following, sneak ahead, and cast the fly a couple of metres or more in front. When dry-fly fishing, let the fly sit on the surface, without movement. When nymphing or fishing a wet fly or small feathered lure, it is worth trying the induced take, as described on page 148.

Good patterns for cruising trout include wet flies that resemble water boatmen and diving beetles. If weed beds are present, damselfly nymphs are a good choice. Cruising trout will take a wide variety of patterns, and in many cases it is just matter of trying something and seeing if it works. Nevertheless, the imagination should not run completely riot. Keep in mind that cruising trout have plenty of time to inspect their prey, so be fairly conservative with regard to colour and size of fly. Drab, natural browns, greens, greys and black are good choices, and it pays to use smaller flies than what might be used for drift-feeding fish in faster water: sizes 14 and 16 are pretty good bets. Use unweighted or lightly weighted nymphs and wet flies: the thing to aim for in a submerged fly pattern is neutral or near-neutral buoyancy, which makes the fly hang in the water column or very slowly sink. There is nothing more unnatural than a weighted fly quickly falling through still water.

Spinning is usually not very effective on trout cruising backwaters and river margins. Clear, smooth, shallow water and the spookiness of the trout all work against the spin-fisher. However, bait fishing can be effective, if light line and minimal weight are used and the angler stalks the trout and casts the bait lightly in its path. This kind of fishing can be as exciting as stalking trout with the fly.

Ambush feeding

Although trout may spend most of their time drift feeding on comparatively small invertebrates, they are opportunistic predators and will attack larger prey such as small fish, frogs and mice. Large drift-feeding trout will often vigorously pursue and strike a lure or wobbler. In the lower reaches of rivers, where small native fish are most common, trout can become very piscivorous, especially in spring and early summer during the whitebait season. At this time of year some trout will be found chasing whitebait and smelt in the slow water at the margins of tidal pools, but where the current is faster they will lie in favourable positions to ambush their prey. In faster water, whitebait and smelt swim up along the banks, and it is here that the trout lie in wait. Just as with drift feeding, the trout will be found where they can gain some protection from the main force of the current. Bank extensions and behind boulders and snags are favourite spots.

In clear rivers, big trout may stay under cover for most of the day, then emerge at night to hunt forage fish. They can sometimes be encountered moving into the shallows to feed under the cover of darkness.

It is important to know the best tides to fish for trout feeding on whitebait and smelt. Some rivers fish best on the incoming tide; others on the outgoing tide. Canterbury rivers such as the Rakaia, Rangitaita and Opihi, which enter the sea via steep, fast guts, generally fish better on an incoming tide. The outgoing tidal currents in these river mouths are too fast, but the bait and smelt come upstream with the incoming tidal push. Rivers that have a lower gradient and sandy mouth, such as the Waimakariri, fish better on the outgoing tide. On the incoming tide the river is too slow or pushes upstream, with the result that the baitfish and the trout are not concentrated along the bank as when the current increases on the outgoing tide. Because there are no hard-and-fast rules, an angler who is unfamiliar with a river is well advised to seek local information on the best tides and times to fish for trout in the tidal reaches.

A special kind of ambush feeding by trout occurs every three to five years in rivers and lakes in New Zealand's back country. The beech (*Nothofagus* spp.) forests seed profusely at about this frequency, following warm summers. This process, termed 'masting', results in a considerable fall of beech flowers, leaves and seeds to the forest floor. This bounty stimulates population explosions of insects and mice; with the mice feeding on the insects as well as the seeds. It is during the mice plagues that some of the largest trout (over four and a half kilograms) are caught by anglers in the back country. Some large trout appear to target the mice and rapidly pack bulk on their already long frames. Some mice undoubtedly fall into the water, but others appear to intentionally embark on expeditions to the other bank; they are adept swimmers. Proof of the benefits to trout in targeting mice is seen in the bulging bellies of trout that have been caught following a night of mouse gluttony. It is not uncommon to find fifteen or more mice in a single trout's stomach.

Fishing strategies for ambush-feeding trout in rivers

Ambush-feeding trout can provide great fly and spin fishing. Lures imitating whitebait and smelt worked up along the bank or behind snags can invoke smashing strikes. One of the best times is just after a flood, when the river is dropping and the water is clearing but still discoloured. This is when the whitebait and smelt will most likely be running and the trout become bold in the discoloured water. You may see disturbances on the surface as the whitebait panic under attack, or trout will be seen swirling on the surface. Sometimes, in clearer water, trout may be spotted from the bank as they dash out from cover or up from the bottom after their prey. You should then quietly sneak upstream a few paces and draw a lure over the spot.

A very effective method for taking trout feeding on whitebait and smelt is livebait fishing with smelt, using either fly or spinning gear. If spinning gear is used, a light weight should be added. In some situations split shot will be all that is needed, but in deep, fast rivers heavier weights often are necessary to fish the bait along the bottom.

Feeding behaviours and fishing strategies

The same live-bait technique can be used with bullies for bait, hooked through the lower lip. This technique is deadly in the lower reaches of rivers draining into Lake Ellesmere such as the Selwyn and LII. Although big trout will leave their cover at night, it still pays to concentrate casting around snags. Even with spinning gear the bait is best worked back to the rod in a continuous retrieve, rather than cast and left in one spot. When a trout takes the bait it usually gives a light tapping sensation, upon which the angler should let out some line to give the fish time to take the bait fully in its mouth before setting the hook. Bait fishing in this manner will appeal to the active angler, as it can be much more interesting than the traditional 'heave and leave' technique. For those intent on relaxation, a rod, forked stick and deck chair may be more compelling.

Traditional feathered lure patterns used for trout in New Zealand rivers fall into two categories: those that represent smelt and whitebait (Hope's Silvery, Red Shadow, Grey Ghost, Dorothy, Taupo Tiger and Jack Spratt); and those that represent bullies ('killer' patterns such as Mrs Simpson, Hamill's Killer and Kilwell No. 1 and No. 2). There are scores of other traditional and more modern patterns to choose from, or on which to base new creative 'cocktails'.

When choosing a fly or creating a new pattern, consider the shape and behaviour of the trout's prey. Bullies are large in the head and taper toward the tail. They are bottom dwellers and swim with a short darting motion. Fish a bully pattern near the bottom and retrieve the line in a series of short (ten to twenty centimetres), smooth pulls. Whitebait have thin, elongated, transparent bodies and generally swim near the surface, at least in the slower currents. When attacked by trout they dash for the surface in a scattering panic. A whitebait fly pattern is, therefore, usually fished higher in the water column, sometimes on the surface, and usually with a moderate to fast retrieve. Sometimes it can help to actually fish the fly across the surface, making a wake that attracts the trout. In fast currents the little fish hug the bottom or banks, so this is where you must present your fly. Adult smelt are more heavy-bodied and fully coloured than whitebait, and flies intended to imitate them reflect this difference, but the fishing technique is similar to that for whitebait.

With all the above flies, when not fishing directly to snags, boulders and bank projections, the technique involves casting across the current and slightly downstream. The line is mended if necessary to sink the fly to the desired depth, then fished in an arc back to the bank. Once the line has straightened, the fly can be worked up along the bank and directed to hesitate and swing over likely feeding lies of trout waiting in ambush.

Two anglers making good use of bank-side cover while spotting in the river below.

The artful science of trout fishing

Dusk or after dark are the times to fish for mice-marauding trout, during the mice plagues. Again, bank extensions, over deep water, can be good places, but the best spots to concentrate on are deep pools. Big trout seek the security of deep water in pools during the day, but become bolder after dark and will feed at the surface and in the shallows. A deer-hair mouse, fished with plenty of movement, on a floating line is a popular bet for tempting these fish. Fishing live mice adds to the sense of expectation, but first you have to catch your mouse. They can be secured to a hook with rubber bands. However, be aware that the mice are not willing subjects in these proceedings and readily bite!

I FIRST BEGAN stalking trout with a baitcaster, not with a fly rod as I do now. This visual pursuit was on the banks of the Clutha River, in the lower tidal reaches where the smelt ran close to shore in great numbers.

My father taught me a method of bait fishing that he used most successfully. The local whitebaiters would willingly give him fresh smelt for bait, which he would secure on two small treble hooks about six centimetres apart at the end of his line. Then, forty centimetres from the bait, he would attach a thin cylinder of lead. He gently tossed this rig slightly upstream into likely waters. By the time that the bait drifted down level with him it would be nudging the river bed, where most fish awaited drifting food.

While I enjoyed this method of fishing, it lacked the visual excitement of stalking fish. So while my father probed distant depths, I would frequently sneak upstream to where I knew the fish fed close, ambushing shoals of smelt that hugged the banks.

I can recall dozens of these solo forays where a particular trout was targeted, but one occasion stands out because of the size of the fish involved. Its exact dimensions I'll never know — it never reached the net. Even considering that the event took place nearly forty years ago and the inevitable 'growth' of fish that get away, I swear that this one was about four kilograms.

I watched the fish feeding for some time before I sought it with bait and line. It fed where the river flowed fast against a jutting bank. Tight shoals of smelt would pass within centimetres of the edge, right on the surface, trying to avoid the strongest current. The trout would wait until they reached a certain point, then slash about through the shoal, which dispersed in panic. The trout would engulf the odd fish but also wound some, which would then drift downstream. After this frenzy the trout would return and prey on the easy pickings.

It was by imitating one of these injured, floating smelt that I hooked the fish. I waited until it had completed one of its raids and was searching and circling downstream. I lobbed an unweighted smelt into the current and let it drift away freely, using an open spool. The monstrous fish rose to the bait. I snapped the spool closed, set my own jaw, then set the hook.

Like all really big fish when hooked, it dived for the river bed. Then began my long vigil while the trout patrolled slowly upstream and down, reluctant to leave the depths. Only after prolonged pressure was I able to ease it toward the surface. It was then, when I got it really close, that I became fully aware of its size.

I can still see the battle's end. Two parts of a treble hook were firmly embedded in the fish's jaw. One part, pointing forwards, remained dangerously free. As the fish continued its dogged battle it brushed past a submerged branch. The free hook became embedded in the wood. No doubt alarmed by this impediment, the trout shook its giant head and, to my horror, the hooks ripped from its mouth. The enormous shape then just melted gradually from view. I had experienced the best and the worst of sight fishing.

CHAPTER NINE

Feeding behaviour in lakes and fishing strategies

DISTINGUISHING BETWEEN trout feeding behaviour in lakes versus rivers can be arbitrary because, depending on current, trout may exhibit the same behaviour in either environment. In slow reaches of rivers, trout can be expected to feed much the same as they do in lakes.

The main feeding behaviour trout exhibit in any particular lake depends upon whether the food source is primarily littoral-based (invertebrates living on the bottom) or limnetic-based (forage fish swimming in the water column). Most lakes provide a combination of both food chains, but often one type predominates. In order to employ the appropriate fishing technique, anglers need to either use local knowledge or sort out for themselves what category a particular lake falls into.

Trout exhibit three kinds of feeding behaviour in still waters: benthic browsing, still-water-column feeding and pursuit feeding. In lakes that have plenty of invertebrates and also support forage fish, the same trout may employ all three behaviours in littoral habitats. Usually, however, when good weed beds are present, trout can be expected to be browsing invertebrates off the bottom and off the weed beds, and casually taking some of the more active invertebrates from the water column. Snails are often the staple prey, with cased caddis also common. The more active invertebrate prey include damselfly and dragonfly larvae and water boatmen. Surface prey, including adult aquatic and terrestrial invertebrates, can also be important, especially from December to February.

Lakes in which trout feed predominantly on invertebrates taken from the bottom and in the water column provide excellent fishing all season, mainly because the trout are usually in relatively shallow water where they can be sighted and cast to directly, or where they reveal their location by rising to emerging nymphs or to surface prey.

Benthic browsing and still-water-column feeding have already been discussed. However, fishing strategies for fish feeding in these manners are more varied in lakes than in rivers.

The artful science of trout fishing

Lake-edge cruisers

For me, one of the most exciting fishing experiences is stalking cruising trout around the margins of lakes, especially when they are rising. The regular 'slurp, slurp' of a big brown trout casually taking natural flies from the surface under overhanging willows, inexorably making its way to the gap where my fly rests on the surface, is guaranteed to make the adrenaline surge. This kind of fishing is even better with a mate to act as a spotter. Two anglers working as a team can more easily keep track of a fish as it mooches along its feeding beat. Because large brown trout often cruise within a metre or two from the bank, it is possible to end up eye to eye with the fish, able to see every spot, every detail and every movement. The best part is when the trout's eye moves to fix on your fly, then in slow motion the fish glides over and up, pushes its neb through the surface, rolls back down and the fly is gone. In that heart-stopping moment time is suspended. The only thing in the universe is the trout and the irresistible urge to strike. You fight back the urge and patiently count – 'one, two, three' – then lift the rod to tighten firmly into a heavy fish. Briefly, there is weight but hesitation at the other end of the line, as though the trout is unaware that it has been hooked. Then all hell breaks loose. The rod pulls down viciously and the reel screams as the trout plunges away over the drop-off. The rattle and tap, tap, tap of the backing knot as the fly line curves away into the deep. The trout rising up and up, finally to end its run with a swirl on the surface way offshore. Compared with those first thrilling seconds, the rest of the encounter is a

A feeding brown trout cruising close to shore.

Feeding behaviours and fishing strategies

mechanical to-ing and fro-ing, gradually working the fish back to the shore.

A feature of lake-edge-cruising brown trout that the angler can use to advantage is that they are creatures of habit. They feed for long periods along the same beat, often cruising along the shore to a particular spot, then moving out over the drop-off to appear at the beginning of their beat and begin the circuit again. Some move back and forth along the shallow littoral, always within range of a cast. To spot these fish it is best to keep well back from the water's edge with the sun at an angle that allows good visibility through the surface glare. Polaroid sunglasses are a must in this situation. A slope down to the lake shore provides the best opportunity for spotting because the angler is looking from an elevated position. Otherwise you need to make use of cover such as bushes, trees and rocks. If these are not present, you should walk very slowly with the utmost caution and be prepared to sink to your knees and freeze when a fish is seen.

Once a fish is located, it is best to back off a little and observe from a safe distance. The aim is to figure out the trout's feeding beat, then get ahead of the fish, unseen, and ambush it next time it swims past. If you have a choice of places from which to ambush, select a position with good visibility in the direction you expect the fish to come from, and with some cover to hide behind. By watching the fish you can guess how far out from the bank it will be when next it appears, and place the fly accordingly. Once the cast is made, drop the rod tip to the ground so the trout can't see it moving or flashing.

Surface glare and shade can make spotting at the water's edge impossible and in this situation a spotter companion is essential. The constant relaying of information to the angler about where the fish is and what it is doing adds to the mounting excitement.

Sometimes a trout is encountered that has a feeding beat under a continuous line of willows or overhanging bush, presenting no obvious clearing from which a cast can be made. This calls for a little imagination and daring. You may be able to climb out over the water on an overhanging branch and present the fly by dapping – dropping the fly on to the surface and keeping absolutely still. This can be incredibly exciting, but the really difficult part begins when the trout is hooked. Usually the initial run of the trout is played with the rod upside down, the line careering off under the overhanging branches while the angler attempts to climb out. If two anglers work as a team, and all goes according to plan, the rod can be quickly passed from one to the other, keeping a tight line on the fish and allowing the angler in the tree to make an orderly dismount.

An elevated position offers a better view of lake-edge possibilities.

Two good surface flies for lake-edge cruisers – Blue Blowfly and Green Beetle.

When lake levels are high, trout can sometimes be found feeding in very shallow water, taking advantage of flooded terrestrial insects and worms. They can often be located by watching for the disturbances they make at the surface, and by their fins and tails breaking the surface. Because they are engrossed in feeding, these trout can be relatively easy prey to a careful angler.

Blind fishing

Blind fishing is casting and retrieving a fly or lure without first sighting a fish. This technique can be employed in a wide range of conditions and by anglers with varying skill and experience. The exciting part is the unexpected, often sudden take. I say 'take' rather than 'strike' because often the trout takes the fly gently or almost imperceptibly. But that in itself is challenging: learning by experience to detect the soft take.

Blind fishing does not just target browse-feeding trout. The fish may be concentrating on invertebrate food but will quite readily take a wet fly intended to mimic a forage fish, or take an insect imitation when feeding on fish. Also, despite the term, blind fishing is not necessarily a matter of chance. Experience can reduce the chance factor, and the odds can be improved by fishing at the best times and in the best places.

Blind fishing in lakes can be productive at any time of day, although the best times are usually dusk and dawn, corresponding with peak feeding activity (more about that later). In daylight, blind fishing is difficult if the surface is flat calm. I have already mentioned how in these conditions the fly line breaking the surface is easily seen from under water, in the surface mirror. When the sun is out and the water surface is calm, it is best to concentrate on spotting trout and executing a careful ambush rather than ambitiously casting here and there, which risks putting the fish down. The best time for blind fishing is when a light breeze scuffs the water surface and the ripples on the surface break up the sunlight into an erratically moving dappled underwater mosaic. This probably makes wet flies and lures more difficult to see. One second they are illuminated, and the next inconspicuous. This may heighten the attack response to movement by trout – but, as mentioned in Chapter Four, is only my guess to explain why fish are easier to catch in these conditions.

A nymph or small wet fly fished slowly on a floating or intermediate-sinking line over shallow weed beds can be deadly in these conditions. This highlights one of the key features of a successful angler: being prepared to adapt to the conditions.

During my doctorate research, living at Lake Alexandrina to conduct my fieldwork enabled me the luxury of choosing the best conditions to go fishing. By trial and error I soon learnt that when a breeze scuffed the surface on a bright day, the fishing could be hot. I have a particularly vivid memory of one sunny December day when I wandered down to the lake for my lunch break, fly rod in hand. A light breeze was blowing from the east, rippling the surface and giving me quiet confidence in the combination of intermediate-sinking line and size 8 Mrs Simpson I had chosen back at the hut. I eased the old clinker boat out from its shed, rowed a hundred metres across the shallow flats and anchored off a point within casting distance of the shore. There was no sign of fish activity at the surface, but within half a dozen casts I had a strong pull and was into the first rainbow. Ten minutes later I brought a fat two-kilogram fish to the net and released it. Within five minutes I felt another vicious tug and had the second strong fish. The action went on like that until I stopped fishing an hour and a half later with a tally of six. I have fished in the same spot on other days, but in calm conditions, for longer periods without a single take.

When fishing over shallow weed beds during the day, you can improve your chances by fishing to clearings in the weed. Trout like to patrol the edges of weed beds, possibly because their prey is more visible. In hot weather, clearings in the weed beds made by cold-water springs are favourite spots.

Don't be in a hurry to retrieve the fly. A very slow twitching of a nymph or wet fly is all that is required. Allow time for the fly to sink the leader in order to avoid surface drag on the retrieve.

A key point overlooked by many anglers is the importance of matching the fly line to the depth and weather conditions. It is advisable to have a range of fly lines of various sinking speeds, on spare spools or spare reels. I usually carry a floater, an intermediate-, and slow-, medium- and fast-sinking lines to cover all options. If there is little or no breeze, or if I am casting downwind over shallow water, I often use the floater. But the intermediate-sinking line copes with wind better. The problem with a floating line is that the wind blows a belly in it during the retrieve, so when a fish takes, you do not have a direct line of pull to feel the take and set the hook. The intermediate line lets you keep in direct contact with the fly and, by sinking the fly better below the roughened water surface, it may be more visible to the trout. It has been my experience that an intermediate line will normally outfish a floater in breezy conditions.

A cardinal rule with blind fishing is to present the fly at the depth where the trout are. A selection of sinking fly lines allows you to achieve this. Let me illustrate this point with another fishing experience from Lake Alexandrina.

A balmy February evening promised good fishing conditions as the creaking oars slowly carried the three of us down the lake. Phil and Wally were visitors to the lake and I was 'guiding' them to one of my favourite fishing spots, a shallow, weedy bay with a clearing formed by springs. I had a hunch that the recent warm weather would have encouraged trout to congregate in the cool spring water. Our excitement mounted as a trout swirled while I anchored the boat. I had told the others that the water was shallow and suggested they use a slow- or intermediate-sinking line. However, Phil had brought only a floater, and Wally a medium sinker. My offer of the intermediate sinker rigged on my rod was politely refused. We were all using similar killer pattern flies, so what was to follow had nothing to do with fly choice.

Phil cast his floater across the spring and began a slow retrieve, closely followed by Wally's medium sinker. They had recovered two-thirds of their lines by the time I sent my fly out over the water. After waiting for the fly to settle, the third slow pull of my retrieve was answered by a sharp tug and a two-and-a-half-kilogram rainbow launched into the air. After a spirited ten-minute tussle the first fish was in the boat. Phil and Wally expectantly cast again. Wally was forced to retrieve at a fairly fast rate to avoid snagging the weeds, but Phil could vary his retrieve. By the time I had unhooked the rainbow and got my gear organized, they had completed about three casts with no result. Another trout boiled on the surface as I cast again. No response this time, but on the next cast I hooked up again. Wally began to get a little tight-lipped, but still refused the offer of the intermediate line. Over about an hour I caught three rainbows, was broken by another and had another solid tug with no hook-up. Phil had one strike on the floating line. By the time my

Feeding behaviours and fishing strategies

repeated offer of the intermediate line was finally accepted, the bite time was over.

I knew from experience that the intermediate line in this spot could be allowed to sink for thirty to sixty seconds, and then slowly retrieved without snagging the weeds. When trout are concentrated in a relatively small area, both horizontally and vertically (the spring in this case), this technique, combined with the correct line, prolongs the time that the fly is in the strike zone.

This story also shows how it is important to understand the seasonal distribution of trout in lakes in relation to physical conditions such as water temperature and food. In midsummer, when the water is warm, you need to fish deep during the day, or else fish cool-water inflows such as spring creeks or springs beneath the surface of a lake. This is where local knowledge enhances your chances of success.

Where a cool stream enters a lake, the first thing to figure out is the location of the cool plume, and its behaviour in relation to wind and waves. The plume does not always run straight out into the lake: it may run at an angle or parallel to the shore. Local anglers will already have this figured out, and watching them will give the visitor a clue where to fish.

A canoe serves as a manoeuvrable and quiet fishing platform on lakes.
Karen Shearer

Many anglers are tempted to immediately wade out deep to begin fishing. However, if you are first there it pays to hang back from the water's edge and try a few casts in the shallows. Trout sometimes edge their way really close inshore when there have not been other anglers scaring them off.

Some anglers take the issue of water temperature seriously enough to carry thermometers, and it does not take long to assemble a useful personal database on a favourite lake, matching diary catches and fishing location against temperature. As we saw in Chapter Five, trout will avoid water temperatures greater than 19°C. They may still move into warmer water but only for short periods. Temperatures above 22°C can be expected to strongly affect trout distribution. This can be a bad or good thing, depending on how flexible an angler is about technique and gear selection. If you have the knowledge to find the fish, and the gear to present the fly or lure to them, you can experience some very good fishing because temperature gradients concentrate trout.

If you draw a blank on trout during the day, because they are inaccessible to your gear or too hard to catch, then dawn and dusk are when you should concentrate your effort. The evening is an especially magical time to fish. The trout often come up to feed near the surface and move into the shallows, and become bolder with the onset of darkness. That is when they are most vulnerable to the angler, whether fishing from the shore or from a boat. I prefer it to dawn, because I can look forward to the fishing getting better and better as the light dims, whereas at dawn the fishing will usually only get worse as the day becomes brighter.

A recent radio-tracking study of trout in Lake Otamangakau showed this very pattern. The rainbow trout stayed deep during the day and came up to the surface and into the margins at dusk and through the night. This mirrored the fishing patterns of anglers who said they had most success with wet flies in the evening when fishing from the shore or near to the surface during dusk and into the night.

Fishing strategies for pursuit-feeding trout

Browse- and pursuit-feeding behaviours by individual trout often are exhibited together, especially in lakes with a diverse prey including invertebrates and forage fish. In these situations a trout that is mooching in the shallows feeding on benthic invertebrates can be enticed to attack a small wet fly imitating a forage fish. However, in lakes with a poor shallow littoral invertebrate fauna and a predominantly limnetic food chain, most trout will be locked into a forage-fish pursuit-feeding mode.

Feeding behaviours and fishing strategies

There is a fairly limited range of forage fish available to trout in New Zealand lakes. In the central North Island lakes, and some further north, smelt are the main fish prey. Other lakes generally have only bullies. Koaro (whitebait) are often also present but not usually as abundant as smelt. Occasionally, others such as goldfish will be present too. Lake Aniwhenua is one such place where, in summer, trout chase goldfish in the shallows. Generally, however, either smelt or bullies or both will be the main forage fish. Trout will forage offshore on smelt for most of the year in the limnetic zone, except from November to January, when spawning smelt move inshore to spawn. When trout are pursuing smelt they often slash the surface as the shoals of smelt attempt to flee. You should retrieve relatively fast and be prepared for savage takes.

Two anglers survey prospects on a South Island lake.

The artful science of trout fishing

A lake-edge pusuit feeder on the lookout for bullies but also willing to take a green-beetle imitation . . .

. . . falls to a successful strike.

Trout feed on bullies usually in a more measured fashion. Adult bullies live on the bottom, so they can dart into cover to avoid the trout. Brown trout can often be seen moving fairly slowly over the bottom, then darting forward to seize a bully. When sight fishing or blind fishing in this manner, the retrieve is usually very slow and it can be useful to impart an irregular twitch to the fly. When sighting cruising trout feeding on bullies, a killer fly such as a Mrs Simpson or Hamill's Killer cast out and allowed to sink to the bottom in the path of the fish can be very effective. If the trout is choosy, leave the fly until the fish is almost upon it and then give it a twitch. The trout will often pounce on the fly as a reflex action.

In South Island lakes, post-larval bullies move into the shallows to settle on the bottom in late January and February. This migration may be earlier in the warmer North Island lakes. Whatever the timing, it is possible to see clouds of small bullies suspended in the water column and on the bottom just out from the edge along the deeper banks, especially in the shade of trees. Brown trout get quite animated feeding on them, and can be seen patrolling the shoreline and bursting into the clouds of little fish. Unfortunately, trout feeding in this manner can be quite difficult to catch. A small killer-pattern fly (no larger than size 10) will sometimes work if laid out in ambush and twitched to attract attention.

A deadly method for catching trout feeding on bullies, either in lake or river, is to spin for them using live bullies for bait (see pages 152–53).

In the Canterbury high-country lakes, koaro whitebait can be found shoaling mainly during January but also right through until March. Trout feed on them in much the same manner as they feed on smelt. They actively pursue them in the limnetic zone, and often along the drop-off at the edge of the littoral zone. If you see trout slashing the surface in these lakes, it is a pretty sure bet they are chasing koaro whitebait. They will take a whitebait or smelt fly retrieved rapidly, but the hard part is getting the fly to the fish. Rainbows especially can be so unpredictable in their movements that it can be a frustrating task to land the fly in their path. They can be seen slashing the surface in one spot and then several metres away a few seconds later. Despite the frustration, fishing for 'whitebaiting' trout in the South Island lakes can be as exciting as for smelting trout in the North Island lakes.

Another rather amazing type of pursuit feeding is seen when trout chase flying damselflies. Usually it is the younger, fitter fish that exhibit this behaviour. The trout appear to be able to see the damselflies flying above the water surface, and they chase after them, sometimes catching them in midair. These trout present a real challenge to the angler but can be caught on dry flies tied to resemble adult damselflies. These are usually tied with red bodies extending well beyond the bend of the hook.

The variety of fishing techniques for pursuit-feeding trout in lakes includes wet fly, harling, spinning, jigging, trolling and, in some places, bait fishing. Using a combination of these approaches, the angler can target trout over various depths and conditions. Early in the season, the cooler surface waters encourage trout to

Damselflies are targeted by pursuit-feeding trout and sometimes are taken in midair.

stay within range of wet fly and harling gear. Later in summer they spend more time in deep water, so are usually only accessible to the wet-fly, harling and shore-based angler early in the morning and in the evening.

Besides temperature, another reason trout may be found in the surface waters at dawn and dusk is because they are following the nocturnal movements of plankton and forage fish. In the warmer parts of the day trout feed deeper, and this necessitates deep-water spinning and jigging or lead-core, wire or downrigger trolling. Deep-water trolling, especially lead- and wire-lining is not everyone's cup of tea. The gear is very insensitive and does not do justice to the fighting qualities of trout: much of the fish's energy is expended fighting the weight of the line rather than being transferred directly to the rod and the angler. Nevertheless, if you want to catch fish in deep lakes, lead-lining is an effective technique. The reality is that you should either adapt to the conditions or restrict your fishing activity to the appropriate time of day for the technique you are willing, or able, to use.

Downriggers offer an improvement over lead and wire lines. They present the gear down deep and allow the fighting qualities of the trout to be experienced. A downrigger is essentially a winch that lowers a heavy metal ball to a predetermined depth, and this is trolled under a boat. An ordinary monofilament line, with lure attached, is attached by a snap to the wire so that it can pull free when a fish strikes. This allows the angler to use a light rod without the encumbrance of a heavy line.

The introduction of downriggers to New Zealand did not come without some debate: because they can be fished at greater depths than lead lines, there was concern about the potential mortality of trout released. To investigate this matter, DOC Taupo undertook a study in which trout were caught by both downrigger and traditional methods, and then kept in netting cages at the surface. Survival rates were similar for both groups. After this reassuring result downrigger fishing was made legal on Lake Taupo in 1994, but the length of the cable is restricted to forty metres.

In deep lakes the success of the various methods discussed above varies with season, and DOC's angling surveys on Lake Taupo demonstrate this point. During spring and early summer, Lake Taupo anglers have similar success with harling, lead lines, wire lines and downriggers. As the summer progresses, the shallower trolling methods (harling and lead-lining) become less effective than deep trolling with wire lines and downriggers. The seasonal depth distribution of rainbow trout is responsible for this pattern (see page 110).

In spring many trout move into the shallows each night to feed on spawning smelt. During the day they may remain in the shallows or move a short distance over the drop-off. These fish are equally available to all of the four fishing methods mentioned above. As summer progresses and the surface waters heat up, the trout move deeper. Echo-sounding surveys have found many trout a hundred metres or more deep during summer, where they are out of reach of all legal fishing methods (except perhaps jigging). Fortunately, some remain around the thermocline, the zone of rapid temperature change between the warm surface and cooler bottom waters. By late summer this zone is usually at about thirty metres, and by late autumn it will be even deeper, beyond the reach of harling and lead-lining gear. Harling techniques fish the lure within five metres of the surface, and lead lines fish down to about fifteen metres. The catch rate for these methods falls in late summer in Lake Taupo because most trout are beyond reach of the gear. Downriggers and wire lines are the most consistent performers at this time of year. A downrigger with forty metres of cable out may just reach the thermocline at thirty metres, allowing for the fact that the cable does not hang vertically but extends down at an angle behind the boat.

Flies for pursuit-feeding trout

The range of wet-fly and lure patterns available to catch pursuit-feeding trout is too large to exhaustively cover here. However, some principles can aid in selecting an appropriate fly for the circumstances. These include size, shape, colour, contrast, flash and movement. It is generally better to use smaller flies and lures by day than by night, except when fishing very deep water where a larger size helps compensate for the dim light. Colour combinations of yellow and black, and yellow and blue are attractive to trout (see page 61 for more on this). In surface waters, black provides good contrast, and red is another preferred colour. Yellow and orange are good choices when fishing deep, as they retain their intensity at depth and contrast well with the background. For the same reasons they are also good choices if the water is discoloured. Some thought should, however, be given to the colour of the forage fish: for example, if smelt are present, a flashy silver fly or lure would be a sensible choice for shallow water or fishing near the surface. Actually, even when smelt are not present, silver and flash works well, although not at depth because there is not enough light to reflect a flash off the surface of such a lure.

When fishing for selective brown trout in edge waters, bold colours and maximum contrast in the fly or lure are not so good, as they may spook the fish. In this situation drab colours, in keeping

The artful science of trout fishing

A smelt-imitating fly. When wet the body will become thinner and shaped more like a natural smelt.

with the cryptic nature of bullies, are more appropriate. Bullies are best imitated with short, bulky, killer-pattern flies, fished with a slow, jerky retrieve. Smelt flies need to be slim and sparsely tied, preferably with a transparent hue. Synthetic materials such as Flashabou and Crystal Flash can be incorporated to give a very lifelike appearance. Narrow flashy lures are also good smelt or juvenile koaro imitations.

Movement in flies can be imparted by the retrieve and also by the materials. In recent years, marabou has been appearing in more and more flies for this reason. It provides a lifelike movement and fluttering, even with the slowest of retrieves. Soft hair flies have traditionally been tied for movement and are still useful in this regard.

Night fishing on lakes
When fishing at night, size and shape of the fly or lure, and speed of retrieve, are the most important considerations. Large and bulky wet flies are good, fished with a very slow retrieve. A novel way of attracting the attention of trout at night, which has gained popularity with lake anglers in recent years, is to use luminescent flies. These glow in the dark and are recharged every few casts by shining a torch or discharging a camera flash at them. It is quite a sight to watch a line of anglers casting luminescent flies in the dark. It can appear as if fireflies are streaking back and forth as the anglers false cast. The innovative spin fisher will find that the same luminescent synthetic materials can be attached to wobblers and blade spinners.

There is no doubt that night fishing is very effective, often yielding a much higher catch rate than daytime fishing, at least to the shoreline angler. Nevertheless, it does not appeal to all anglers. Those who do not do much night fishing usually are plagued with tangles.

With experience, one develops a feel for the fishing gear at night. It is possible to keep track of the proper functioning of the fly line and rod by feel and sound. At the first hint of an imbalance in the rod or line, or an unusual noise from the fly line and leader moving through the air, stop the cast and check for tangles. It is also a good idea to shorten the cast length as it gets dark: this reduces the chance of tangles or a fly embedded in the back of your head.

I prefer to fish during the day and the change of light in the evening. When I do fish at night I prefer to do so from a boat, with company. The social aspect can definitely help to while away the time when the fishing is slow. I have fished with some memorable characters at night from a boat on Lake Alexandrina. One in particular comes to mind. In my impressionable student days at the lake I was often visited, usually out of the blue, by the late John Bull, then head ranger of the South Canterbury Acclimatisation Society. John would arrive late in the day, often with one of his fishing buddies, but in time to have a good feed, and invariably with a bottle of whisky in hand. The prising of the top from the bottle was usually followed by the pronouncement that 'it won't be wearing that hat again tonight!' After dinner cooked on the coal range and washed down with a few chasers, John would assemble his fishing gear with the expectation that I would proceed to row him all over the lake for the night's fishing. John was not the most co-ordinated of anglers, especially in a boat, having suffered for years with a Parkinson's-type neural disorder. That trait, combined with pitch darkness and the whisky (with a dash of lake water), made for some hilarious and precarious incidents, but we certainly caught a lot of trout. We would yarn for hours, sometimes until two in the morning, about characters of days gone by and of the present, acclimatisation society and catchment board politics, and big trout caught and lost.

Large trout, especially browns, are often caught at night when they lose their daytime wariness, but experience still can make a difference. The take of a big brown on a wet fly at night is often felt as just a gentle tightening of the line. An experienced angler will strike immediately to secure a hook-up, but it is all too easy to react too late.

Sometimes night fishing will turn up the unexpected. I recall hooking in shallow water a very large fish that bored away with my line time and time again with formidable power. I spent a good thirty minutes with the fish circling the boat, out there somewhere in the black. The pattern was consistent with a huge brown, and my fishing buddy and I began to speculate on its weight. There was no doubt in our minds that we were about to see a double-figure fish – and we

The artful science of trout fishing

did: finally, after several abortive attempts, I drew the great bulk of a ten-kilogram-plus longfin eel into the torchlight!

Spawning trout – a special case

Another significant fishing opportunity is that offered by spawning trout congregating in lakes. From autumn to spring they may be found congregating off stream mouths on their way to spawn. In lakes where winter fishing for spawning trout is legal, these fish present a special fishing opportunity because they are concentrated and vulnerable to angling. As we saw in Chapter Two, even though spawning trout may not feed very much, they will still take a fly, spinner or bait.

The Rotorua area presents unique opportunities to fish for spawning trout, owing to the prevalence of hatchery liberations in several of the lakes. Hatchery trout tend to congregate at the points of liberation around the lake edges. The first thing that a visiting angler should do when planning a winter fishing trip to this district is to contact the Eastern Fish and Game Council for details of the location of liberation sites and the months that trout are expected to return there.

When trout run up tributaries to spawn, they generally occupy deeper water than resident fish. They hug the bottom as much as possible, mainly to conserve energy. The key to success when fishing for spawning trout is, therefore, to fish deep, using either heavily weighted nymphs or fast-sinking lines with wet flies. In the larger Taupo tributaries nymph anglers often use a two-fly rig consisting of a large, heavily weighted nymph (a 'lead bomb') to get to the bottom, with a small, unweighted dropper nymph. The latter is commonly a trout-egg imitation such as a Glo-bug, but conventional nymphs such as Hare and Copper will also take fish.

The other key to success is to wait for a fresh, which stimulates the trout to run up the rivers. They will readily snap at flies and lures in the discoloured water following a fresh. In normal and low-flow conditions trout will congregate in pools, and these are naturally the best places to concentrate fishing effort. However, it is less well known that at higher flows, during and immediately after a fresh, trout can be encountered in shallower water: in the tail-outs of pools, and runs, and often close to the river margins. This was 'discovered' in a recent DOC radio-tracking study of rainbow trout in the Tongariro, and confirmed what some old hands with an intimate knowledge of the river already knew.

It is not just in the spawning season that trout move into shallow water during and after freshes: they may also do it during spring and summer. A case in point is the lower and middle Wairau River, near Blenheim. Here anglers believe there is a high proportion of sea-run

Release of juvenile hatchery rainbow trout at the Lake Okataina boat landing, Rotorua. The trout return to the release point when they mature and provide anglers with a hot spot to focus their fishing efforts.

Fish & Game NZ – Eastern Region

Feeding behaviours and fishing strategies

brown trout that move progressively up the river in spring and early summer. After a fresh, these fish can be found in shallow margins and lined up in shallow chutes of rapids, at the heads of drop-offs into pools and runs.

But let's get back to fishing spawning runs. Brightly coloured flies are popular, especially for rainbows. Oranges and reds are the most common colours employed. Some anglers believe these colours work because they match orange trout eggs, which are eaten by trout on the spawning grounds. But there is another reason. Reds and oranges are recognised among trout and salmon as aggression colours. Males in particular display these colours, more so as they near the spawning grounds and approach spawning condition. A flash of red or orange can therefore be expected to elicit an aggressive snap.

A good place to fish for migrating trout is at mouths where the fish congregate before running upstream. Wet-fly fishing with a feather or hair lure is very effective. In the daytime the trout

A pair of anglers setting out down a well-worn lakeside track.

are most likely to stay fairly deep, just over the drop-off, so a fast-sinking or sinking-head line is needed. At night, however, the trout become bolder and may slip up over the drop-off, often into quite shallow water if the stream is fairly small. Floating lines can be quite effective in these situations.

Remember not to wade directly into the water upon arrival. Trout often will be nosing up into the shallows, so it pays to 'fish your feet first'. I recall one night in April fishing the shallow mouth of a creek in Lake Alexandrina. By being careful not to stomp about, and keeping false casts to a minimum, I was able to pick up a few fish that took the fly right under my rod tip. Every half-hour or so there would be a heavy swirl beside me as a trout nosed its way into the stream water flowing over the wide, shallow delta. That was a very exciting fishing experience.

Pre-spawning fish usually are in prime condition and fighting fit; in fact, generally the best time to catch large, heavy trout is from late summer to autumn and winter, when the fish put on weight for the coming season. If you are after trophy fish, this is a point to bear in mind; and it applies to both lakes and rivers. I have seen some anglers kill large bags of post-spawning trout early in the fishing season from lakes and tributaries. This seems to me to be a waste, as the fish are usually thin with washed-out white flesh, and not good fare. It is more sensible to release the fish to allow them to recover and provide top sport and table fish later in the season.

PART FOUR

Conservation and management

The artful science of trout fishing

IN DECEMBER 1993 my brother Ho and I fished a fine little stream in North Canterbury. While it drained quite steep country, it still had frequent deep, green pools along its length, with bedrock exposed in many places. It was an ideal environment for trout, as our catch for the day demonstrates. We fished for six hours and in that time saw sixteen trout, all in the pools or associated pockets, and landed seven. The smallest weighed just under two kilograms, with the others weighing from three to well over four kilograms. These figures alone attest to the quality of the fishery, and it was certainly one that we valued very highly.

A few days later a severe storm threatened, so we broke camp and sought the comforts of home. That proved to be wise because next day there were reports of flash floods in North Canterbury. I particularly recall seeing television pictures of water racing through the streets of Kaikoura after a stream had breached its banks.

It wasn't until early 1994 that I learned the storm had devastated 'our' trout stream. I returned to the locality in early March of that year. Along the entire length of the stream the pools had been completely filled with small, choking pebbles and sand. The water was no longer sparkling or clear. It now carried a load of sediment and was obviously continually discoloured despite late-summer low flows. After finding and landing just one very lean trout, I departed and haven't been back since. However, I do hope that several years of more moderate flows will assist the pools to develop and deepen once more. Then the trout will return – and so will I.

Obviously, the environmental deterioration just described was extremely rapid and could be attributed to one natural flood event. But in the last forty years I have witnessed the demise of many other streams as their banks and beds have been altered or the water quality (or quantity) has changed in response to land development.

PERSONAL EXPERIENCES such as that described by Les highlight the fragile nature of trout habitat and just how critical habitat quality is. While we can do little to moderate the impacts of natural flood events, we ought to be able to mitigate human impacts on the rivers supporting our fisheries – if there is the will to do so.

Protecting habitat is the key to preserving our trout fisheries. Though stocking may appeal as a cure for perceived lack of trout, it deals only with the symptoms and not the causes of fish population decline; usually the cause is destruction, or slow degradation, of habitat. This is a universal lesson learnt by fisheries managers in Europe and North America where our trout originate. Widespread

Debris piled high from one shore to another demonstrates the power of many New Zealand streams in full flood.

declines in wild trout and salmon in these continents followed massive changes in land use, vegetative cover, wetland drainage and river control. New Zealand is promoted abroad as having a clean, green image, but the reality is that we have been repeating the same mistakes as other countries. Land-use change and resulting degradation of our lowland freshwater ecosystems and fisheries has actually proceeded at a more rapid pace here than overseas.

The managers of our trout and salmon fisheries are well aware of the central importance of maintaining habitat for the continued existence of these fisheries. That is why they invest a great deal of time and effort in habitat advocacy. Without that effort it is certain that we would all have fewer places to fish, and fewer trout to catch.

The following chapters introduce the New Zealand freshwater sports fishery management agencies, what they do and the issues they face.

CHAPTER TEN

Sports fishery management in New Zealand

Fish and Game New Zealand has statutory responsibility for the management of sports fish and game birds in New Zealand. The organisation is essentially a transformation of the former acclimatisation societies, which were reformed by the Conservation Law Reform Act 1990, but with more clearly defined and audited management functions. The acclimatisation societies began to form in the 1860s and were involved first in the liberation of exotic species throughout New Zealand, and later fish and game bird management. See R. M. McDowall's *Gamekeepers for the Nation* for an excellent historical review.

Fish and Game New Zealand is financially independent from the New Zealand government; it is entirely funded by licence revenue. However, its responsibilities as prescribed in the Conservation Act must be performed to the satisfaction of the Minister of Conservation. Its overarching function is 'to manage, maintain and enhance sports fish and game resources in the recreational interests of anglers and hunters'.

Fish and Game New Zealand comprises twelve regional councils and a national council situated in Wellington. Council members are elected by licence holders and employ professional managers and fisheries and resource officers. This model gives anglers considerable influence on the management of their trout and salmon fisheries.

The Department of Conservation (DOC) is also involved. In addition to its responsibilities for preserving indigenous freshwater fisheries, DOC is also charged with protecting recreational [salmonid] fisheries and freshwater fish habitats. In particular it is responsible for managing the Lake Taupo trout fishery. When the Conservation Law Reform Act 1990 was drafted, it was not possible to include the Taupo district within Fish and Game's jurisdiction because existing legislation defined a unique relationship between the Crown and the local Maori iwi, Ngati Tuwharetoa, pertaining to the management of the Lake Taupo fishery. Ngati Tuwharetoa has legal ownership of the bed of Lake Taupo and its rivers. In return for providing public access to, and use of, Lake Taupo and its rivers, the iwi is paid by the government an amount equivalent to half of the revenue received from fishing and boating fees and shares decision-making with the Minister of Conservation in setting the classes and fees for fishing licences. Since this contract is between Ngati Tuwharetoa and the government, management of that fishery had to remain the function of a government department, not an independent agency such as Fish and Game New Zealand.

Because of its quality, international reputation and attendant tourism infrastructure, the Lake Taupo fishery generates the largest income of any single trout fishery in New Zealand, and thus receives the most intensive management and research effort.

While the Lake Taupo fishery is comparatively well funded, the same cannot be said for the rest of New Zealand's trout and salmon fisheries. With the exception perhaps of the Rotorua lakes, the others are starved for cash. It could be argued that the licence revenue which alone supports Fish and Game management throughout New Zealand is woefully inadequate to support the effort required to research, conserve and manage our internationally renowned trout and salmon fisheries. The funding is also out of proportion to the benefits that accrue from the fisheries and conservation of their habitats to the wider community and economy, and related forms of recreation.

Currently, Fish and Game New Zealand's total annual revenue from fishing licence sales is about $4.5 million, while total licence revenue received by DOC Taupo is about $1.5 million.

Trout fishing is used as a drawcard by the New Zealand tourism industry and contributes significantly to the economy. In 1991 the economic value of freshwater sports fishing in New Zealand was estimated at $145–231 million per annum. The Taupo fishery alone was worth about $61–97 million (NBR, 1991). The government receives 12.5 per cent goods and services tax from fishing-licence revenue, and various taxes from the economy generated by freshwater fishing (for example, sporting goods and boat sales, fuel, vehicles, accommodation and guiding fees). None of this is invested back into management of the fisheries. A minimal amount, less than $500,000, is currently invested in research directly related to trout fisheries, and no government research investment is being made in wild salmon fisheries. This compares with more than $5 million that the government invested in salmonid research in the early 1980s. The decline in research funding has occurred at a time in New Zealand's history when there are unprecedented pressures on our trout

Conservation and management

and salmon fisheries from increased tourism, and environmental impacts from water abstraction, hydroelectric power generation, and agricultural and other pollution. Moreover, since the advent of the Resource Management Act in 1991 there is now a greater requirement for scientific information on the effects of some of these activities on our fisheries.

The place of stocking

Some anglers who feel the fishing is not as good as it used to be believe stocking to be the solution. However, fisheries managers nowadays are not very sympathetic to this view. Why is this so? What are the pros and cons of stocking?

The world-class fisheries that we enjoy in New Zealand owe their existence to the persistent stocking efforts of the early acclimatisation societies. Successes in the late 1880s led to more and more effort in stocking existing fisheries and extending the range of trout at the beginning of the twentieth century. This was particularly so for brown trout, which were spread far and wide into almost all accessible waters – further assisted by this species' sea-running tendency, which enabled them to colonise rivers that were not stocked and no doubt to this day helps them repopulate rivers after flood or drought. Less effort was put into acclimatising rainbow trout throughout the country, and this species never established sea-running stocks. This latter fact, regrettably, has denied Kiwi anglers the thrill of pursuing steelhead (sea-run rainbows), which display awesome strength and speed when hooked.

The first serious challenge to the acclimatisation societies' preoccupation with stocking came in the 1920s and 1930s from scientist Derisely Hobbs, who worked for the societies' research committee and later the Marine Department. Hobbs set about evaluating the success of natural reproduction by trout and the need for and effectiveness of trout stocking. His studies indicated that natural reproduction in most New Zealand waters was very good – quite sufficient to sustain wild populations. With this in mind, and when the natural mortality of released fish was taken into consideration, most of the stocking efforts could be shown to be insignificant.

As a result of this research, in the 1930s and 1940s Hobbs challenged the accepted practice of hatchery releases, and as a result there was a steady decline through the 1950s and 1960s. Some societies bucked the trend in the 1970s and 1980s as Hobbs' message grew fainter with the passing of time. But more recently, in most regions, there is even less interest in stocking by modern-day fishery managers. Reasons include the costs of running fish

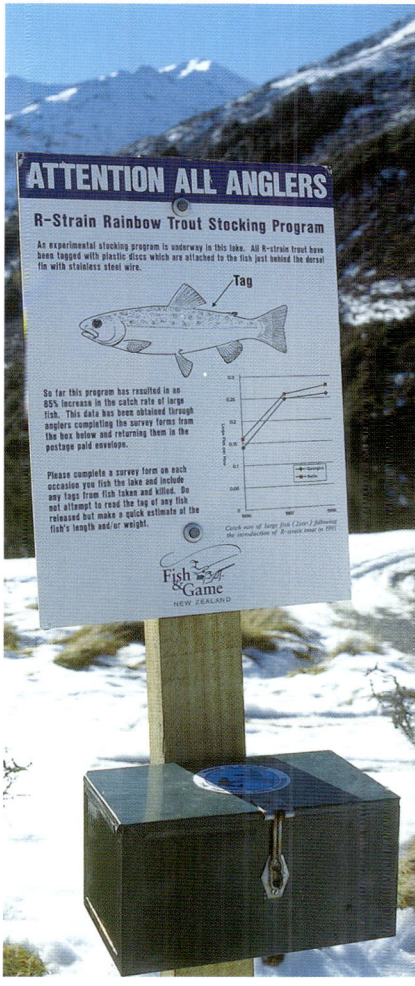

A notice at Lake Selfe, in the Canterbury back country, informing anglers about a stocking experiment with R-Strain rainbow trout – the progeny of fast-growing river-resident fish.

hatcheries, a greater awareness among Fish and Game managers and councillors of the cost-benefit of stocking, and a shift in management focus toward habitat protection.

Nowadays, most remaining hatchery-release programmes are for lake systems, like the Rotorua lakes, that have inadequate natural spawning waters but are popular with anglers. The futility of stocking rivers in which trout are already established is now widely recognised. The economics of stocking finally put an end to many of the remaining stocking activities in New Zealand, and now this is usually the key factor in deciding whether or not new stocking initiatives get off the ground.

Perhaps the following will convince the reader of this fact. The cost of yearling brown trout from a hatchery has been estimated by Fish and Game New Zealand at about $5–6 per fish. After release into a river, the stocked trout might experience an annual survival rate of 20–50 per cent. This means that for every hundred yearling trout released, only four to twenty-five may survive several years or more to reach maturity, depending on the river and flood and drought conditions. If we measure the economics of stocking in terms of the number of adult trout available to the angler, and their contribution to reproduction, then by this stage each trout has cost between $26 and $162. Recent cost-benefit analysis undertaken on some of the stocking programmes has come up with some sobering figures. Each stocked trout caught by anglers cost between $64 and $195 in Otago, a region that has its own hatchery with attendant lower costs of fish transport (50 per cent less than, say, for Nelson). In Taranaki the cost-benefits are even worse: each stocked trout caught by anglers was estimated to cost a staggering $436.

The planting of eyed ova has, in the past, been raised as an alternative, but this is equally expensive. Eyed ova cost about $60–250 per thousand, depending on how they are obtained, plus planting costs. Assuming the egg boxes are planted in a favourable location most eggs will hatch, but this is not guaranteed; for example, siltation can cause high mortality. In any event, it is commonly the case that over 95 per cent of the fry will be dead by the end of the first year. This figure is based on several studies estimating natural mortality. On average, a thousand eggs will produce about one to three adult trout, meaning that the real costs of planting eyed ova work out to be $20–250 per fish, at least as bad as the costs of stocking yearlings.

These cost-benefits of stocking are clearly unsupportable in the context of the present price of an annual adult fishing licence of only $88. An angler who catches a stocked trout is in effect receiving a huge subsidy from other anglers. If a Fish and Game council were to seriously consider stocking in light of these economics, they might as well sell raffle tickets in place of fishing licences.

The cost per fish escalates when anglers catch only a small percentage of the stocked trout. Only when the return rate to anglers is high can stocking be justified; for example, when there is good productive habitat for rearing trout but spawning habitat is limited. Couple that with high angling pressure, and return rates can be high enough to make stocking a viable option. A case in point is Eastern Fish and Game's stocking of the Rotorua lakes with fish raised at the Ngongataha hatchery. These fish supplement the very limited recruitment from wild stocks, and the lakes provide excellent trout habitat and growing conditions. The low stocks of wild trout, the good habitat and high fishing pressure result in a good return to anglers. The average return of hatchery fish to the angler is estimated to be at least 18.6 per cent. Since the total cost of raising and stocking has been estimated at only $1.82 per fish, the cost of each fish caught works out at between $6.45 and $9.78.

Anglers sometimes argue for stocking to bolster trout populations that are perceived to be in decline owing to deteriorating habitat. This argument is unsound because natural mortality is so high that few released trout are caught. Furthermore, impaired habitat quality is likely to increase natural mortality even higher. To some extent this argument depends on what features of the habitat are impaired. For example, if only the spawning gravels are degraded, then artificial stocking might be warranted. However, to be more than a temporary fix it would need to be followed up by spawning-habitat enhancement. Spawning gravels are often degraded by siltation, which also means the invertebrate food supply of trout is likely also degraded by smothering. So the released trout still may not do well, owing to food limitation. This highlights the need to understand the various factors limiting a trout population before proceeding with expensive stocking programmes.

A situation in which hatchery releases to rivers might be justified is where angling pressure is so high that a significant proportion of the hatchery fish are caught soon after release, before most of the fish are lost by natural mortality. This is essentially a 'put-and-take' fishery, equivalent to many of the river-stocking programmes in the United States subsidised by government agencies and patronised by hordes of anglers. In the New Zealand context, the user-pays fisheries-management regime, together with the comparatively low fishing pressure on our rivers, means that this kind of stocking programme cannot be justified.

Research in the United States has shown that hatchery trout

A juvenile brown trout gets a new home following a trip in a fish tanker. Fish such as this one that have been salvaged from drying rivers on the Canterbury Plains can provide good returns to anglers when released in high-country lakes that have limited spawning habitat. Alternatively, Fish and Game staff sometimes release them in the nearest permanent water body.
Ross Millichamp

in rivers can be detrimental to wild populations by interbreeding and through competition. Unless hatchery trout are carefully bred from wild stock taken from the river or lake into which they are to be released, they may be ill-adapted to survive in the wild. This situation is more important in North America and Europe (the native range of our trout species), where populations are more likely to have evolved traits specific to local environmental conditions. The management agencies have only recently become aware of the importance of avoiding mixing of stocks to preserve native biodiversity. This is less critical in New Zealand, where the trout have been introduced (and comparatively recently) so are less likely to have evolved significant differences between populations. Nevertheless, recent research has revealed that chinook salmon in New Zealand have developed some genetic and morphological differences in the thirty-odd generations that they have been at large here.

Wild trout like this are more aggressive than hatchery-raised fish, which are not used to territorial behaviour.

American research has shown that when hatchery trout are released on top of an existing river population of wild trout, the latter may experience reduced growth and survival, caused by competition for feeding positions. The wild trout initially are more aggressive than hatchery trout and try to fight off the intruders. Wild trout are keenly aware of each other's territories and dominance status, and generally minimise infighting by respecting each other's territorial boundaries, but every now and then a trout will 'try it on' with its neighbour. Because hatchery fish are reared in crowded conditions where food is comparatively unlimited, they are less aggressive than wild trout. They have not learned to play by the unwritten code of territorial behaviour. Once released into a river in which wild trout are already present, the hatchery trout blunder into the wild fishes' territories, ignoring the aggressive behavioural signals, and fights result. The sheer numbers of hatchery trout swamp the wild trout, with the latter becoming exhausted from incessant fighting and high stress levels.

If put-and-take fisheries are to be contemplated at all, it makes sense to locate them on small artificial lakes and ponds near or in cities, not on rivers. Some anglers look down their noses at the idea of put-and-take reservoir fisheries. These are elitist views, out of touch, I venture to say, with a large sector of the angling community. One only has to consider the popularity of put-and-take 'take a kid fishing' days organised by Fish and Game, DOC and community groups to appreciate the demand for this kind of fishing in New Zealand.

For those new to the sport of trout fishing, or with limited means for transport, or the physically handicapped, put-and-take fisheries can offer rewarding angling opportunities. A friend in Toronto

Conservation and management

regularly fished a series of artificial ponds on the outskirts of this busy city. Phil is retired now, and during one of my visits he was crippled with a knee complaint and a crook shoulder, the latter a painful reminder of tumbling down a bank of the Ahuriri River on a previous fishing adventure in New Zealand. Phil graciously invited me to accompany him on a trip to fish 'the ponds', a privilege for which he paid a not-insubstantial annual fee (considerably more than a New Zealand trout fishing licence). We drove over a grass and dirt track up to within ten metres of Phil's favourite pond. After assembling his gear he limped over to a handy stump upon which he perched for most of the afternoon, and from which he could survey the water and cast to trout. The surroundings, while artificial, were very picturesque and serene. No concrete ponds here: they were all earth-lined, with reeds and submerged aquatic weeds and grasses and trees gracing the banks. My wife spent a pleasant afternoon exploring the area and watching the plentiful birdlife, while Phil and I went about the serious task of fishing. There were plenty of rainbow trout, but they were no pushovers. Light leaders and small flies were required for success, and the water was clear enough to see the refusals. The afternoon was very rewarding in terms of scenery, catch rate, quality of fish, and challenge. There were enough opportunities to experiment with flies and technique, and to learn something. The experience left me in no doubt of the value of artificial put-and-take fishing ponds.

A Fish and Game release of hatchery-reared fish from a tanker. Stocking trout and salmon into lakes, such as this one, that have inadequate spawning habitat can provide cost effective returns to anglers.

Fish & Game NZ – Central South Island Region

Do hatcheries pose a disease risk?
Hatchery liberations, as opposed to the mere presence of hatcheries, can pose a disease risk. Although acknowledged as theoretically possible by management agencies, the significance of disease introduction to wild populations by hatchery fish has only recently been fully appreciated. This has come about through the realisation that whirling disease has seriously compromised trout populations in some rivers in the United States.

Whirling disease is caused by a microscopic parasite, *Myxobolus cerebralis*, which attacks cartilage of growing trout, producing skeletal deformities, particularly of the head. Other symptoms include a darkening of the tail, a loss of equilibrium and frenetic tail chasing, and mortality, mainly in young fish. The tail-chasing symptom is what gave rise to the name of the disease. Tubifex worms, such as those commonly sold for pet-fish food, are an intermediate host used by the parasite. These worms live in the mud of river bottoms and play an essential role in the *M. cerebralis* life history. Of the salmonids, rainbow trout are the most susceptible to whirling disease, while brown trout are largely resistant to it.

Prior to the mid-1990s whirling disease was considered to be mainly a problem confined to hatcheries, where high densities of trout could encourage outbreaks. This encouraged complacency amongst hatchery managers and Fish and Wildlife staff, and exacerbated the spread of infected hatchery stock into rivers and lakes throughout many states in the United States. The practice of indiscriminate hatchery releases came to an abrupt end with the discovery in the mid-1990s that whirling disease was responsible for severe declines in rainbow trout populations in the famous Madison River of Montana, and in parts of the Colorado River. As a result, hatchery sanitation is now taken more seriously in states known to harbour whirling disease, and inter-catchment stocking policies are much more conservative.

Now there is a growing interest in wild-trout management in the United States and among anglers from that country. In fact, the opportunity to fish for wild trout now is one of the key ingredients that make the New Zealand trout-fishing experience attractive to North Americans.

The whirling disease experience in the United States is a timely lesson for New Zealand. A key point arising from that experience is that disease should not be overlooked as a factor that can limit trout populations, even wild populations. Most freshwater fisheries ecologists and managers in New Zealand have little or no first-hand experience with major fish diseases. When investigating trout populations we tend to concentrate on habitat features and angling impact, because those are the areas in which our experience is based. The same occurred on the Madison River: research efforts were first directed at flows, water quality, water temperature, fish habitat change and fishing pressure before scientists experienced with fish disease identified whirling disease as the culprit.

Fortunately, New Zealand is free of most of the debilitating diseases that plague Northern Hemisphere trout and salmon populations. But whirling disease is present in some parts of the South Island, and there have been two outbreaks in South Island hatcheries. The first was in 1971 at the Otago Acclimatisation Society's hatchery on the Waitaki River; the second, and more severe, outbreak was in 1980 at the then Ministry of Agriculture and Fisheries hatchery at Silverstream, on the outskirts of Christchurch. These scares contributed to the closure of both hatcheries, although Silverstream has resumed some limited operations related to salmon research and production in recent years.

The Silverstream outbreak led to a survey of whirling disease in other waters and hatcheries throughout the South Island. So far the disease has been found in only a few locations in Otago and Canterbury, and there is evidence that it has been spread by both human and natural transfer between catchments.

Wild brown trout populations in New Zealand probably are not at risk from whirling disease because they are resistant. Whether wild rainbow trout populations in the South Island are affected by whirling disease has not been investigated. In fact, our knowledge of natural variations in populations of both rainbow and brown trout throughout New Zealand and the importance of the various limiting factors generally is poor, mainly because of lack of research.

CHAPTER ELEVEN

Conserving the habitat

WE OFTEN HEAR the days of yesteryear referred to as the 'golden age' of fishing and hunting in New Zealand. Why is it that older anglers often complain that fishing today is poorer than in the past? No doubt there is an aspect of human psychology at play in these remarks. The mind tends to selectively recall the best fishing trips, and numbers get exaggerated over time. That said, I still believe there is some truth behind this angling folklore. My own experience attests to it, as does what is known of historical changes of the land and fresh waters of New Zealand since the introduction of trout and salmon.

I grew up fishing on a spring creek only ten minutes' walk from my home on the northern outskirts of Christchurch. My memories from those boyhood days, about forty years ago, are of a clear stream running over a gravel bed between banks of watercress. There were plenty of beautifully coloured, though not very big, brown trout. Half-kilogram fish were about average, and a whopper might be twice that size. For my mates and me, that stream was our training ground. There we progressed from spin fishing, through drifting a worm under a cork float, to fly fishing. We had individual names for the 'lunkers' that scornfully refused our first attempts with crude fly-fishing gear. My first fly outfit consisted of a supple eight-foot (2.3-metre) split-cane spinning rod with a hand-me-down cheap fly reel from my father, spooled with limp green backing. Yet I learnt to catch trout with it in that little spring creek.

As the years slipped by, I was attracted by new and bigger waters downstream, and then further afield, beckoned by an adventurous spirit born in the wild places around that spring creek where I spent so much of my youth.

Now, with adult eyes, I see the lower reaches of that same spring creek. The waters no longer run clear but all too often are grey. Where cress once flourished, trampled banks ooze mud and are littered with wire and plastic – signs of agricultural and urban 'progress'. Concrete culverts discharge milky-grey washings and the

The artful science of trout fishing

flotsam of suburbia. Once-prolific beds of the Canadian pondweed *Elodea*, which supported an abundance of freshwater shrimps, are now replaced by green slime on a thick bed of silt – in part, the legacy of a drainage board's over-enthusiastic efforts with dragline and herbicide for aquatic-weed control. This process was a testament to the bureaucratic indifference of successive catchment and drainage boards, and regional and district councils, to environmentally sustainable catchment management.

Not far from that spring creek, chronic pollution from industry and sewage has been allowed to foul the river that my father and I fished for salmon.

Also in the span of my forty-year fishing career I have watched algal blooms appear in my favourite lake after Rural Bank loans encouraged the local farmer to develop wetlands for intensive stocking. Around the country I have seen too many stream banks trampled and fouled by stock; silage pits, dairy sheds and industry discharging their wastes to rivers; carcasses, agricultural chemicals and rubbish tipped down banks; and the lifeblood of rivers drained for irrigation, or dammed and diverted for hydro power.

The next time you are fishing on river or lake, take time to contemplate the question: will it be like this in ten years' time, or for the next generation of anglers? One thing is clear from the history of trout fishing in this country and elsewhere: streams, rivers and lakes are fragile environments. The documented and anecdotal accounts of habitat loss warn us not to take our sport for granted.

The price of economic progress in New Zealand and elsewhere has been the loss of many small trout streams, wild rivers, lakes and wetlands that once supported abundant trout. In some places this process has proceeded at an almost imperceptible pace measured over the span of generations; in others it has been surprisingly fast.

Point-source pollution such as a factory outfall is very obvious when it is bad, so it attracts attention from anglers and the public. Prior to the 1980s, New Zealand did not have a very good record of preventing and controlling industrial pollution. Less obvious, and therefore less well known, is the effect of wide-scale agricultural development on rivers, lakes and wetlands, and their trout fisheries, but there is a growing awareness that the impact has been huge, especially on our lowland rivers. A recent survey of angler perceptions indicated that there has been a widespread decline in these fisheries. This has been very insidious and it is the most difficult to deal with. Insidious because it has occurred slowly enough that generations have grown up accepting as normal that our catchments and the rivers that flow through them are degraded. The land- and water-management practices that have

Point-source pollution of New Zealand rivers is not as prevalent now as it was prior to the 1980s. Nevertheless, warnings such as this are still fairly common on our lowland rivers.

Fish & Game NZ – Central South Island Region

Conservation and management

caused the damage are ingrained and, until recently, were sanctioned and encouraged by government.

This is not to say that all change has been slow. With the recent expansion of intensive dairy farming, several examples have arisen of rapid deterioration of spring creeks. Clear, gravel-bottomed creeks that supported good trout fisheries have changed into muddy ditches choked with aquatic weeds, just six months or so after the surrounding sheep farms were converted to intensive dairying. The irony here is that the same farmers that caused the damage now complain to the regional councils that these choked 'drains' are a flood-control problem that should be addressed with public money! This is an example of inappropriate catchment management whereby a few land developers benefit at the expense of the wider community.

With larger rivers, the main reason it has taken so long for the public of New Zealand and land and water managers to appreciate the scale and magnitude of the impact is because change has been cumulative. As more subcatchments are developed for agriculture, and stocking of the land intensifies, more tributaries become degraded. This in turn results in a gradual deterioration of the receiving waters, the larger rivers. Trout anglers 'vote with their feet' in response to poorer returns and aesthetics. In New Zealand we have been fortunate that until now there have been plenty of other places to go fishing. The situation continues on a downhill slide to the point where the fact that a river once supported a vibrant trout fishery is often a distant memory of the old, and a surprise to the new generation.

Another contrbuting factor is that New Zealand's low population and wide-open spaces have made us complacent about the state of our rivers and lakes. Towns and cities spend millions of dollars on sewerage, and rightly so. But what about those millions of sheep and cattle spread out over the countryside? We overlook the fact that cows and sheep have to shit too, and where does *that* end up? In our rivers and lakes of course!

To put this in perspective: one cow produces the contaminant-loading equivalent to about four people. The contaminants here are largely nitrogen and phosphorus, the main nutrients required by plants — including algae and waterweeds in rivers and lakes. Cadmium is another contaminant, leaching from farms as a result of superphosphate fertiliser application.

Intensive dairy farming causes the worst nutrient pollution. For example, some of the early research into dairy expansion in Southland showed that waterways in intensively farmed dairying areas had nitrogen concentrations up to five hundred times the

Cows are more inclined to urinate and defecate when they step into a stream. Their trampling damages the stream bed and banks, and releases sediment. Little wonder that most of our lowland rivers now run turbid and are no longer fit for contact recreation and drinking.

Fish & Game NZ – Southland Region

Careless stock management practices like this one are unfortunately still all too common in dairy farming districts in New Zealand. The resulting damage to banks, sediment and nutrient run-off degrades trout habitat, water quality and the river ecosystem.

Richard Fitzpatrick

natural level, and phosphorus up to a hundred times. Some dairy farms have as many as 4,000 cows; the nutrient pollution from a farm this size is equivalent to a town of 16,000 people. If a new town this size were proposed anywhere in New Zealand, a lot of attention would be given to resource planning and consents to deal with sewage. But few people bat an eye when land is converted to new dairy farms.

The complacency of New Zealanders about our 'clean, green image', and the fact that our small population has a comparatively minor impact on the environment, is ill-founded. New Zealand's economy still depends heavily on agriculture, which vies with the tourism industry as the country's highest earner. In the year 2000 the total livestock population in New Zealand, including dairy cows, beef cattle, sheep and deer had an estimated nitrogen and phosphorus contaminant loading to streams, rivers and lakes equivalent to a population of at least forty-four million people. In order to earn export dollars and material wealth from agriculture, we maintain the livestock for a much larger population, not simply enough for our own seemingly insignificant four million people, and we suffer the environmental costs of doing so.

Regional and district councils miss the bigger issue when they concern themselves mainly with point-source discharges. They would require a resource consent for a discharge from a dairy shed, but ignore the fact that 70–99 per cent of the nitrogen and 40–90 per cent of the phosphorus entering rivers from dairy farms may be in the form of non-point-source run-off. Most regional and

Deer also trash trout streams through overstocking, trampling and wallowing.

Fish & Game NZ – Southland Region

Conservation and management

district council staff don't know how to deal with this issue, and only recently have there been signs that some authorities are beginning to take the issue seriously. There is widespread belief that nothing can be done about land-use intensification, and this further contributes to the inaction of regional and district councils.

Regional councils have been slow to consider the cumulative environmental impacts of the expansion in intensive farming, and are often loath to place limits on such 'development' because of the economic benefits. There are signs of a change in attitude by some of the regional councils, but it appears that this has only come about after highly publicised lobbying by Fish and Game New Zealand and the Ecologic Foundation, with their 'dirty dairying' campaign.

Uncontrolled expansion of dairy farming not only risks severe water-quality degradation, but also places excessive demands on water for irrigation in traditional dry-stock farming regions such as Canterbury and Otago. The result in Canterbury has been an unprecedented demand for new irrigation schemes that source their water from nearby rivers or from wells. Some of the new dairy farms make massive demands on our public water resources. For example, a 3,000-cow farm proposed in Canterbury required 560 litres per second – as much as a city of 65,000 households. This 'water rush' has precipitated major battles between Fish and Game and irrigation companies formed by consortiums of farmers. Not only must the water supply be secure, but it is most needed at the time of year when river flows are lowest and temperatures are highest, so that aquatic life is under the most stress. This compounds the effects of pollution from nutrient run-off and dairy sheds. The low rainfall and river flows in dry-country regions means that there

Irrigation demands in dryland regions such as Canterbury have made massive demands on public water resources. As a result, surface and ground waters have been depleted and polluted (the latter from nutrient-rich water leaching through the ground).
Ross Millichamp

The artful science of trout fishing

is less dilution of pollutants than in traditionally wet dairy regions. The result is enriched rivers and polluted groundwater.

Of course, not all farming practices are bad, and dairy farming does not have to be environmentally unsustainable. For example, intensive farming has less impact in high-rainfall regions such as the west coast of the South Island, where nutrients are flushed off and diluted more quickly. Also, most West Coast catchments have larger proportions of their area in native bush. All this helps mitigate the impacts of farming. Nevertheless, even in that region there have recently appeared ominous signs of trout-stream deterioration associated with dairy-farm expansion.

The impacts of farming on waterways are still only partially understood, and the intensity of effects varies from place to place. Rainfall, geology, soil structure and management practices all influence the pollution load emanating from farms. The challenge ahead for the farming industry and land- and water-management agencies is to decide how much development is enough. Just what type and intensity of farming is compatible with healthy rivers and lakes, and vibrant sports fisheries?

Sediment run-off is another major symptom of careless land use often associated with agriculture and forestry. Destabilisation of the land surface, combined with periodic natural storm events, can lead to significant increases in silt, sand, gravel and rocks entering rivers. An increase in a river's bedload can lead to a widening and shallowing of the channel. This fills in pools and other deepwater habitat essential to adult trout, and erodes banks, with the loss of associated overhanging cover. For example, a study in North America found that when sand was added to a natural pool, reducing the volume by half and the area of water deeper than 0.3 metre by two-thirds, trout numbers fell to a third of the previous level. It can take decades for a river channel to regain its equilibrium, and it may never return to its original state if the changed land use continues.

Dairy farming and trout fishing need not be incompatible, but their co-existence will require changes to farming expectations and management practices.

Accelerated erosion of fine materials causes rivers to run turbid and smothers their beds in silt and sand. This can make them useless for trout spawning and impairs their ability to support aquatic invertebrates, the food of trout. Species most affected by sedimentation and organic pollution are mayflies, stoneflies and some of the caddisflies that drift in the water column. These are the insects that sustain the drift-feeding behaviour of trout, and which fly fishers exploit. The elevated water turbidity reduces the feeding opportunities for trout by making it more difficult for them to see their prey.

I have undertaken computer modelling that shows the effect of chronic elevated turbidity on visual feeding, alone, can seriously

Conservation and management

limit the food intake of trout and slow their growth. This, combined with the reduction in numbers of insects, may undermine the viability of drift feeding by trout. It may mean that drift feeding becomes profitable for the trout only at certain times of day, such as at dusk, when some species of caddisflies synchronise their emergence (hatches). Elevated turbidity also reduces fly-fishing opportunities by denying the angler the chance to sight fish. Reports by anglers of deterioration in river fishing associated with land development indicate that angling quality may be impacted by turbidity and sedimentation long before an obvious change is seen in the trout population.

The following is a list of land-use impacts that have affected our rivers and lakes. They are too numerous to discuss here in detail. Instead, I introduce them to give the reader a feel for the overwhelming pressures bearing upon trout habitat, the very foundation underpinning our trout fisheries.

A nice balance between natural and developed land uses, preserving good trout habitat and pleasing aesthetics.

- Wetlands have been extensively drained throughout New Zealand. This reduces water storage in catchments, increasing flood-flow levels and reducing base flows in receiving rivers. The former can increase the scouring frequency of riverbeds, with damaging consequences for trout eggs and fry and the aquatic insects that trout eat.
- Extensive native-forest clearance across New Zealand has had similar effects – reducing water storage, increasing flood frequency and bedload, and increasing stream temperatures through the loss of shade.
- Intensive stocking of farmland and grazing of riparian margins has accelerated erosion and nutrient leaching. As a result, rivers running through agricultural land now often run turbid for prolonged periods after floods, and excessive nutrient enrichment stimulates unsightly growths of periphyton (slime).
- Point-source pollution from dairy sheds is also a continuing problem. In recent years much research and management effort has been invested in improving dairy-shed waste management using small on-farm settling and oxidation ponds and spray irrigation of effluent. This means less ammonia in our streams and rivers, but nutrient enrichment and faecal-coliform pollution are still big problems. Dairy-farm oxidation ponds vary greatly in their effectiveness at reducing faecal coliforms, and particularly nutrients.
- Nutrient leaching has also contributed to the eutrophication of lakes in agricultural catchments. This stimulates algal blooms and deoxygenation of bottom layers, reducing aesthetics and

The artful science of trout fishing

River-control works often create artificial channels and reduce trout habitat.
Fish & Game NZ – Wellington Region

Isolated pools provide trout with a temporary refuge from river drying, but eventually many fish succumb to stranding or lack of oxygen before the river resumes flowing. Water abstraction for irrigation has prolonged these critical periods in small rivers draining dry-land regions such as Hawke's Bay, Nelson–Marlborough, Canterbury and North Otago.
Cawthron Institute

habitat capacity for trout and their prey (including both invertebrates and forage fish).

- Exotic forestry can have similar effects to native-forest removal during the land clearance and roading stage prior to planting and during logging. In dry catchments growing forests can lead to significantly reduced water flows, and cause small streams to dry up completely where once they flowed all year round – an issue for trout-spawning and fry-nursery areas. Culverts and fords associated with forest roads can impair trout passage, which can reduce spawning and the abundance of trout in headwater fisheries.
- Urbanisation has encroached upon riparian margins of rivers. Urban development increases the amount of impermeable land in a catchment. This accelerates rainfall run-off, increasing the intensity and frequency of flooding, which in turn widens and shallows stream channels. The flood-control works that follow, and which encourage even more encroachment of riparian margins, often reduce habitat complexity because they do not take into consideration the needs of stream life such as trout. Then, too, there is the problem of toxic substance run-off and leaching from urban areas.
- The encroachment of agricultural development and associated buildings on riparian margins and river flood plains results in similar pressures to 'tame' rivers with engineering works. Sometimes these control works have had unforseen consequences because they have been done with inadequate understanding of river form and function. In many places in North America for example, river managers now realise that river control works done in the past to stabilise channels and reduce flooding have in fact had the reverse effect. There has rarely been any independent review of the appropriateness of river control management in New Zealand.
- Gravel extraction from rivers for road and construction aggregate can have similarly unpredictable long-term effects. It alters fish habitat, disturbs aquatic insect populations and can smother downstream populations in silt, a particular problem during low flow.
- With the widespread development of land for agriculture, and a drive for even more intensive operations to improve farming economics, there has arisen an insatiable demand for irrigation water. This is especially so in dry regions such as the east coasts of the South and North Islands and in Nelson, and has placed heavy demands on surface and ground water resources. Inadequate long-term land- and water-resource planning by regional

and district councils has led to the overallocation of resource consents to take water from river catchments. There are now many examples around the country where the flow of otherwise good trout rivers is reduced each summer to well below the natural low flows, with the result that long-term trout-habitat capacity is severely impaired.

- Hydroelectric-power development has had similar impacts on some rivers whose flows have been diverted or stored. Hydro development is very visible and has radically changed many rivers and lakes in both the North and South Islands. One major impact has been the barriers created to trout and salmon migrations. There is no denying that the overall impact of hydro development has been negative for river fisheries, but the effects have not been all bad. There has been some compensation by the creation of very good reservoir fisheries and some good tail-water river fisheries.

A diver monitors juvenile rainbow trout below the Rangipo Dam on the Tongariro River. Hydro-power and irrigation dams have mixed effects on salmonid fisheries. They have extinguished several migratory trout and salmon populations in New Zealand and degraded some river fisheries. On the other hand, they have provided some excellent reservoir fisheries and, in some situations, have been compatible with continued high-quality river fisheries.

Cawthron Institute

The above makes depressing reading. This list could be written for any temperate industrialised nation in the world. New Zealand, in its short period of European colonisation, has experienced the same kinds of abuses, limited only by the low population and large amount of land too rugged to develop.

We only have to look to North America for the severe consequences of neglecting catchment-wide processes in misdirected land development. And it is here that, as a consequence of past mistakes, significant progress has recently been made on how to go about the research into and management of land and water on a catchment scale. Considerable effort has also been spent there on river restoration, several examples of which have been stimulated by active campaigning by Trout Unlimited (TU).

TU recently began a high-profile restoration programme on the Blackfoot River, which was made famous by Gordon McLean's book *A River Runs Through It*. Much has been learnt on this and other rivers in North America regarding how to undertake community-watershed restoration. In the case of the Blackfoot, this is in response to degradation by agriculture, mining and forestry (see Williams et al. 1997). It is fitting that environmental degradation of a trout river made internationally famous in popular press and film should attract the attention of community and government agencies, and remedial action be taken.

There is a small river just north of Wellington, draining into Pauatahanui Inlet, that in its own way lays claim to international fame for its trout fishery. It too has suffered environmental degradation related to agricultural development, and the fishery is almost lost. To most people the Horokiwi is like any of the many small streams running through agricultural land throughout the country. Probably too, very few anglers are aware of its international reputation – based not on its fishing but on a ground-breaking scientific study of its fishery undertaken in the 1940s by K. Radway Allen, a Marine Department scientist whose research was partly funded through a fishing-licence levy by the acclimatisation societies.

Over the intervening years the Horokiwi's trout fishery has wasted away – why, no one knows for sure because no research or monitoring was undertaken during its decline. But a recent investigation by NIWA suggests that land-use change and unchecked agricultural development was the cause. The history of the Horokiwi exemplifies the deterioration of New Zealand lowland trout streams, and highlights the indifference of rural communities and regional councils to the environmental impacts of past and present land-use practices. It is ironic that politicians and government bureaucrats in Wellington have taken so long to recognise the issue when they have such a good example virtually on their doorstep.

The above paints a gloomy picture of the care taken of the nation's freshwater heritage by former generations. Fortunately, there appears to be a growing awareness of the need for better environmental stewardship by central government and local communities. A case in point is the small spring creek on the outskirts of Christchurch that I described fishing as a boy. In recent years a community group has been formed with the aim of protecting the stream from further environmental degradation, and it has been active in riparian enhancement and wetland restoration. Similar land- and stream-care groups have been forming throughout the country, encouraged by central and local governments.

The role of Fish and Game New Zealand in habitat conservation

I often hear anglers criticising Fish and Game councils and their staff, complaining about the cost of licences, not enough stocking and not seeing rangers in the field. This demonstrates an ignorance of the real issues threatening their sport and how Fish and Game councils actually are serving licence-holders' interests.

Unbeknown to many anglers who complain about trivialities, a struggle is going on behind the scenes to conserve the environmental integrity of the remaining rivers, lakes and wetlands that support their fisheries. The foremost organisation in this effort is Fish and Game New Zealand; formerly this work was done by acclimatisation societies. No other agency has had a greater role in advocating freshwater environmental conservation, and campaigned more suc-

Opposite: *Pristine places such as this are highly valued by New Zealand anglers and those from overseas.*

cessfully for sensible environmental law in this country. All paid for, I might add, by angler and game-bird licence revenue.

The acclimatisation societies were instrumental in the Wild and Scenic Rivers legislation in 1981 – an amendment to the Water and Soil Conservation Act 1967. They, and their successors the Fish and Game councils, have been the most vigorous environmental group seeking water-conservation orders for the protection of rivers throughout New Zealand, making three-quarters of all applications. They also had a significant role in lobbying for the enactment of the Resource Management Act (RMA) in 1991, which brought about improved environmental management in New Zealand. The RMA is New Zealand's key environmental legislation governing the use of natural resources, including fresh waters. Fish and Game councils ensured the inclusion of section 7(h) in the RMA, which requires regional and district councils 'to have particular regard for the protection of habitat of trout and salmon'.

The RMA is seen by many as a revolutionary piece of law that goes a long way toward putting environmental values on a more equal footing with economic development. In particular, anyone seeking to develop or use the environment is now expected to 'avoid, remedy or mitigate adverse environmental effects' of their activities. In many ways the RMA has made it easier for Fish and Game staff to advocate conservation of trout and salmon habitat and recreational values, because the law specifically embodies these values.

More recently, Fish and Game even successfully tested the sovereign right of Parliament to make laws applying to all peoples of New Zealand. This was related to a highly controversial case in Taranaki, where Maori claimed that customary fishing rights guaranteed under the Treaty of Waitangi extended to trout, an introduced species, and would enable them to fish without a licence in some circumstances. Regrettably, while the Crown funded the Maori case, no support was provided to Fish and Game to cover its legal costs. The Department of Conservation fisheries section performs similar advocacy and management functions within the Taupo district.

Since the establishment of Fish and Game New Zealand and the Department of Conservation in 1990 there has emerged a new breed of fisheries staff in this country, well educated and very knowledgeable in environmental law, especially the requirements of the RMA. They spend countless hours researching submissions and attending hearings for regional and catchment plans and water-consent hearings, to ensure that regional and district councils set appropriate conditions for conserving trout and salmon habitat.

Without their vigilance, and that of informed and dedicated Fish and Game councillors, the overwhelming pressures of developers would erode New Zealand's freshwater habitats at a much greater rate. Even so, these efforts are still being frustrated by many regional and district councils that refuse to interpret the RMA in such a manner as to halt the cumulative loss of trout, salmon and native fish habitat.

At present, one of the biggest challenges facing water and fisheries managers in this country is sustainable land and water management at the catchment and regional level. There is a wealth of knowledge both here and overseas on the ways that poor land-management practices impact on aquatic habitats and the life they sustain, including trout. However, to those with a passion for trout there has been a frustrating inertia among most regional and district councils in applying this knowledge to educate and regulate landowners in best land-management practices. In bureaucratic circles many of the right words are being said but little effective action is being taken at the catchment scale. To be fair, the problem is formidable, especially in agricultural areas. Just how do you go about getting hundreds of landowners, with varying interests in what happens outside their farm boundaries, to commit to changing their land- and stock-management practices to reduce the impact they have on streams and rivers for the common good? The problem is especially daunting when you consider that most farmers are unwilling to change unless it can be proven this will not cost them.

An interesting twist to this story is that some of the markets for our agricultural products may end up being a major factor forcing primary producers to clean up their act. In order to gain entry into the lucrative European and North American markets, our primary industries will likely have to demonstrate that their products have been grown and processed in an environmentally sustainable way. Unfortunately, countering this trend is the recent refocusing by the New Zealand dairy industry on Asian, Latin American, Russian and Middle Eastern markets. Here the interest is in low-cost, high-volume production of milk powder and other bulk products for customers with little interest in environmental sustainability. Nevertheless, to its credit Fonterra – New Zealand's largest dairy co-operative – recently proposed an accreditation system requiring its members to meet environmental standards for milk production on farms. Ironically, Federated Farmers – New Zealand's farming lobby organisation – opposed this enlightened initiative.

CHAPTER TWELVE

Indigenous conservation and trout fisheries management: an uneasy tension

IN THE YOUNG COLONY of New Zealand in the late 1880s, introducing exotic species was a common practice, as in other colonies and in Britain itself. Acclimatisation societies were particularly active; their establishment in New Zealand followed from their popularity in Britain and elsewhere in Europe.

The establishment and spread of brown and rainbow trout in New Zealand was due to the vigorous stocking efforts of the acclimatisation societies. The initial introductions were preceded by the passing of legislation in 1867 to allow the importation of trout, and in the same year the first introductions were made. The eggs came from Tasmania, where brown trout had been recently introduced from England. Several further introductions were made from various sources, including England, Scotland, Germany and Italy.

Rainbow trout were introduced to New Zealand from California. There is some doubt about when the first introductions occurred and where in California they came from. The earliest consignment appears to have arrived in 1877, but the main and best-documented one was in 1883. Other shipments were made in the late 1880s and in 1930.

Stocking by the acclimatisation societies in the late nineteenth century was encouraged and subsidised by provincial and central governments. In the early 1900s the newly formed Marine Department was directly responsible for the successful introduction of chinook salmon, and the recreational salmon fisheries that developed on the east coast of the South Island. So the introduction of many of these exotic animals and plants, trout and salmon included, did not occur by happenstance or the isolated efforts of eccentric individuals, but rather as an organised, sustained programme with government and public encouragement and co-operation.

Nowadays, the introduction of exotic species receives mainly bad press, owing to the disastrous impacts some have had on native fauna and flora. Examples include rabbits, possums, deer and weeds such as gorse. This overlooks the fact that many introduced species have become accepted and valued additions to New Zealand's fauna and flora, both feral and domestic, ranging from trout and salmon to game birds and domestic livestock. On the other hand, community attitudes to deer and other big-game animals are mixed: they are valued by hunters and deer farmers but vilified by conservationists, who hold the preservation of indigenous biodiversity to be paramount.

It is all too easy to think poorly of the settlers and colonial governments for so enthusiastically acclimatising exotic species when the impact of some of these on the native fauna and flora has proved so devastating. The settlers also had devastating direct impacts on the bush and wetlands, which they cleared and drained for pastoral farming. Today, conservationists mourn the loss of 'natural New Zealand', the ancient Gondwana relic, and cherish what little remains of it. But we have the benefit of hindsight; the colonists did not. We should not judge our forebears by the standards of today. We can hardly criticise their actions from the comfort of our living rooms, just perhaps their over-enthusiasm in so thoroughly modifying the landscape, the fauna and flora.

The colonists found themselves in a foreign land where little was familiar, so they set about modelling farms and gardens on those from their homelands, and 'enriching' the native fauna and flora with familiar and desired exotic species. It was early recognised that New Zealand was richly endowed with cold-water rivers, lakes and wetlands. Yet the colonists saw little in the way of useful sporting fish in them – although they recognised eels and whitebait as food sources. This is not surprising because our native fish fauna is comparatively sparse, and many species are small, cryptic and often few in number – although whitebait can be seasonally abundant. Charles Hursthouse summed up the general opinion in 1857: 'Just as New Zealand forests are destitute of game, so are its rivers destitute of fish . . . they boast no single fish worth the angler's catching . . .' Spackman's 1892 account of angling in New Zealand states: 'Twenty-five years ago not one of these rivers had the least interest for the angler . . . the rod of the fisherman never cast a shadow on their waters; every one of these mighty rivers, every one of the thousands of creeks and streams that flow into them . . . were tenantless and profitless to the sportsman.'

So in the late 1800s and early 1900s private individuals, acclimatisation societies and government agencies set about introducing trout and salmon to these 'virgin' waters. Their efforts with brown and rainbow trout, and chinook salmon, were spectacularly successful and resulted in the establishment of world-renowned fisheries. Moreover, the fishing was available to the common man, an egalitarian aim of the acclimatisation societies.

Until recently, the impacts of these foreign fish on our native fauna went largely unnoticed. Trout and salmon very much defined the fisheries and conservation values of our fresh waters. Native fish, apart from whitebait and eels, were regarded as an academic curiosity. This situation has changed radically over the past twenty years, however, owing to the rising popularity of indigenous conservation philosophy. In government circles this has resulted in more research and conservation-management effort on native fish and aquatic biodiversity.

There is little doubt now that trout have had impacts on native fish, probably also on native aquatic invertebrates and, in some special situations, even on the function of stream ecosystems. Little was known about the impacts of trout on native fish before the 1990s. Research on the subject had lagged behind similar research on the native terrestrial fauna. Moreover, it has been only since the 1970s that New Zealand's native fish fauna has been reasonably well described and life histories of most of the species understood. This has been due in large measure to the prolific research and publishing efforts of R. M. McDowall (see Selected References).

Comparatively speaking, New Zealand's freshwater fish fauna is rather sparse. As of the year 2000, thirty-five native species had been identified, some just recently. The Department of Conservation (DOC) considers that almost a third of these are threatened by habitat loss or by introduced species. Since European settlement, twenty-one introduced species have been added to the fish fauna, making a total of fifty-six. About half of our native fish species are sea-migratory, or diadromous.

Our freshwater fish fauna is small and has a high proportion of sea-migratory species, for a variety of reasons. Partly these are because New Zealand has been geographically isolated from other significant land masses by vast distances and long periods of time. They are also related to its turbulent geological history, including marine submergence, ice ages, rapid mountain building and erosion, and volcanic activity. According to McDowall, 'this turbulent history would undoubtedly have caused significant amounts of extinction. It is probable that much of our fauna is derived by dispersion of marine-tolerant life stages across the Tasman Sea from eastern Australia.'

The earliest recognised impacts of trout on native fish were in New Zealand's best-known trout fisheries, Lake Taupo and the Rotorua lakes. There, trout were responsible for severe declines in populations of the little galaxiid koaro. It was probably the same following trout introduction in many other lakes throughout New Zealand. Koaro are one of the five galaxiid species that make up New Zealand's famous whitebait runs. The sea-migratory koaro, which runs up rivers from the sea each spring, also occurs as land-locked populations in lakes.

The evidence for decline in lake populations of koaro following introduction of trout is largely anecdotal, but nonetheless compelling. For instance, the phenomenal sports fishery that developed in Lake Taupo within thirty years of the introduction of trout in 1887 is believed to have been because koaro were an abundant food source. In fact, koaro were previously so prolific that they provided an important traditional fishery for Ngati Tuwharetoa. By 1912, however, trout had so depleted the koaro that trout size and condition plummeted; the plentiful bags of huge trout that were a feature of the early fishery became much rarer. The fishery went through several rocky years, with size and condition of trout temporarily improving in response to periodic netting efforts, and changes to the regulations, to reduce trout numbers. The Taupo fishery was finally stabilised in the 1930s when common smelt (another small native fish) were introduced to the lake to provide an alternative food supply. This action was modelled on a similar successful restoration of the trout fisheries in some of the Rotorua lakes earlier that century. It is now believed that common smelt compete with koaro and probably exacerbated their decline in Taupo and in other lakes to which they were introduced to support trout populations. Koaro still exist in most of these lakes but in greatly reduced numbers.

Land-locked populations of koaro occur also in many tarns and small lakes scattered over the South Island high country. Many of these water bodies are trout-free, but unfortunately some anglers see them as an opportunity to create new fisheries known only to them and their mates. A few fry tossed into one of these tarns can produce trophy trout within a few years, grown fat by gorging on koaro. This may sound appealing but it is ecologically reckless behaviour. Given that trout are already so widely distributed, the remaining trout-free water bodies have special scientific and ecological importance. For that reason it is a breach of the Conservation Act and Fisheries Regulations to release trout into waters not already inhabited by them. When anglers behave in this manner it undermines the credibility of the entire angling community in the minds of conservationists.

So far we have dealt with trout impacts in still water. In order to understand the impacts of trout on native fish in streams and rivers, it is necessary to distinguish between fish that reside in fresh

An angler surveying excellent trout water in the upper Taieri River. Small tributaries in the surrounding hills provide refuge for threatened stream-resident galaxiids where waterfalls prevent upstream invasion by trout.

Inset: The Otago roundhead galaxias is one of the galaxiids vulnerable to predation by brown trout.

R. M. McDowall

water for their entire life history and those that migrate to and from the sea.

The stream- and lake-resident species are more prevalent and diverse in geologically old regions of New Zealand, such as parts of Otago. Because they are stream-resident for their entire life histories, these species are most at risk from trout. In fact, the clearest evidence for impacts of trout on native fish in running water comes from research on some recently discovered stream-resident galaxiids in Otago. In the late 1980s and 1990s a research team from the University of Otago began studying fish distribution in the Taieri River catchment. They soon realised that some of the small native galaxiids they found were in fact a new species. This sparked an intensive investigation of other streams in the Otago and Southland regions, with the result that several new species were discovered. To the untrained eye, and even to experienced fish biologists, most of these species are very similar in appearance. In fact, the taxonomic separation of the various species has relied on genetic research. The researchers noticed that the first of these species discovered in the Taieri catchment had very restricted geographic distribution – they were most abundant in small streams above waterfalls. This they attributed to predation by brown trout, although competition for space and invertebrate food may also be occurring. Wherever trout were abundant the galaxiids usually were absent or uncommon.

Many of the streams in which the impacts of trout on Otago galaxiids have been studied have comparatively stable flows, and as a result the trout are abundant and stunted. This explains why the small galaxiids are at such risk of predation. However, stable flow regimes are not the norm in New Zealand streams and rivers, most of which have unpredictable, frequent floods. This is probably the main reason why trout densities are low by North American standards. On the other hand, native fish have evolved within this unstable environment. It is unlikely, therefore, that the impacts of trout on native fish have been as severe in these types of rivers as they have been in the catchments inhabited by Otago galaxiids. Recent research on native fish and trout distribution in the upper Waimakariri River catchment has supported this view: resident native galaxiids and bullies were most abundant in the unstable streams with fewest trout.

Not all stream-resident native fish are as vulnerable to trout as the Otago galaxiids. For instance, upland bullies are widespread and abundant in most streams and rivers throughout the South Island, co-occurring plentifully with trout despite being on their menu. The reason for the upland bully's success probably lies in its prolific breeding capacity – it spawns multiple generations per summer – and the fact that it hides from predators among the rocks and gravels of the river bed.

Resident native freshwater fish are most vulnerable to predation and competition impacts from trout because they live their entire lives in the same stream or river. Sea-migratory native fish species, on the other hand, are able to escape the attentions of trout when they are in the ocean. Moreover, these species are believed not to home to the streams in which they were born, unlike trout and salmon. The ocean provides a means of dispersing their populations among the plethora of streams and rivers around the coastline; although there may be some regional separation resulting from coastal currents. While trout pose a risk to any native fish that migrate back into rivers heavily populated by trout, some will always find their way into trout-free rivers and streams. Moreover, even within catchments supporting trout, some migratory native fish can find local refuge in habitat unsuitable for trout, such as small headwater tributaries, once they have run the gauntlet of trout predation in the lower river. Several of these migratory species have an impressive ability to climb wet surfaces, enabling them to get past waterfalls and other obstacles that are barriers to trout. The point already made about unstable flow regimes suppressing trout populations and thereby reducing the predation and competition pressures on native fish, also applies to these migratory species. So the combination of migratory life histories, trout-free refuges and variable flow regimes have enabled sea-migratory native fish to persist in reasonable abundance, despite the widespread distribution of trout.

Nevertheless, some migratory native fish have declined since European settlement. These include the five galaxiid species that make up the whitebait runs (inanga, koaro, banded kokopu, giant kokopu and short-jawed kokopu), plus longfin and shortfin eels. Although the acclimatisation of trout coincided with the declines in these species, trout are not thought to be the main or even a major cause. The decline in eels can be blamed squarely on commercial fishing and habitat loss. The acclimatisation societies may also have contributed with their culling efforts prior to the 1970s. Habitat degradation is believed to have been the main reason why the large galaxiids declined. Trout predation may have contributed: after all, there is no denying that trout readily eat galaxiids, both whitebait and adults. However, the potential impact of trout predation needs to be placed in context of the millions of whitebait also removed every year by recreational and commercial fishing for this delicacy.

Despite the various known impacts of trout on native fish, most species are still fairly abundant and distributed widely around the country – especially the sea-migratory species. There are some concerns over the restricted distribution of some resident galaxiids, especially in Otago, and the role of trout in this, but these are localised conservation issues related to small, mainly headwater streams. In fact only one native fish species is known to have become extinct since European colonisation, the grayling. Again, while this coincided with the acclimatisation of trout, and trout are implicated in their decline, habitat change also is considered a likely factor in the grayling's demise. To what degree trout may have contributed is unknown. There have as yet been no species extinctions attributed to trout, but this cannot be taken to mean none occurred. Little was known of the native fish fauna during the early years of the colony, so species could have vanished without ever being recognised.

Very little research has been undertaken into the impact of trout on aquatic invertebrates in New Zealand. However, as these are the staple diet of trout in most waters, it would be surprising if there were no impact. Robin Tillyard, one of New Zealand's early entymologists, suggested as long ago as 1920 that aquatic insect populations had declined because of trout predation. Trout target large and active invertebrates, and over time this could select against these types in localised fauna. Recent research has corroborated overseas studies showing that trout can affect the behaviour of some mayflies. It appears that mayfly nymphs can smell the odour of trout upstream, and as a result they feed less on the exposed surfaces of stones, and drift less often, during the day than at night. In a related study on a Taieri River tributary this effect was shown to result in the proliferation of periphyton (algal slime) on the stream bed. In a nearby stream where galaxiids but not trout were present, mayflies grazed more freely on the periphyton during the day, as well as at night, cropping it short. This was the first study in New Zealand to demonstrate, as has been shown in the Northern Hemisphere, that trout can fundamentally affect stream-ecosystem function. Nevertheless, the effect is likely to be confined to streams where stable flow allows periphyton, and trout populations, to attain high biomass.

To summarise: trout have impacted native fish and other aquatic life. They clearly have reduced the local abundance of some species, and currently are thought to be an extinction threat to local populations of a few stream-resident galaxiids.

Whether they can be said to have reduced biodiversity depends on how you define this term. At a national level, biodiversity may mean species richness – the number of species throughout the country. By this measure there is no evidence that trout have reduced national biodiversity, as they have not been shown to have caused extinctions. However, a broader definition of biodiversity takes into account not only the number of species, but also their abundance, and how these combine and fit within ecosystems in their natural state, at both national and local level. By this measure, trout can be said to have reduced indigenous biodiversity by depleting some native fishes, and probably also aquatic invertebrates, and influencing the function of stream ecosystems. However, these changes have mostly gone unnoticed, and not negatively influenced the public's appreciation and use of fresh waters. This 'out-of-sight, out-of-mind' attitude towards native fish, in contrast to the obvious glamour and value of trout, perhaps explains why trout remain especially favoured exotic species in the minds of most politicians and bureaucrats.

Is the special status of trout in New Zealand deserved?

Trout fishing has become part of our national outdoor heritage, passionately pursued by about 160,000 licensed anglers. It also attracts overseas anglers, many of whom are among the biggest spenders to visit our land. In the year 2000, about 47,700 international visitors went freshwater fishing in New Zealand. They spent

Conservation and management

$199.4 million, an average of $4,179 per visit – 42 per cent more than the average visitor spend of $2,934 (Tourism New Zealand, unpublished data).

The tourism value of trout fisheries was recognised very early by government. From its inception in 1901, the Department of Tourism was actively involved in some of the introductions and in promoting trout fishing. Various government departments with tourism mandates managed the fisheries in Taupo, Rotorua and Southern Lakes districts throughout most of the twentieth century, and Taupo is still managed by DOC. The New Zealand tourism industry continues to push trout fishing in its international promotions. The high profile and tourism value of the fishery has been responsible for much of the government's political support of trout, right up to the present day.

The quality of New Zealand's fishing waters attracts local and overseas anglers alike.

The artful science of trout fishing

It is interesting to contrast the history of attitudes to trout and deer. Both were introduced by acclimatisation societies; both are highly valued for recreation; and both have tourism value. Yet wild deer are defined by government policy as pests, while trout are defined (indirectly) as desirable species. For years deerstalkers have looked longingly at the way trout fisheries are managed here, despairing that deer populations were not officially valued likewise and managed as a resource. Why then the special treatment of trout?

Deer have always received much greater attention than trout from conservationists concerned about the preservation of indigenous flora and fauna – or, in today's conservation-speak, the preservation of indigenous biodiversity. The reasons for this are that, traditionally, the most interest has been in terrestrial environments, and deer have had highly visible and dramatic impacts on valued native forests and grasslands and, in turn, some native fauna, most visibly birds.

But the real political pressure for action to control deer began with the threat to agriculture. First, in the 1920s, farmers woke up to the fact that the ever-increasing deer herds were competing with domestic stock for their valuable pastures, and demanded deer control. Then they were joined by the Forest Service and catchment boards, which became ardent anti-deer campaigners because they believed that deer were responsible for the severe erosion widely visible in the high country, a paradigm that was only de-bunked in the 1980s. Accelerated erosion in critical areas of the high country had been considered a serious flood risk to farmland, towns and cities downstream.

So the real threat from the 'deer menace' was to New Zealand's economy, not to indigenous biodiversity. The result was that first protection of deer was lifted in 1930, then they were declared noxious under the Noxious Animals Act 1956. Later still, they became treated as pests under the Wild Animal Control Act 1977, a statute that remains to the present day. Even after scientists concluded that deer did not accelerate high-country erosion, the juggernaut of anti-deer policy continued under the increasingly popular banner of 'conserving indigenous biodiversity'.

This latter development is particularly relevant to the place of trout in modern New Zealand. Unlike deer, trout have never threatened our economy. To the contrary, they have added substantially to it through their contribution to tourism. However, if government policy toward introduced animals is now to be measured by the yardstick of impact on indigenous biodiversity, is this special status of trout in New Zealand so secure?

Conservation and management

As we saw earlier, trout have indeed had impacts on native fish and other aquatic life. However, the available evidence, albeit sketchy, suggests this has not caused extinctions of native species. Unlike those of the terrestrial environment, plants and animals of aquatic environments are largely hidden from view. Proselytising conservationists have a much easier task convincing the public that native trees and furry or feathered creatures are worth preserving. The public can walk among them and touch them, and can notice the changes caused by introduced animals. Native trees contribute to spectacular vistas, either collectively as native bush, or as individuals in the case of giant kauri. Not so for native fish. They remain a furtive mystery beneath the distorting window of the water's surface. Their own secretive and cryptic nature obscures them further, even to those who take the trouble to look with mask and snorkel.

People relate to lakes and rivers as parts of landscapes. Their contact with them is confined mainly to the surface. They swim and boat on the surface, and fish through it, but they do not easily relate to what is underneath, apart from the fish they pull up on the end of a line. Moreover, the public does not relate well to small, slimy animals such as native fish, but appreciate trout because they are large, powerful, colourful – and even edible. Trout and salmon have always been, and continue to be, the fish that the public sees and values in fresh waters. This is why trout define the conservation and fisheries values of lakes and rivers in the minds of the New Zealand public and international visitors.

Nevertheless, some conservation policies appear at odds with the special status of trout. Indigenous biodiversity conservation philosophy is on the ascendancy in New Zealand and now underpins key conservation policies adopted by government. This has caused an uneasy tension with Fish and Game's interests in conserving and managing natural ecosystems for the sustainable harvest of introduced, and native, animal populations.

In 1992 the New Zealand government signed the International Convention on Biodiversity, and ratified it in 1993. This obliges New Zealand to develop national strategies, plans and programmes to conserve and sustainably use biodiversity. Our government has chosen to interpret biodiversity to mean *indigenous* biodiversity. As part of the planning process to honour its obligations to the convention, government adopted the New Zealand Biodiversity Strategy in February 2000. Theme 2 of that policy document is relevant to the place of trout in New Zealand, requiring that 'Introduced fish (including sports fish such as trout . . .) and introduced game (such as ducks) are managed so that they do not pose threats to

It would be difficult to contemplate a stream like this devoid of trout.

The artful science of trout fishing

indigenous species of plants and animals.' This is consistent with the central policy of the Biodiversity Strategy – that indigenous fauna and flora take precedence over introduced species.

This philosophy has long underpinned conservation policy for national parks, but in an even more extreme form. Section 4 (2b) of the National Parks Act 1980 states that 'Except where the [National Parks and Reserves] Authority otherwise determines, the native plants and animals of the parks shall be as far as possible be preserved and introduced plants and animals shall be as far as possible exterminated.' The intention of this policy – to exterminate introduced plants and animals – raises serious issues because some of our best river trout fisheries occur in national parks – the very fisheries promoted by the tourism industry as embodying adventure tourism in '100% Pure New Zealand'. Despite such policy, trout are tolerated in national parks through a special dispensation by the National Conservation Authority, recognising that introduced sports fisheries provide an established and valuable resource that pre-dates most of the national parks.

A spectacular spot in Fiordland where a pristine natural environment can be enjoyed by visitors, who may also see big trout cruising in crystal-clear waters.

One wonders, however, how long such goodwill may last. Until policy clearly defining the valued status of trout in natural ecosystems is enshrined by act of Parliament, trout in national parks will be subject to the whim of conservation politics. Ironically, one of the reasons why Lakes Rotoroa and Rotoiti were included in Nelson Lakes National Park in 1954 was to preserve their trout fisheries, because at that time no other legal mechanism existed to protect these water bodies.

The following point made in the Biodiversity Strategy is also relevant to trout:

> On the basis of current knowledge about the interaction between trout and indigenous freshwater biodiversity the New Zealand Biodiversity Strategy does not promote a significant reduction in the current distribution of trout. However, in some places (at the margins of their distribution) where trout threaten indigenous species, or the natural character of pristine ecosystems, they may need to be reduced or removed.

Talk of reducing or removing trout may alarm the angling community, but if it is confined to the margins of the distribution of trout, as stated, then it should not significantly affect angling opportunities in New Zealand. For example, anglers have little to fear from the control or removal of trout in a few small Otago streams used by threatened galaxiids. These waters are scarcely worth fishing and are not significantly contributing spawning and fry rearing to valued downstream trout fisheries.

However, it is the opening phrase – 'On the basis of current knowledge' – in the above quote that is more thought-provoking. It implies that significant action against trout is not promoted because there is *currently* insufficient evidence of impacts by trout on indigenous biodiversity to warrant it. So what happens if and when evidence does arise that trout have significant impacts on indigenous biodiversity in rivers or lakes supporting major trout fisheries? In keeping with the central theme of the Biodiversity Strategy the implication is that DOC would be encouraged to control or eradicate trout in the affected waters. This would conflict with the interests of anglers, Fish and Game and the tourism industry, not to mention DOC's own recreational fisheries protection mandate.

This dilemma raises the question about whether we really want trout in this country; or do we simply tolerate and exploit them because they are already here and can't be eradicated? After all, this has long been the unofficial attitude of government towards feral deer. This view could justifiably be challenged because it undervalues the proven economic, recreational and social significance of trout (and salmon) in New Zealand. Weighing up the pros and cons of this matter, R. M. McDowall wrote in *Gamekeepers for the Nation*:

> . . . it is quite possible that, even if it had been known that some introduced species would have harmful impacts, a decision to bring them here might still have been made, to obtain the benefits that have resulted. Here the establishment of brown and rainbow trout are prime examples; these species have had quite significant harmful impacts on the indigenous fish fauna, yet so great are their benefits to anglers and tourism that it would be a difficult decision to remove them and restore the aquatic ecosystems that have been affected by trout.

Regardless of the common sense of this view and its acceptance in the past, conservation-lobby groups favouring indigenous biodiversity have become more strident in their opposition to introduced animals. The new generation of university biology graduates, natural-resource planners and conservation officers have been influenced by the ideology of indigenous conservation, and encouraged to be sympathetic to native fauna and flora and to view introduced animals as pests. Middle bureaucrats and conservation lobbyists now often snidely refer to trout as 'aquatic possums' – a barbed analogy between trout and the introduced Australian brush-tailed possum, which has had devastating impacts on native forests.

I view this change in conservation ideology and politics with some concern because I believe it misrepresents the interests of those who most use fresh waters in New Zealand. Like it or not, trout and salmon are icon fish that define the fisheries values of our rivers and lakes. Some people, perhaps Maori in particular, may argue that eels have, or should have, this status. Regardless, there is no denying that trout and salmon dominate the images of our freshwater fisheries promoted in New Zealand and abroad. They also exceed all other freshwater fisheries in recreational and commercial* significance, and income generation. Moreover, social surveys show that trout and salmon angling are the most popular active recreational activities on New Zealand's rivers and lakes.

From a personal perspective, I cannot and would not like to contemplate a New Zealand without trout. Like many before me, I was first drawn to explore our wonderful rivers, lakes and mountains by the trout (and deer) there, and this is still true. This naturally led to an appreciation of our native flora and fauna. As Thomas McGuane wrote in *The Longest Silence*: 'It is not given to every soul pining for the natural world to be a naturalist. Most of us require a game to

---

* There are no commercial wild fisheries for trout and salmon in New Zealand. Commercial usage in this context refers to economic gain through guiding and charter-boat fishing.

The lure of trout inspires anglers to explore New Zealand's rivers and lakes.

play, whether hunting, bird-watching, angling, or sailing, and each create superb opportunities to observe the weather, the land under changing light, the movement of water.'

Trout are so much part of the outdoor culture I have experienced that my New Zealand would be incomplete without them. Because of trout, rivers fascinate me. Trout give rivers and lakes mystery and potential, inviting exploration.

CHAPTER THIRTEEN

Managing angling

THERE ARE TWO MAIN ELEMENTS of recreational fisheries management. First, management of habitat and the fish. If the habitat is managed well, fish populations should be vibrant; otherwise, in some special situations, additional stocking can be beneficial. Second, there is managing anglers, traditionally done by regulating bag and size limits to conserve fish stocks. More recently, however, there has become a developing awareness among recreational fisheries managers, in New Zealand and in the Northern Hemisphere, about the need to understand and manage the angling experience.

Although of primary concern to fisheries managers, an understanding of fisheries management should be of interest also to anglers. After all, angler-management initiatives require the co-operation of anglers, either by obeying regulations or by voluntary action.

Angling pressure

We often hear the comment that trout are not as big or not as plentiful as in 'the good old days'. Is there any truth in this assertion, or is it simply that anglers have selective memory? The latter is a proven fact. Anglers' recall of number and size of fish they have caught, or number of fishing trips they have taken, has been found to be unreliable over time periods greater than three to four months. People have selective memories, and anglers are no exception. We tend to recall events that are most memorable – usually pleasant rather than unpleasant events. The exceptional bags or the largest fish are etched on our memory. The many days spent catching few or no trout are lost from conscious thought because they are ordinary. Another effect of time on anglers' memories is to unintentionally exaggerate the size of fish. This should not be taken as confirmation of the notion that 'all fishermen are liars': it simply is a fact of human nature. Well-kept angler diaries can overcome the problem of recall, but they often omit crucial information such as catch per hour.

That aside, there are valid reasons why the fishing nowadays

The artful science of trout fishing

A small but satisfying brown trout.

may not be as good as yesteryear, at least in some places. As fishing pressure increases on any fishery there is the likelihood that the size of fish will decline. And if fishing pressure is very high, so too may the number of fish decline as the larger, older fish are cropped. This point was raised as early as 1932 by Edward Percival, Professor of Biology at Canterbury College (now the University of Canterbury), as a possible reason for a perceived decline in the size of trout in New Zealand, and specifically in the Oreti River, Southland. Trophy trout may well have been more common during the establishment phase of our trout fisheries, and during the frontier phase of our back-country river fisheries in particular. Anglers who first explored our virgin trout waters were fishing to previously unexploited stocks, which must have included a higher proportion of large old trout than they do today.

Habitat degradation as a result of land and urban development may also have contributed to a reduction in fish size, by degrading the food and feeding conditions of trout. The impact of trout themselves on the native fish populations that were once so prolific in New Zealand (see pages 205–10), would have further reduced trout growth rates.

Many of New Zealand's back-country rivers have relatively low trout populations. In these, even low angling pressure has the potential to impact trout numbers and size if the catch is killed, as we will see later.

Size and bag limits

The idea behind a minimum legal size (usually called a size limit) is to protect fish until they are old enough to have spawned at least once and thereby contribute to maintaining the population. The size limit therefore needs to be set a little larger than the average size at first spawning. This has not always been the case in New Zealand. Size limits sometimes have been set arbitrarily, without being based on an understanding of growth rates and size at maturity. Moreover, usually a single size limit has been applied to an entire region. When I first started fishing, about forty years ago, the size limit in my home province of Canterbury was ten inches (twenty-five centimetres). I believe the same size limit applied to most regions of the South Island in those days. The flaw in this is

Killing a large trout like this has more impact on the fishery than the death of a smaller fish.

that trout grow at different rates in different waters. A size limit of twenty-five centimetres might protect trout until maturity in one waterway but be too low in another. In fact, the high growth rate of trout in most New Zealand waters actually makes a size limit of twenty-five centimetres ineffectual for protecting trout through first spawning. In many parts of New Zealand trout exceed thirty or even forty centimetres by the time they first spawn, at two or three years of age. A twenty-five-centimetre size limit may be more appropriate in Southland or inland Otago where cooler waters retard trout growth. However, in the north the size limits ought to be higher if protection for trout through to maturity is the aim.

In some areas trout grow so fast that whether or not the size limit achieves the aim of protecting them to maturity depends on variation in growth rates between years. The following example illustrates this point. In late 1995, spawning rivers of Lake Taupo were badly affected by sediment from ash falls and mud flows caused by the eruption of Mt Ruapehu. This also coincided with bad floods in the spring of 1995, just when most rainbow trout spawning was completed. The Department of Conservation (DOC) anticipated a weak year-class, and so raised the size limit from thirty-five to forty-five centimetres in 1997 to reduce the harvest of fish born in 1995 and 1996. However, the ash fall had an unforeseen beneficial effect on the productivity of the lake. As a result, the trout grew so quickly that many had exceeded the forty-five-centimetre size limit by the spring of 1997 so they could be caught and kept by lake anglers six months before the fish had their first chance to spawn, or be caught by river anglers, in the following winter.

A 'slot limit' can be used to protect trophy fisheries. This is a kind of size restriction whereby only fish of a prescribed length range (usually middle-sized fish) can be killed. The aim is to protect both the younger fish until maturity, and the large trophy trout. This type of restriction is a compromise between catch-and-release and harvesting regimes.

In recent years most Fish and Game councils have dispensed altogether with conventional size limits, and now rely entirely on bag limits to conserve trout stocks and equitably share the total take of fish. If the bag limit is set at a sensible level for stock conservation, then a size limit is superfluous. If anglers choose to take fish, they have a choice of either keeping a small trout or releasing it in the hope they will catch another, larger one. The taking of small fish should not be viewed as a threat to a fishery, provided that the bag limit is set at an appropriate level. Killing small fish has less effect on the population than killing larger trout (see page 32).

Mature trout generally experience a lower rate of mortality than small trout. They have survived the sieve of natural mortality and have attained a body mass sufficient to make a significant reproductive contribution to the population. When an angler kills a mature trout, this reproductive potential is lost from the population. This logic only holds true when post-spawning survival and recovery of condition are sufficient to allow fish to spawn repeatedly, year after year. Otherwise, the harvesting of fish that have matured and spawned can be encouraged. This has been the view held by the managers of the Rotorua and Taupo rainbow trout fisheries in the past. Rainbow kelts in these lakes can be slow to recover condition and, as a consequence, post-spawning mortality can be high (30 per cent or more). Moreover, angling pressure in Lake Taupo is high. Consequently, DOC's management of this fishery in the past intentionally focused on the harvest of maiden trout. However, recent scares of overharvest and decline in the trout population have caused DOC to change its view of repeat-spawning trout because these fish help sustain the population of harvestable trout in Lake Taupo.

Prior to 1990 most regions had very liberal bag limits – a total of ten fish per day was not uncommon, and based on the belief that fishing pressure was low in most places. They also reflected the exploitative mentality prevalent amongst Kiwi anglers, many of whom fished as much for the pot as for the pleasure. Most legal-sized trout that these anglers caught were killed and, if surplus to immediate needs, were given away, canned, smoked or consigned to the deep freeze.

Over the past two decades bag limits have been progressively reduced in most regions. Nowadays, limits of four fish on lowland rivers and one or two fish on back-country rivers are the norm. A few rivers now are 'catch-and-release only'. This trend has been in response to the increasing unease among Fish and Game managers and councillors about the vulnerability of our trout populations. Another reason is that imposing lower bag limits places greater value upon the trout resource. It makes the statement that fisheries managers are concerned about the resource. This point can be useful when arguing the case for conservation of trout habitat in resource-consent hearings related to water and land exploitation. This strategy nicely pre-empts the claim sometimes made by land and water developers that angler harvest potentially has more impact than their proposals on the trout resource.

While changes have been occurring in the attitude of fisheries managers toward bag limits, so too have there been changes in anglers' attitudes. In recent years there has been a shift of philosophy towards limiting the kill and to catch-and-release, at least in many waters, and particularly in back-country rivers.

Catch-and-release

The modern-day ethic of catch-and-release (C&R) grew to prominence first in North America. The United States also forged the lead in C&R legislation. In 1934 Pennsylvania became the first state to implement C&R regulations on a trout fishery, and a decade later Michigan imposed C&R restrictions on some of its trout waters.

In North America, the spread of C&R gained impetus through the activities of Trout Unlimited. This organisation, formed in 1960, has actively promoted the philosophy of fishing for sport, not for food, and 'limiting your kill' instead of 'killing your limit'.

In North America, a realisation of the recreational value of sports fish gave C&R both an emotive and economic impetus. The late Lee Wulff, a life-long advocate of fly fishing and C&R, wrote in his 1939 *Handbook of Freshwater Fishing* that 'game fish are too valuable to be caught only once'. We only have to consider the large sums of money that some international tourist anglers spend to catch trout in New Zealand to come to the same conclusion. Some of these anglers may spend $500 per day or more on guiding fees, $1,000 per day on helicopters, $600 or even more per day on accommodation, and $3,000–12,000 on airfares to get here. A moderately good day's back-country river fishing might yield them five trout landed. The value of each fish to the economy is obviously very large – in the hundreds or even thousands of dollars. Furthermore, the value of a released trout increases by the same amount each time it is caught again! This is a simplistic picture – for example, it assumes that tourist anglers are here only for the trout – but it should serve to make us think twice about killing trout for the pot without considering the potential value, and enjoyment factor, of the fish to other anglers.

International fishing magazines and North American tourist anglers introduced C&R to New Zealand anglers. Over the past decade our own national trout-fishing literature has further encouraged the spread of the ethic in this country. A measure of how prevalent C&R is nowadays in New Zealand was revealed by a recent social survey of back-country river anglers in the Otago and Nelson–Marlborough Fish and Game regions, undertaken by Carl Walrond and myself. Of all trout caught by surveyed anglers, 92 per cent were released. Non-resident anglers had the highest return rate – 98.8 per cent – while resident anglers returned 80 per cent – still a high return rate. In recent years there has been much

Anglers can take measures to protect the environment in which they enjoy their sport.

A beautifully marked brown trout being released after careful handling in a net.

talk among Kiwi anglers about increasing angling pressure on our back-country rivers, and this has been to a large degree focused on the effects of tourist anglers. One point is clear from the above: we cannot accuse tourist anglers of threatening the viability of our trout populations. On that matter we should look to our own behaviour.

Under certain circumstances C&R regulations have proven very beneficial for trout fisheries. Spectacular improvements in catch rates and increases in average size have been reported in several states in the United States. Many of these fisheries were traditionally maintained by annual releases of legal-sized hatchery trout, but since the advent of C&R wild recruitment has been sufficient and the releases are no longer necessary.

There are some situations in which C&R has been shown to be an inappropriate management tool, such as in high-altitude, cold-water streams where temperature limits growth and harsh winter conditions result in high mortality. The combination of slow growth and short life expectancy produces stunted fish and leaves little opportunity for C&R to improve catch rate and average size.

The success of C&R can also depend on the level of natural

The artful science of trout fishing

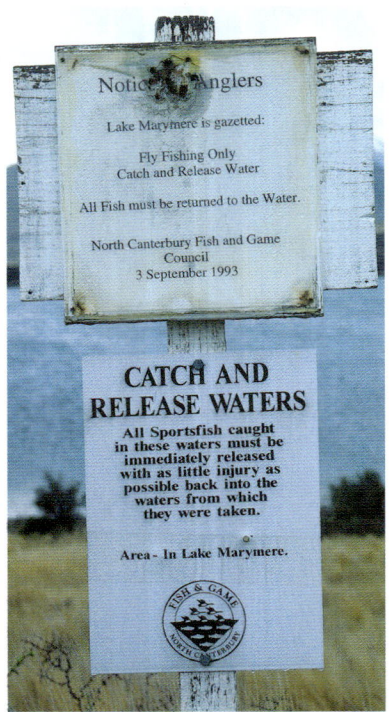

Catch-and-release is mandatory in some New Zealand waters.

recruitment. Where natural recruitment is more than sufficient to maintain the population, taking fewer fish may increase competition and result in smaller trout. This is more critical in lakes, where trout abundance is less limited by competition for space than in streams. Consequently, in lakes increased recruitment will more directly translate to increased numbers of trout and growth rate will suffer accordingly.

The success of C&R also depends on the species of trout present. The best successes have been with cutthroat trout, which are particularly easy to catch. Rainbow trout also cope well with being caught and released, while brown trout generally are regarded as being the most difficult to catch so they respond less readily to C&R regulation. Nevertheless, improvements in brown trout fisheries have been reported in response to some C&R management programmes in North America.

While advocates of C&R are not hard to find, misgivings have arisen among some anglers and fishery managers over the potential effects on the wellbeing of trout and their behaviour. Concerns have been expressed over hooking mortality, sublethal effects on stress levels, reproductive success and growth rate, and behavourial changes affecting angling success.

The general consensus of several studies on the subject is that most trout (90 per cent or more) survive when caught and released. There are records from North American rivers of individual trout being caught and released up to thirteen times. Research showed that cutthroat trout were caught an average of 9.7 times during one season in a C&R section on the Yellowstone River!

My own experience suggests that brown trout are particularly hardy. In a radio-tracking study I was involved with on the Wairau River in Marlborough, 95 per cent of them survived the trauma of being caught, then anaesthetised and surgically implanted with radio transmitters. This stress no doubt was greater than that from simply being caught and released.

Nevertheless, at times C&R can result in fish dying; for example, when they are hooked in the gills or stomach, as is often the case with bait fishing. Extensive handling also decreases their chance of survival, and obviously the longer the fish is removed from the water before release the poorer its chances of surviving.

Trout become more stressed and exhausted more easily when the water is warm, especially above 18°C. The more quickly the trout is played, brought to the net and released, the better will be its chances of survival, especially when the water temperature is high.

When fish are played to exhaustion the concentration of lactic acid increases and oxygen and energy reserves decrease in their blood. They can take considerable time to recover after these events. Measurements on Atlantic salmon have shown that it can take two to eight hours for their lactic acid levels to return to normal, and up to twelve hours to restore their energy reserves. This raises the possibility that reproductive potential may be impaired in fish that are repeatedly caught and released, especially those that are caught on their spawning migration. However, the jury is still out on that one. Studies of Atlantic salmon have shown no difference in egg and sperm viability between fish that have been caught and released and those that were undisturbed.

C&R can affect trout feeding behaviour and, potentially, growth rate. The effect on feeding behaviour probably varies between species, as the following examples would appear to indicate. A laboratory-based study in North America found that brown trout stopped feeding for up to three days after being handled. A similar study on rainbow trout found that most fish resumed feeding within a day after disturbance. These results match my own fishing and research experience with these species, and the experience of fishing guides whom I know.

Other studies have revealed some interesting changes in social behaviour of trout in response to C&R. A study of wild cutthroat trout in a river in Idaho found that the largest, dominant fish were the most likely to be caught, and in three out of four cases the released fish permanently lost its preferred feeding position to another trout.

The interruption of feeding behaviour is likely to affect catchability more than long-term growth. For the latter to be affected, the feeding activity of trout would have to be significantly curtailed by angling disturbance and C&R. Trout are likely to respond to such high angling pressure by simply becoming harder to catch. The fascinating subject of change in behaviour and catchability of trout in response to angling pressure is further discussed on pages 233–41.

One more aspect of C&R needs to be considered: how do anglers feel about it? In many rivers where compulsory C&R has been imposed in North America there has been an initial decrease in angling use, followed by an increase a few years later in response to better catch rates and bigger fish. Most anglers have come to accept C&R where it has been imposed by regulation. Some C&R rivers in the United States have become so popular that they now have major crowding problems, which presents fish and wildlife agencies with the new problem of whether to control angler numbers – and if so, how?

Trout should be released as quickly and gently as possible, preferably without taking them out of the water.

Fortunately, most back-country river anglers nowadays release their catch; otherwise many of these fisheries would be at risk from stock depletion. However, voluntary C&R may not always be sufficient, and some regional Fish and Game councils already impose C&R regulations or a one-fish bag limit on some rivers. A few such rivers are the subject of C&R trials; for example, the upper Oreti, Eglington and Mataura in Southland. Results to date indicate an increase in trout numbers in the Oreti and Mataura C&R reaches relative to neighbouring reaches where standard regulations apply. One- or two-fish bag limits imposed on many back-country river headwaters have a similar effect to C&R, particularly in light of the comparatively low angling pressure on most of our rivers. Anglers often catch more than one or two fish per day in these rivers. Studies of angling pressure on the Caples and Greenstone Rivers, in Central Otago, have shown that most anglers release their catch despite the one-fish bag limit.

I BEGAN FISHING in 1955 as a seven-year-old lad. This was a time when a bag of fish was what one killed and that meant all that were caught – except the 'sprats'. The bigger the bag, the prouder I was to take it home; and the larger the fish, the better. Catching fish was my prime motivation for going to the river in those days, and as I grew I'm certain that my dream of landing a monster was nurtured as well. I witnessed my father landing a six-pounder one day. I looked on in awe. A year or two later I was again present when he netted a nine-pounder. When a ten-pounder finally came his way I was hooked. I had to get one of those too. It took twenty years.

By the late 1970s stalking trout was the only way that I fished, and I loved to explore new waters. It was inevitable that I would eventually 'discover' a stream that harboured trophy trout, and when I did I soon landed my first double-figure fish. While I admired the wariness of the fish (it took nearly an hour of casting to fool it) and marvelled at its power and tenacity, I still 'had' to kill it at the battle's end. It was then quickly despatched to a taxidermist for mounting.

Despite the fact that the taxidermist had completed his craft skillfully, I remember feeling a strange sense of indifference when I collected my trophy. I had always anticipated that a mounted fish I had caught would be something I would be proud of and eager to display prominently. However, it wasn't so. The thing was dead in every sense – its colour, its shape, its feel – it was out of place.

By the time that I had landed my first trophy trout I was a strong

Conservation and management

advocate of the C&R ethic. But I believe that my feelings after having a fish mounted strengthened my resolve for the practice. The fifteen trophies I have caught since have all been eagerly returned to their rightful place – to live and breed, but also to maintain life in the river that they occupied, and continue to attract other anglers.

Over the years my angling focus has altered completely. While catching fish is still important, it is not my main reason for heading to a river. I now feel uncomfortable killing a fish, but when I do take one 'for the pot' it is a smaller fish rather than a large, impressive one that I choose. Size *doesn't* matter!

Perhaps I should feel ashamed of my earlier attitude towards killing fish, though that was common practice in the 1950s and 1960s. However, like other anglers of my generation, I have fished through a time when angling has changed and evolved quickly. Fortunately we have changed too. Anglers taking up the sport today begin with better education and a heightened conservation ethic. If we wish to retain healthy fisheries, and the trophy fisheries that anglers dream of in particular, then we must promote the idea of C&R – especially of the biggest fish.

STALKING LARGE TROUT in solitude, in clear rivers surrounded by spectacular scenery epitomises the New Zealand back-country river experience so prevalent in fishing magazines today and marketed abroad. The catchments of these rivers are still in their natural condition or largely undeveloped, and this has ensured the integrity of the habitat upon which these trout populations depend. Unlike lowland rivers, habitat loss is not a pressing management issue for most back-country rivers. Instead, the issue is the impact of fishing pressure. Back-country river fishing has become very popular over the past twenty-five years as a result of publicity and better access and air and road transport. The decline in lowland fisheries may also have contributed to this trend.

I was very fortunate to have spent six years undertaking research on back-country river trout fisheries during the late 1990s and early 2000s related to angling use and its effects on anglers and trout. Roger Young and Carl Walrond were colleagues working with me on the project, both recent graduates who, like me, are also keen anglers with a thirst for the outdoors. In undertaking this research I have had the pleasure of getting to know some of New Zealand's leading fishing personalities who pioneered back-country fishing techniques and guiding. This work has taken me into some of the most remote rivers in New Zealand to record and experience first-

The artful science of trout fishing

hand the wonderful unique fishing opportunities that this country has to offer.

In the late 1980s New Zealand anglers began voicing concern over increasing fishing pressure on these fisheries. Tourist anglers and guides have been most criticised in this regard, perhaps because they are convenient scapegoats, but also because when they began using helicopters to access remote rivers they were inevitably noticed by ground-based anglers. Reports of altercations between guides and Kiwi anglers, of tourist anglers camping for extended periods on some rivers, and of trout becoming more difficult to catch sustained this smouldering fire of discontent. Calls to control the situation, especially guiding and aerial access, were disputed by guides and other anglers. Part of the problem was that much of the information available on the state of the fisheries was based on hearsay and conjecture – not the stuff upon which Fish and Game councils can base management decisions. In response they, along with the government, commissioned and supported research to address the matter. What follows is a summary of that research effort.

First, what motivates anglers to fish back-country rivers? Our research indicated that the main reasons are to experience peace and solitude, natural environment and scenery, and to be able to spot trout. The actual catching seems to be secondary to seeing trout and having the opportunity to fish for them. The importance of spotting trout is critical to the New Zealand back-country fishing experience, which usually includes a high component of stalking large trout in clear waters.

Anglers reported that the main things limiting or detracting from the back-country angling experience were crowding, lack of time and lack of legal public access. While it was the greatest constraint, 'crowding' is perhaps not the right word in this instance: we are not talking about anglers standing shoulder to shoulder, or even within sight of one another. Probably a more appropriate word would be 'encounter' – and very low levels of encounter at that. Social surveys have shown that anglers have the lowest level of encounter tolerance of all recreational users in the New Zealand back country. Most hope not to see any other anglers over the course of their day's fishing, although they will tolerate a small level of contact: on average, two or three encounters per day. Any more than that and they are likely to become dissatisfied and consider fishing elsewhere. Non-resident guided anglers are the least tolerant: they expect to see no other anglers, and on average will tolerate no more than one encounter per day. This is not surprising when you consider that they usually have been sold the expectation

Helicopters are often used by anglers to access remote waters.

Opposite: This delightful stream on the eastern side of the South Island's Main Divide offers anglers the chance to enjoy the solitude of a wilderness setting.

of fishing in solitude on remote rivers with the high likelihood of fishing to undisturbed trout.

Our angler surveys in the Nelson–Marlborough and Otago Fish and Game districts between 1996 and 1998 showed that angler usage on most back-country rivers was still very low. On most days, and on most rivers, anglers can still expect to encounter no other anglers. There were only a few rivers on which recorded encounter levels were approaching or at tolerance thresholds. Rivers such as the Greenstone and Caples in Central Otago fall into this category, and the comparatively high angler usage of these rivers is encouraged by popular hiking tracks through their valleys. Anglers appear to have a perception of 'crowding' on some rivers that is perhaps exaggerated in relation to actual angling usage. For instance, in our surveys 15 per cent of anglers said they avoided fishing some back-country rivers some of the time because they considered that they would be crowded.

A common cause of conflict on back-country rivers occurs when one angling party 'jumps' another. This term refers to the later-arriving anglers leaving insufficient room for anglers already on the river. In some cases this may arise through ignorance, when anglers are unfamiliar with angling etiquette, but in other situations it can be deliberate. When encountering other anglers fishing a back-country river, you should give them plenty of room to fish upstream. A typical length of river that an angler will fish in the course of a day's fishing is two to four kilometres, and more on some rivers. When an angler 'jumps' another, this inevitably results in ill-feeling. The original angler's chances of catching fish will be lessened by the offending angler disturbing the reach and scaring the fish. Some anglers respond to this intrusion by having words with the newcomer and then pushing in ahead to drive the point home. In order to avoid such altercations, when encountering other anglers it is best to have a yarn with them and ask them how far up or down the river they intend fishing. A typical deal would be for you to walk upstream, avoiding wading the river so as not to scare the trout with your scent, and begin fishing above that point. Usually you can reach an amicable agreement to share the available water and both have an enjoyable day.

Over the past decade or more there has been much talk among Kiwi anglers of trout becoming harder to catch in back-country rivers. Research that I undertook with Roger Young has confirmed this view, particularly for brown trout exposed to fishing pressure. The sensitivity of trout in these rivers to angler disturbance is possibly a unique feature that underlies the low encounter tolerance between anglers. Our back-country rivers are typified by low densities of

Crowding of waterways in the back country detracts from the angling experience.

Opposite: Having reached his destination after a long hike, an angler contemplates the beauty and promise of an undisturbed pool.

large trout that are visible in very clear water. This combination means fishing success is very dependent on the trout being undisturbed. Large trout are very prone to disturbance in clear, shallow waters. Because these fish are relatively few, any disturbance by one angler can severely limit another angler's chances.

We had expert anglers fly fish for trout in a systematic manner to compare trout catchability and sensitivity to disturbance between brown trout rivers with low and high angling pressure, and between wilderness brown and rainbow trout rivers. Essentially we used angling as a research tool to measure catchability and the response of trout to disturbance. By using experienced anglers we were able to factor out the influence of varying skill levels. While the more 'heavily fished' river experienced relatively high pressure by New Zealand back-country river standards, the actual level of use would still be low compared to some of the popular trout rivers in the United States, where dozens, even scores, of anglers may be seen in a day. For example, on our heavily fished river a typical fishing beat of three to four kilometres might host a maximum of two or three angling parties (of one or two anglers) in a day, perhaps on four or five days per week. More commonly, one angling party might visit a reach with the same frequency.

On each of our study rivers, two of the anglers fished for three consecutive days on two or four trips between November and March, accompanied by an observer who recorded the data. Some reaches were fished on each of the three days, others on two of the days. Each day, virgin water was fished to act as a control for comparison with the reaches that were fished repeatedly. The angling approach was that typically followed by most back-country river fly fishers, except that only trout that were spotted from the bank were fished for. In the two rivers in which brown trout were studied, every trout caught was tagged with brightly coloured dart tags, with the colour of the tag specific to each fishing trip. By carefully viewing trout through binoculars to check for tags before casting to them, we were able to ascertain whether each fish had been previously caught by the research team, and if so, when.

Each trout was systematically presented with flies in a predetermined order. The choice of fly patterns was based on the experience of the fishing guides assisting us with the research. If a guide expected the fish would rise to dry flies, we first cast a relatively large, light-coloured attractor dry fly such as a size 12–14 Royal Wulff or Red Humpy. If these were refused, we then presented similar profile but darker patterns such as the Black Wulff and Bluebottle Humpy. If still no response, we switched to smaller, lower-profile, more natural representations such as the Parachute

A headwater pool such as this might contain only one or two trout, and fish-bearing pools are often far apart.

Adams and Hatchmaster. In this manner we systematically varied fly profile, colour and then size. This rationale for fly presentation was based largely on the wide experience of Tony Entwistle, the principal Nelson-based guide participating in the research.

If dry flies were unsuccessful, or inappropriate because the trout was feeding deep, we then tried nymphs. The first choices of nymph presented in most situations in the two brown trout rivers were the common Nelson flies, Nelson Brown and *Coloburiscus* (a dark fly). Both are moderately bulky, hairy, rough-outline patterns. A size 8–12 weighted Hare and Copper nymph was the first choice on the rainbow trout river. This rough, hairy, bulky pattern is a well-known general fly for deep and/or fast water. Lead paste or split shot was added for weight when the fish were very deep. Deep fish were also presented with large, weighted nymphs such as the Buller Caddis and Green or Black Stonefly. If there was no response to these, then smaller, smooth, slimmer nymphs of different colours were tried. These included Pheasant Tail, and Green or Yellow Caddis. These lightly weighted flies were also used for trout feeding in the shallower, slower margins, where rough-bodied flies often perform more poorly, perhaps because the trout have more time to inspect the fly. Smaller flies were also used more regularly on the heavily fished river because the experience of the fishing guides was that this was necessary to have a realistic chance of catching trout. As with the dry-fly selection, the principles that guided the choice, and order of presentation, of nymphs was fly profile, colour and size, but with weight also taken into consideration. Incidentally, this rationale for fly selection provides a sensible basis for anglers to follow in most river-fishing situations, unless previous experience on that water enables you to make an immediate informed choice.

Each fly was presented to each trout at least three times. If there was no response, the next fly pattern in the list was presented, and so on until the trout was either hooked or spooked.

Results from comparing the two brown trout rivers showed a clear difference in behaviour and catchability related to fishing pressure. Trout in the heavily fished river were harder to find and harder to stalk. The anglers saw fewer fish in the heavily fished river, yet drift-diving surveys indicated that numbers were similar in both rivers. The trout were more easily scared in the heavily fished river, with the anglers spooking almost half of them, whereas they only spooked 18 per cent of the 'naive' trout in the remote river.

Trout from the heavily fished river were the most difficult to catch, and less likely to take the first fly offered. They required more presentations of each fly and, as a consequence, took longer to catch, if indeed they were caught at all. The naive trout from the remote river were easiest to catch, while trout that had been caught previously in the remote river by the research team were intermediate between these two extremes. For example, 55 per cent of the naive trout from the remote river were taken on the first cast, compared with about 45 per cent for previously caught trout. Only 29 per cent of the trout in the heavily fished river were caught on the first cast. Trout in the remote river were less discriminating. About 75 per cent of these took the first fly pattern presented to them, compared with 55 per cent in the heavily fished river.

We estimated the size of the trout population in each of the rivers from drift-diving counts, and this gave us the opportunity to estimate the proportion caught by the two expert anglers in the research team. In their book *Stalking Trout*, Les Hill and Graeme Marshall calculated that in a short time even just a few skilled anglers could potentially capture a significant proportion of the trout population in some of our smaller back-country rivers. Expert anglers fishing the remote river during our study caught 30 per cent of the brown trout population by the end of their second fishing trip (after a total of six days' fishing). By the end of the fourth trip (after twelve days) they had caught 40 per cent of the population. By contrast, in the heavily fished river they caught only 5 per cent of the fish after two trips (six days) and 11 per cent after four trips (twelve days). This suggests that trout populations in lightly fished, remote rivers are very vulnerable to angling pressure. Fortunately, as we have already discussed, the high level of C&R voluntarily practised by most anglers provides some measure of protection to these stocks. As fishing pressure increases, the trout become harder to catch, and this too helps protect them. However, even low pressure can have an impact on trout stocks, mainly by decreasing the abundance of older, possibly trophy-sized fish. Many of our headwater rivers have only small trout populations: drift-diving surveys have shown that densities of fewer than twenty adult trout per kilometre are common. Potentially these fisheries are the most vulnerable.

Trout in the remote river exhibited an extreme response to angler disturbance. After the anglers had moved through a fishing reach, a high proportion of the trout hid under cover (boulders and undercut banks) and remained hidden for at least three days. The following will help to illustrate this point. On the first day of each trip we experienced some exceptional fishing. On the best reach one angler might see thirty to forty trout, of which perhaps fifteen would be hooked. On the second day he would see and hook only half that number, and by the third day he would see only a few and be hard-pressed to catch any at all. This rapid reduction was not just caused by trout going into hiding after they had been caught and released, because at least half of the fish seen were not hooked, and some not even fished to. Moreover, drift-dive counts showed that even on the first day, when the most trout were observed by the anglers, they were seeing only about 14–33 per cent of the population actually present. This suggests that even just the anglers walking through a reach caused many of the trout to hide, presumably because they saw or smelt the anglers. The pattern of decline in numbers of trout seen and hooked on successive days on each fishing trip in this remote river is shown below.

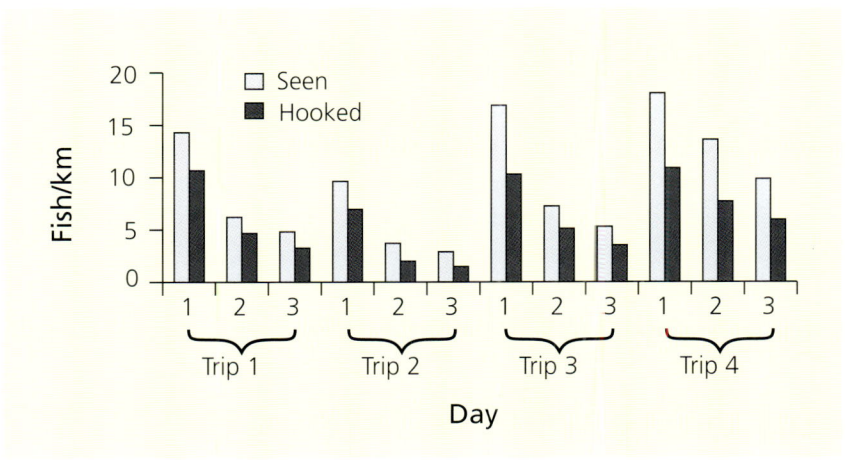

Number of trout seen and hooked by two expert anglers fishing the same section of river over three successive days. Data from four fishing trips to a remote river in Kahurangi National Park, South Island.

We did not see the same kind of extreme response to angler disturbance in the more heavily fished river. There, variations in the numbers of feeding trout seen and hooked seemed to depend more on environmental conditions, such as weather, than on whether or not we had fished there on previous days. For example, we had the best fishing on bright sunny days when water temperature rose steadily during the day. We saw, and caught, far fewer trout when the weather was cloudy and overcast with little variation in air and water temperature.

The above applies to brown trout; rainbow trout seem to be less affected by angler disturbance in remote rivers. They came back on the feed within a few hours of being disturbed by anglers in a remote section of the Rangitikei River that we studied. Most of them were in deep pools that provided secure cover. We even saw some rainbows recommence feeding just half an hour after first being disturbed, and within sight of the angler. Nevertheless, fishing guides contend that rainbow trout in back-country rivers are more difficult to catch now than a decade ago. I was actually surprised at how difficult the rainbows in the Rangitikei were to catch. Footprints and fishing camps along the river's banks suggested that this wilderness river actually receives considerable fishing pressure, at least by New Zealand standards.

Research in Idaho has shown that hatchery rainbow trout become more difficult to catch with exposure to angling. The same study indicated the lesson learned from being caught appears to wane after three to four weeks, at least for rainbow trout, and suggests that angler visits would need to be extremely infrequent for trout to remain naive to angling. Even in New Zealand there can be very few waters, especially rainbow trout rivers, with such low angling pressure.

In the summer of 2001 I had a unique opportunity to see for myself how rainbows unaffected by fishing pressure react to the fly. I received special permission from the Department of Conservation to spend a week in a remote river near Lake Te Anau, studying the behaviour of undisturbed rainbow trout. The river is normally totally unfished because the public are excluded from the area to protect takahe, an endangered native bird. In one day's fishing I had twenty rainbow trout take the fly, of which eleven were large fish (over forty-five centimetres long). All except two took a size 12 Royal Wulff on the first drift. The remaining two took a nymph on the first drift.

The ease at which I could catch these naive rainbows reminded me of a day I spent fishing for beautifully coloured cutthroat trout and brook char in a remote alpine stream in Utah. The fish were absolute suckers for any large dry fly. The fishing was so easy I could let my attention wander over the grand alpine vista, casually casting to lies and keeping only a partial eye on the fly. If I missed a strike, no matter: another fish would oblige within a few minutes. This kind of fishing may sound exciting, but in fact it soon got tedious. The reason is that it lacks the unexpected and it is not particularly challenging. It is fun to experience this kind of fishing if the country, river or species is novel. But in order to sustain one's interest, the fishing needs to present a challenge, a mystery or something new.

The above research has confirmed that angling pressure clearly has an impact on trout behaviour in remote rivers, and especially brown trout. Anglers arriving at a remote river in New Zealand's back country can expect excellent sight fishing providing that the river has been well 'rested'. They should see plenty of large trout, in fishable locations, and find them reasonably easy to catch. They would have an entirely different angling experience and impression of the river than would anglers arriving soon after them. The latecomers might see and catch relatively few fish and gain the impression that the river was underpopulated with spooky, difficult trout. Anglers who are experienced with the more remote New Zealand rivers are aware of this, and so avoid fishing the same reach day after day. Instead, they continually are looking for 'new' – undisturbed – water. Some tourist anglers, and some inexperienced Kiwis, have been known to set up fishing camps and 'thrash' the same area day after day. This is not a good strategy, as it can result in rapidly decreasing return for effort, and encourage the trout to be even more wary of other anglers.

One might expect that, as trout were exposed to more fishing pressure, they would become habituated to the regular presence of anglers and be less likely to flee to cover, or at least would resume feeding more quickly after being disturbed. After all, trout that spend most of their time hiding from anglers are likely to be more hungry, and hunger is a strong motivational force. Certainly, in some popular rivers in the United States trout are surprisingly tolerant of anglers and rafters. I have seen this in brown and rainbow trout in the famous tail-water fisheries of the Green River below Flaming Gorge Reservoir, and the Provo River, Utah. When fishing those rivers, other anglers are always in sight and often within casting distance. There are also scores of rafts, drift boats and canoes to contend with – a floating procession of splashing holidaymakers and anglers. On New Zealand rivers the first hint of such an intrusion would terrify the trout and send them packing. But in these American rivers the fish simply move aside, let the wading angler or

Angling is no longer a male preserve. Women are increasingly finding that trout fishing enriches the outdoor experience.
John Hayes / Les Hill

The artful science of trout fishing

raft pass by, then resume feeding. It is not unusual to be up to your thighs in water casting to fish up ahead and then notice a trout or two drift feeding under your rod tip. In the crowded San Juan River, New Mexico, the trout have learnt to feed on aquatic invertebrates dislodged by wading anglers. Anglers in turn have learnt to stir up the bottom with their boots. This so-called 'San Juan Shuffle' is now an illegal practice.

I suspect that such extreme habituation of trout to anglers is unlikely to occur in New Zealand back-country rivers. These are usually very clear and the trout large in relation to river depth and width, and thus feel exposed and insecure when out feeding. The North American rivers referred to above are comparatively large and the trout smaller. Fish in these rivers usually have the security of deep water close at hand if they need to move out of the way. So although New Zealand back-country trout may become a little less likely to flee the approach of an angler, and recover from disturbance more quickly, they probably always will be comparatively spooky.

Although evidence from research and from experienced anglers is that trout in New Zealand back-country rivers are very wary, there are times when they appear to drop their guard and behave less cautiously; for example, when really 'on the feed', and especially

Trout in New Zealand's clear back-country rivers are often very wary.

just after a fresh. When rivers have been low and clear for a long time, the trout can become wary of being exposed in the open, and very spooky at the approach of anglers. This behaviour can change rapidly during a fresh. When I first heard about this from guides and other experienced anglers, I assumed they meant during the high-flow conditions that exist just as the rivers were clearing. While the fishing can be good in these conditions, my own experience has been that the best time is a day or two later, when the flow has dropped further and the water has completely cleared. If these conditions coincide with the fine, warm weather conditions of an anticyclone, you can anticipate an excellent day's fishing. One of the factors that may encourage trout to feed well when the weather is clear and fine is rapidly increasing water temperature over the course of a day, as I mentioned above.

Another strategy for catching educated back-country river trout is to concentrate on fishing the faster water. Here the fish are more difficult to spot but much easier to catch because they have less time to examine the fly and the surface turbulence makes it harder for them to see the leader or the angler.

In summary, the research on New Zealand back-country river trout fisheries has shown that three things happen as angling pressure increases. First, trout are disturbed by anglers and may hide. This is a serious issue for brown trout fisheries in wilderness locations, but not such a problem in brown trout rivers where angling pressure is high, or in rainbow trout fisheries. Second, trout learn from being caught and released, and become harder to catch. Third, some anglers start to avoid rivers where they can expect to see others, especially if they encounter more than three anglers a day.

It is also now clear what defines the back-country river angling experience and how both anglers and trout respond to increasing angling pressure. Maintaining the quality of the angling experience may require management action on a few rivers where angler-encounter rate is approaching or exceeding tolerance thresholds determined by research. However, contrary to the hype that has surrounded this issue, the problem does not yet warrant intervention on most back-country rivers. Moreover, there is an impressive number of such rivers in this country with free access to all.

Managing the angling experience

Angling pressure on a few back-country rivers has reached the stage where Fish and Game is considering managing angler numbers to ensure the continuation of quality angling experiences. In Otago a balloted permit system is being trialled to control angler numbers during peak fishing months on the Greenstone River.

Another option is to control access — for example, by limiting or prohibiting the use of aircraft — but Fish and Game has no legislative power to do this, and DOC can do this only in areas under its jurisdiction. Indeed, DOC, encouraged by Fish and Game, has already placed controls on helicopter access to some rivers.

Fish and Game has also tried to spread angling pressure by negotiating legal access to and along rivers, and publicising access points with signs and pamphlets. This works well on rivers with road access. It provides alternative fishing spots, especially to anglers who are unfamiliar with a river, thereby taking the pressure off other places.

A permit system is the most equitable way to control angler use. With such a system, the number of fishing days and parties per year is fixed and then split between resident and guided tourist anglers according to various formulas. There are similar systems in North America, such as for steelhead fishing on the Dean River, British Columbia, which favours resident over non-resident anglers, and guided anglers over non-guided. The permit system being trialled on the Greenstone is non-discriminatory — all anglers, regardless of origin, have an equal opportunity to apply for and obtain a fishing permit. Discriminatory regulations are unacceptable to the New Zealand government, which has the final say in approving fishing regulations.

There are two downsides to permit systems. One is that they involve administration and compliance costs. The other is that some of the freedoms Kiwi anglers take for granted would be curtailed. This needs to be put in perspective, though: we are dealing with only a very small number of rivers that may require angler management.

When considering a permit system, fisheries managers need to decide if they wish to manage for some or all three of the angling effects on back-country fisheries: angler disturbance, trout becoming harder to catch, and angler-encounter level. These three effects can be managed by juggling the number of angling parties allowed to fish a river over a season, and the rest period between successive parties. It is probably unrealistic to manage for trout becoming harder to catch, because this would require rivers to be rested for at least several weeks between angling parties. Then there would be so few opportunities to fish that most anglers would lose interest with the ballot and be unwilling to support the cost of administration. If trout get harder to catch, at least anglers can compensate to some degree by improving their technique.

More realistic management goals for permit-regulated back-country rivers would be: first, to provide sufficient rest periods

Angler Access signs are erected by regional Fish and Game officers after negotiation with landowners.

between angling parties to minimise the effects of disturbance; and second, to set the number of angling parties at a level where each party has enough room to fish and not encounter one another often enough to become dissatisfied. The latter will probably become the main criterion for setting limits on the number of anglers on a river. A rest period of at least three days between angling parties would be necessary for remote brown trout rivers. A shorter rest period would suffice on the more heavily fished brown trout rivers and on rainbow trout rivers. The latter can be fished more frequently without having a major effect on trout behaviour and angling opportunities.

Minimising trout disturbance is important too because the perception that 'they' are disturbing 'our' (or 'my') fish affects the level of encounter that anglers will tolerate. Angler surveys and other research suggest that the optimum would be to keep the level of angler encounters at one or zero per day on remote brown trout rivers. However, one or two angler encounters per day is an appropriate management goal for rainbow trout rivers and accessible brown trout rivers.

Positive management action is necessary if we are to maintain the quality of the angling experience on the most sensitive back-country river fisheries. Otherwise we will see a progressive deterioration in the quality of the fishing experience. Uncontrolled increase in angler use will undermine the very features that attract us to these rivers – solitude, unspoilt environment and the chance to see and catch good numbers of large trout. Already some river fisheries are on that slippery slope.

Social surveys have shown that back-country river anglers want various rivers to be managed in different ways. They want to have the opportunity to fish the full spectrum of rivers, from those with easy access beside roads where it is accepted that they will probably encounter other anglers, through to wilderness rivers offering solitude and no disturbance from helicopters. The challenge facing Fish and Game New Zealand is how to set up management initiatives that provide and maintain this range of experiences within its financial resources, and with the continued support of anglers. If and when Fish and Game is successful in this endeavour, this will herald a new level of sophistication in fisheries management in New Zealand.

The other major challenge facing Fish and Game New Zealand and the wider angling community is how to stem the deterioration of our lowland river fisheries. Anecdotal accounts of declines in lowland fisheries abound throughout the country, but there is little hard documented evidence other than from survey of angler perceptions. Environmental decline is perceived to be the main cause, largely associated with agricultural development. There is no shortage of scientific evidence documenting the poor water quality and ecosystem health of our lowland rivers. An urgent need exists for research to understand the cause and extent of deterioration in these fisheries. Water and fisheries management in New Zealand needs to move beyond conservation of habitats that remain after exploitive industries have taken their toll. River restoration and fisheries enhancement are needed to replace such rearguard action.

Agricultural and other land development, and hydro power demands will continue to expand, further stressing our trout and salmon fisheries. We need to be able to define what level of development is compatible with healthy rivers and healthy sports fisheries. Until then, fisheries managers will continue to be on the back foot when advocating habitat conservation, and our lowland rivers will continue to become less attractive places for trout and anglers.

More on the angling experience: why we fish

Reasons why anglers fish have challenged the minds of writers throughout angling history. The reasons are many and varied, and change over the course of an individual's lifetime angling journey.

The obvious answer is that we go angling to catch fish. At the most basic level, catching fish to eat motivates most of us at some point on our angling journey. However, it may come as a surprise to some readers to learn that when trout anglers have been asked this question in surveys, they often rate other aspects of fishing as more important than catching trout. Usually, when one begins trout fishing, actually catching fish is the prime motivation. However, over time anglers gain fulfilment from their sport in other ways. Fishing

Angling takes us to places of breathtaking beauty and grandeur.

can be contemplative, an escape from the business of modern life. It can offer simplicity – a mind in harmony with nature. On the other hand, habits from our busy lifestyles can flow through to the way we conduct angling – frenetically driving us on to the next pool and the next fish.

Other anglers are motivated by curiosity and the thirst for novelty and adventure. This is what drives many of them to see what is beyond the next bend in the river. A related motive is the satisfaction that comes from learning – adapting to changing circumstances, seeking and applying new knowledge – and experiencing success accordingly.

Angling can encourage a striving for technical skill and biological knowledge, offering continued challenges over an angler's lifetime. Similarly, some anglers rise to the challenge of perfecting the arts of fishing, such as casting and fly tying.

There is no doubt that angling is exciting. The anticipation of the strike followed by a crescendo of erupting water cascading from

The artful science of trout fishing

a leaping trout and the scream of the reel: this is pure addictive excitement.

For some anglers a competitive streak drives their involvement in their sport and interaction with other anglers. Others seek companionship through fishing. For males fishing can be a substitute for directly communicating emotions and friendship. It is an emotive experience in which feelings and thoughts are shared simply through fishing together.

Aesthetics can be important too. Angling takes us to pristine places of breathtaking beauty and grandeur. It encourages an appreciation of natural surroundings, of lakes and rivers, and of the beauty and force that emanates from a glistening, live trout.

Eventually, for some anglers, a river or lake can become a place of belonging: where life is framed within landscapes of natural form and permanence of time; where thoughts and spirit are focused by water's sound and movement, by changing light and colour, in wild places; and where memories linger.

SELECTED REFERENCES

Allen, K. R. 1951: The Horokiwi Stream: A study of a trout population. *NZ Marine Department Fisheries Bulletin* No. 10.

Allen, K. R. 1952: A New Zealand trout stream – some facts and figures. *NZ Marine Department Fisheries Bulletin* No. 10A.

Allen, D. M.; McFarland, W. N.; Munz, F. W.; Poston, H. A. 1973: Changes in the visual pigments of trout. *Canadian Journal of Zoology* 51: 901–14.

Berners, Juliana 1496: *A Treatyse of Fysshynge with an Angle*. Boke of St. Albans, Westminster.

Calabi, S. 1990: *Trout and Salmon of the World*. The Wellfleet Press, Secaucus, New Jersey.

Cryer, M. 1991: *Lake Taupo Trout Production: A four-year study of the rainbow trout fishery of Lake Taupo, New Zealand*. Department of Conservation, Science & Research Series No. 26.

Davies, P. E.; Sloane, R. D. 1987: Characteristics of the spawning migrations of brown trout, *Salmo trutta* L., and rainbow trout, *Salmo gairdneri* Richardson, in Great Lake, Tasmania. *Journal of Fish Biology* 31: 353–73.

Denton, E. J.; Gray, J. A. B. 1988: Mechanical factors in the excitation of the lateral lines of fishes. pp. 595–617 in: Atema, J., Fay, R. R., Popper, A. N.; Tavolga, W. N. (eds.), *Sensory Biology of Aquatic Animals*, Springer-Verlag, New York.

Favro, L. D.; Kuo, P. K.; McDonald, J. F. 1979: Population study of the effects of selective fishing on the growth rate of trout. *Journal of the Fisheries Research Board of Canada* 36: 552–61.

Ginetz, R. M.; Larkin, P.A. 1973: Choice of colours of food items by rainbow trout (*Salmo gairdneri*). *Journal of the Fisheries Research Board of Canada* 30: 229–34.

Hayes, J. W. 1984: Competition between brown and rainbow trout in Scotts Creek, a spawning tributary of Lake Alexandrina. PhD thesis, University of Canterbury, New Zealand.

Hayes, J. W. 1987: Competition for spawning space between brown (*Salmo trutta*) and rainbow trout (*S. gairdneri*) in a lake inlet tributary, New Zealand. *Canadian Journal of Fisheries and Aquatic Sciences* 44: 40–47.

Hayes, J. W. 1988: Comparative stream residence of juvenile brown and rainbow trout in a small lake inlet tributary, Scotts Creek, New Zealand. *NZ Journal of Marine and Freshwater Research* 22: 181–88.

Hayes, J. W. 1995: Spatial and temporal variation in the relative density and size of juvenile brown trout in the Kakanui River, North Otago,

New Zealand. *NZ Journal of Marine and Freshwater Research* 29: 393–407.

Hayes, J. W.; Stark, J. D.; Shearer, K. A. 2000: Development and test of a whole-lifetime foraging and bioenergetics growth model for drift-feeding brown trout. *Transactions of the American Fisheries Society* 129: 315–32.

Hill, L. 1997: *Stalking Stillwaters*. The Halcyon Press, Auckland.

Hill, L.; Marshall, G. 1985: *Stalking Trout: A serious fisherman's guide*. The Halcyon Press, Auckland.

Hill, L.; Marshall, G. 1991: *Catching Trout*. The Halcyon Press, Auckland.

Hughes, N. F., Hayes, J. W., Shearer, K. A., Young, R. G. 2003: Testing a model of drift-feeding using 3-D videography of wild brown trout in a New Zealand river. *Canadian Journal of Fisheries and Acquatic Sciences* 60: 1462–76.

Hursthouse, C. 1857: *New Zealand or Zealandica: The Britain of the south*. Stanford, London. 2 vols.

Jowett, I. G. 1990: Factors related to the distribution and abundance of brown and rainbow trout in New Zealand clear-water rivers. *NZ Journal of Marine and Freshwater Research* 24: 429–40.

Jowett, I. G. 1993: Models of the abundance of large brown trout in New Zealand rivers. *North American Journal of Fisheries Management* 12: 417–32.

Jowett, I. G. 1995: Spatial and temporal variability of large brown trout abundance: a test of regression models. *Rivers* 5: 1–12.

Jowett, I. G.; Richardson, J. 1989: Effects of severe floods on instream habitat and trout populations in seven New Zealand rivers. *NZ Journal of Marine and Freshwater Research* 23: 11–17.

Logan, H. 2001: Gondwana invaded: an address on distinctive features of managing indigenous biodiversity in protected areas in New Zealand. *Journal of the Royal Society of New Zealand* 31: 813–18.

Maclean, N. 1976: *A River Runs Through It*. University of Chicago Press, Chicago.

MacCrimmon, H. R. 1971: World distribution of rainbow trout (*Salmo gairdneri*). *Journal of the Fisheries Research Board of Canada* 28: 633–704.

MacCrimmon, H. R.; Marshall, T. L. 1968: World distribution of brown trout, *Salmo trutta*. *Journal of the Fisheries Research Board of Canada* 25: 2527–48

McMichael, G. A.; Kaya, C. M. 1991: Relations among stream temperature, angling success for rainbow and brown trout, and fisherman satisfaction. *North American Journal of Fisheries Management* 11: 190–99.

McDowall, R. M. 1990: *New Zealand Freshwater Fishes: a natural history and guide*. Heinemann Reed/MAF Publishing Group, Auckland.

McDowall, R. M. 1994: *Gamekeepers for the Nation: The story of New Zealand's acclimatisation societies 1861–1990*. Canterbury University Press, Christchurch.

McDowall, R. M. 1994: *Trout in New Zealand Waters: The biology and management of trout in New Zealand's lakes and rivers.* Fish and Fowl Series No. 4. The Wetland Press.

McDowall, R. M. 2000: *The Reed Guide to New Zealand Freshwater Fishes.* Reed Publishing (NZ) Ltd., Auckland.

McDowall, R. M. 2003: Impacts of introduced salmonids on native galaxiids in New Zealand streams: a new look at an old problem. *Transactions of the American Fisheries Society* 132: 229–38.

McGuane, T. 1999: *The Longest Silence: A life in fishing.* Jonathan Cape, London.

Meehan, W. R. (ed.) 1991: Influences of forest and rangeland management on salmonid fishes and their habitats. *American Fisheries Society Special Publication* 19.

Mylechreest, P. 1978: Some effects of a unique hydroelectric development on the littoral benthic community and ecology of trout in a large New Zealand lake [Waikaremoana]. MSc thesis. University of British Columbia, Canada.

National Research Bureau 1991: The economic worth of recreational fishing in New Zealand. Recreational Research Report. NRB, Auckland.

Page, M. J. 1986: The distribution, feeding, and growth of brown (*Salmo trutta* L.) and rainbow trout (*Salmo gairdneri*) in Lake Alexandrina. MSc thesis, University of Canterbury, New Zealand.

Percival, E. 1932: On the depreciation of trout-fishing in the Oreti (or New River), Southland. *NZ Marine Department Fisheries Bulletin* No. 5.

Roberts, B. C.; White, R. G. 1992: Effects of angler wading on survival of trout eggs and pre-emergent fry. *North American Journal of Fisheries Management* 12: 450–59

Rosenbauer, T. 1988: *Reading Trout Streams: An Orvis guide.* Nick Lyons Books.

Rosgen, D. 1996: *Applied River Geomorphology.* Wildlands Hydrology, Pagosa Springs, Colorado.

Rowe, D. K. 1984: Factors affecting the foods and feeding patterns of lake-dwelling rainbow trout (*Salmo gairdneri*) in the North Island of New Zealand. *NZ Journal of Marine and Freshwater Research* 18: 129–41.

Rowe, D. K.; Chisnall, B. L. 1995: Effects of oxygen, temperature and light gradients on the vertical distribution of rainbow trout, *Oncorhynchus mykiss*, in two North Island, New Zealand, lakes differing in trophic status. *NZ Journal of Marine and Freshwater Research* 29: 421–34.

Rowe, D. K.; Scott, D. 1989: Effects of climate warming on trout fisheries in northern New Zealand. *Freshwater Catch* 41: 3–4.

Scott, D.; Hewitson, J.; Fraser, J. S. 1978: The origin of rainbow trout, *Salmo gairdneri* Richardson, in New Zealand. *California Fish and Game* 64: 200–09.

Scott, D. 1964: The migratory trout (*Salmo trutta* L.) in New Zealand. I. The introduction of stocks. *Transactions of the Royal Society of New Zealand* 4: 209–27.

Smith, D. C. W. 1990: The biology of the rainbow trout (*Salmo gairdneri*) in the lakes of the Rotorua district, North Island. *NZ Journal of Science* 2: 275–312.

Spackman, W. H. 1892: *Trout in New Zealand: Where to go and how to catch them.* Government Printer, Wellington.

Southland Regional Council 1993: Southland diary farm expansion, Environmental Impact Assessment. Report prepared by Robertson Ryder & Associates, Dunedin.

Stephens, R. T. T. 1984: Smelt population dynamics and predation by rainbow trout in Lake Taupo. PhD thesis. University of Waikato, New Zealand.

Stolz, J.; Schnell, J. (eds) 1991: *Trout, The Wildlife Series.* Stackpole Books, Harrisburg, Pennslyvania.

Sutton, Roger. 2002: *Keeping Faith with Fin and Feather: People and imperatives in wildlife management.* Privately published, Invercargill.

Tillyard, R. J. 1920: Report on the neuropteroid insects of the hot springs region, New Zealand, in relation to the problems of trout food. *Proceedings of the Linnean Society of New South Wales* 45: 205–13.

Walton, I. 1653: *The Compleat Angler.* Weathervane Books, New York.

Williams, J. E.; Wood, C. A.; Dombeck, M. P. (eds) 1997: *Watershed Restoration: Principles and practices.* American Fisheries Society, Bethesda, Maryland.

Wulff, L. 1939: *Handbook of Freshwater Fishing.* J. P. Lippincott, New York.

Yerex, D. 2001: *Deer: The New Zealand story.* Canterbury University Press, Christchurch.

Young, R. 1999: Catch and release: A review of overseas research and implications for New Zealand. *Cawthron Report* No. 523. Prepared for Fish and Game New Zealand.

INDEX

acclimatisation societies 28–29, 84, 171, 179, 181, 187, 198, 200, 203–05, 209
age 26, 32–33, 48
age structure 32–33, 79
agriculture / agricultural 127, 181, 189–192, 194–95, 197–98, 201, 212
agricultural development 84, 196–97, 244
alevin 26–28
algae/algal 76, 84, 86–87, 102–04, 146, 191, 195, 210
algal blooms 40, 102, 190, 195
Allen, K. Radway 22, 28, 31, 198
angler disturbance 238–40, 242–43
angler encounter 230, 233, 241–44
angling pressure (see also fishing pressure) 45, 52, 130, 183, 219, 220, 223, 225, 227–28, 234, 236, 239–42
angling use/usage 233, 242–43

back-country rivers 26, 32–33, 39, 48, 87, 124–27, 129, 133, 135, 139, 143–44, 220, 223–25, 228–30, 233, 236, 238, 240–41, 243
bag limit 221–23, 228
bait fishing 37–38, 42, 67, 152–54, 167, 226
benthic invertebrates 123, 125, 164
Big Fish Programme 46, 48–49
biodiversity 184, 204–05, 210, 212–16
Biodiversity Strategy 213–15
blind fishing 160–62, 166

brown beetle 39, 136
bullies 29, 37, 88–89, 92, 104–05, 111–14, 152–53, 165–67, 170, 208

caddisflies 87–88, 92, 114, 148, 157, 194–95
camouflage 62–63
cannibal trout 30–31
catchability 227, 234, 236
catch-and-release (C&R) 37, 120, 222–28, 236
catchment boards 171, 212
channel shape 82, 84, 86
cicadas 39, 131
clothing 63–64
competition 184, 208–09, 226
conservation 198, 200, 203, 205, 209, 212–16, 222, 244
Conservation Act 179, 206
cover 18, 22, 41, 50, 52, 60, 63, 68, 70, 73, 77, 79, 82, 84–85, 89, 93, 96–97, 101, 107, 109, 114–15, 135, 143, 150, 152–53, 159, 194, 237–39
cruising trout 36, 114–18, 120, 133, 148–51, 158–59, 166

dairy/dairy farming/dairy industry 190–94, 201
dam(s) 29, 190
damselflies 40, 114, 148–49, 157, 167
Daphnia (see water fleas)
deep trolling 41
deer 192, 204, 212, 215–16
Department of Conservation (DOC) 29, 35, 168, 172, 179–80, 184, 200, 205, 211, 215, 222–23, 238, 242

depth 41, 52, 62, 75, 82–83, 89, 91–92, 95, 99, 102, 105, 110, 129, 140, 142–43, 146, 153, 161–62, 168–69, 240,
diadromous 205
disease 28, 31, 186–87
district councils 190, 192–93, 196, 200–01
downrigger 41, 168–69
dragonfly 113–14, 157
drift diving 36, 59, 68, 80, 83, 91, 236–37
drifting invertebrates 46, 87, 90, 125, 137
drought 28, 51, 75, 80, 181–82
dry-fly fishing 34, 36, 39, 53, 60, 139, 142, 150

economic value 180, 224
eels 29–30, 88, 204–05, 209, 216
eggs 24–28, 30–33, 47–48, 77, 172–73, 182, 195, 203, 227
energy/energetics 46–48, 91, 96, 103, 111–12, 123–26, 130–32, 172, 227
enrichment 84, 87, 194–95
epilimnion 101
erosion 84, 87, 127, 194–95, 205, 212
exotic species 203–04
eutrophication 76, 102–03, 195
eye(s) 57, 60

false casting 59, 144, 170, 174
feeding 38, 41, 46, 52, 67–68, 76–77, 89–94, 96, 106, 109, 111, 114, 118, 120, 123, 126–27, 129–31, 134–35, 137, 139, 141–42, 144, 147–48, 151, 154, 157, 159–60, 164, 167, 184, 220
   ambush feeding 151–52
   benthic (bottom) browsing 120, 148, 157, 160, 164
   drift feeding 46, 76, 89, 91, 120, 123–24, 126–28, 135, 139, 146, 151, 194–95, 240

   pursuit feeding 157, 164, 167, 169
   selective feeding 52, 87, 131–32, 134
   still-water-column feeding 148, 157
feeding lies 87, 91, 96, 98–99, 120–21, 130, 143, 146–47, 153
fertiliser 84
Fish and Game 48, 85, 172, 179–80, 182–85, 193, 198, 200–01, 213, 215, 222–24, 228, 230, 233, 242–44
fisheries management 219, 244
fishing pressure (*see also* angling pressure) 52, 133, 183, 187, 220, 223, 229–30, 236–38
floods 18, 23–24, 28–31, 35–36, 38, 51, 72, 79–84, 86, 92, 137, 152, 176–77, 181–82, 195–96, 208, 212, 222
flood control (*see also* river control) 191, 196
flow 31, 35, 37, 80, 82–84, 86, 91–92, 94, 133, 140, 187, 196–97, 208–10, 241
fly fishing 36, 38, 67, 152, 189, 195
food 10, 22, 27, 29, 33, 36, 46, 50–51, 61, 73, 77, 82, 86, 92, 96, 99–106, 108, 111–12, 115, 123–26, 132, 146, 157, 163, 183–84, 194–95, 206, 208, 220
forage fish 47, 104–05, 111–12, 114, 151, 160, 164–65, 168–69, 196
foraging area 125, 128, 132
foraging cost 46–47
forestry 194–97
fresh 24, 35, 137, 172–73, 241
fry 26–28, 30–32, 50, 87, 126, 132, 195–96, 206, 215

galaxiids 104–05, 114, 206, 207–10
genetic 45, 184, 207
gradient 80–81, 86, 89, 126, 151

grayling 209
gravel extraction 196
green beetle 40, 97, 112, 118, 160, 166
growth 29, 31, 33, 45–47, 49–50, 77, 103, 111, 184, 195, 220–22, 225–27

habitat 22, 39, 51, 75, 77, 79, 81–82, 84–87, 89, 91, 93, 97, 102–03, 105, 123, 140, 146, 148, 176–77, 179, 182–83, 186–87, 189–90, 194–98, 200–01, 205, 208–09, 219–20, 229, 244
harling 167–69
harvesting 222–23
hatchery 172, 183–86, 225
headwaters 22, 26, 47, 82, 87, 123, 144, 196, 208–09, 228, 237
heron 28, 29
helicopter/aerial access 45, 230, 242, 244
Hobbs, Derisely 181
homing 67
Horokiwi Stream 22, 28, 31, 197
hydroelectric power 86, 108, 181, 190, 197, 244
hypolimnion 101–03

inanga 37, 39, 88, 209
induced take 148
introduced animals 204–05, 213–14, 216
irrigation 86, 190, 193, 196–97
invertebrate drift 124, 128
invertebrates 31, 36–37, 39, 47, 80, 82–84, 86–88, 90–93, 105–08, 111, 123–24, 127, 135, 148, 151, 157, 160, 164, 183, 194, 196, 205, 208–10, 240

jigging 167–69

koaro 37–38, 40, 112, 114, 165, 167, 170, 206, 209

kokopu 209
koura (freshwater crayfish) 104, 112–14, 125

Lake Alexandrina 24, 27–28, 36, 106–09, 111, 113–15, 161–62, 171, 174
lake morphology 102, 104
lake-outlet rivers 80, 83, 148
Lake Tarawera 26, 48–49, 102
Lake Rotorua 41, 103
Lake Taupo 35, 102, 106–08, 110–12, 168–70, 179–80, 205–06, 211, 222–23
Lake Waikaremoana 106–09, 111–12
land development 176, 194–95, 197, 244
land management 201
land use 84, 177, 193–95, 198
lateral line 64–65
lead lining 41, 168–69
life cycle 21, 34, 50, 88, 104
life history 34, 47, 207, 209
limnetic zone 103–04, 108–09, 111–13, 157, 164–65, 167
littoral zone 103–09, 111–14, 157, 159, 164, 167
longevity 33, 47
low flow 23, 76, 83–84, 86, 91, 121, 172, 193, 196–97
lowland rivers/streams 33, 39, 127, 131, 135, 190–91, 198, 223, 229, 244
lure 63, 67, 76, 129, 139, 142, 150–53, 160–61, 164, 168–70, 172–73

McDowall, Robert M. 179, 205, 216
mayflies 11, 84, 87–88, 121, 131–132, 134, 136, 149–50, 194, 210
mesotrophic 103
metalimnion 101–02
mice 152–54
microhabitat 101

midges 87–88, 92, 112–13, 131, 134
migration 22–24, 27, 29, 33, 47, 50–51, 67, 167, 173, 197, 207
migratory 17–18, 205–06, 208–09
mortality 27–28, 45, 77, 168, 182–83, 186, 223, 225–26
movement (by anglers) 63–64
movement (by fish) 22–23, 41, 51–52, 57, 109

native fauna/flora 203–05, 212, 216
native fish 88, 151, 201, 204–10, 213, 220
navigation 67
night fishing 62, 170–71
nutrients 76, 84, 101–02, 191–95
nymph fishing 63, 129, 135, 139, 142, 150, 172

oligotrophic 102–03
optimal foraging 132
otoliths (fish ear bones) 33, 64
oxygen 75–76, 101–03, 105, 195–96, 227

pelagic 111
Percival, Edward 220
periphyton 84, 87, 104, 148, 195, 210
permit system (for angler management) 241–42
photic zone 105
piscivorous 151
plankton 80, 102, 104–05, 168
　phytoplankton 104–05, 109
　zooplankton 102, 104, 109
pocket water 91, 96, 146
Polaroid sunglasses 143, 159
pollution 75–76, 181, 190–95
pool (eye) 90, 93–94, 135, 138, 141, 143, 147
predation 38, 105, 111, 207–09
predators 26, 28–29, 57, 60
prey detection 57, 126–27
production 77, 84, 105, 123–24

productivity 49, 84, 102–03, 105, 107–08, 111, 222
profundal zone 104

radio tracking 23, 111, 164, 172, 226
redd 25–26, 28
redd superimposition 28
regional councils 86, 190–93, 196, 198, 200–01
Resource Management Act (RMA) 75, 181, 200
riparian/riparian vegetation 84–86, 195–96, 198
river-/stream-resident 22, 39, 49, 207–10
Rotorua lakes 46, 48–49, 102, 111–12, 114, 180, 182–83, 205–06, 211, 223

sea-migratory 205–06, 208–09
sea-run 17, 38, 41–42, 49–51, 172, 181
scales 33
search image 132
sediment / sedimentation 73, 176, 191, 194, 222
shag 28–29
sight (*see* vision)
sight fishing 89, 143–44, 147, 155, 166, 239
silt 27–28, 31, 84, 87, 182–83, 190, 194, 196
size limit 45, 221–22
smell 67–68, 70, 210
smelt 18, 24, 38–39, 41–42, 88–89, 92, 104–08, 111–14, 151–55, 165, 167, 170, 206
snails 86, 88, 92, 104, 112–13, 148–50, 157
Snell's circle 58–59
sound 64, 66, 70
space 27, 29, 50–52, 77, 83, 86
spawning 19, 23–28, 31, 33–39, 47–49, 62, 67, 138, 142, 172–74, 182–83, 185, 194, 196, 215, 221–23, 227

spin fishing 37–38, 67, 70, 142, 151–52, 167–68, 170, 189
spotting 93, 115, 141, 143–44, 146, 152–53, 159–60, 230, 234
spring-fed rivers/spring creeks 80, 83, 148, 163, 189–91, 198
stalking 93, 114–15, 117–18, 151, 154, 158, 228, 230
steelhead 17, 19, 22, 51
stress 184, 226
stock/stocking (livestock) 190–91, 195, 210, 212
stocking (fish) 176, 181–83, 185, 198, 203, 219
stocking (economics) 182–83
stoneflies 84, 87–88, 194
streamer flies 137
strike zone 129, 163
survival 27–28, 182, 184, 226

tagging 23
taste 67
temperature 19, 21, 24, 26, 36–37, 39, 41, 46–47, 75–77, 84, 92, 101–03, 105–06, 128, 133, 136, 163–64, 168–69, 187, 193, 195, 225–26, 238, 241
terrestrial insects/invertebrates 39, 111, 114, 131, 136, 138, 157
territorial 32, 96, 99, 120–21, 184
thermocline 76, 101, 110, 169
tides/tidal 38, 41–42, 88–89, 123, 151–52, 154
Tillyard, Robin 209
tourism 180–81, 211–12, 214–16, 224
trophy trout 26, 34, 45–46, 49, 51–54, 206, 220, 222, 228–29, 237
trolling 167–68

Trout Unlimited 197, 224
turbidity 62, 96, 112, 114, 123, 127, 194–95

urbanisation 189, 196

velocity (of water) 75, 82, 89–92, 126, 128, 135
velocity refuge/shelter 89–90, 92, 96, 124–26, 147
velocity shear/shear zones 90–91, 93–96, 147
vibrations 64–65
visibility (underwater) 59–60, 112
vision 57–62, 130

water abstraction 181, 196
water boatmen 88, 148–50, 157
water clarity 84, 102, 121, 127, 130
water conservation order 200
water fleas (*Daphnia*) 104, 112–13
water management 190, 194, 210, 244,
water quality 75, 102, 176, 187, 193, 244
wet-fly fishing 63, 150, 160–61, 164, 167–73
wetlands 84, 177, 190, 195, 198, 204
whirling disease 186–87
whitebait 38–41, 88–89, 92, 104, 112–14, 151–53, 165, 167, 204, 206, 209
wilderness rivers 32, 230, 234, 238, 241, 244
wild and scenic rivers legislation 200
willow grub 39, 126, 134
wire line 41, 168–69